Real Estate P.24

OTHER BOOKS BY KIRIL SOKOLOFF

The Thinking Investor's Guide to the Stock Market

The Paine Webber Handbook of Stock and Bond Analysis

Investing in the Future:
10 New Industries and over 75 Key Growth Companies
That Are Changing the Face of Corporate America

Is Inflation Ending? Are You Ready? (with Gary Shilling)

STREET SMART INVESTING

STREET
SMART
INVESTING

A Price and Value Approach

to Stock Market Profits

George B. Clairmont
and Kiril Sokoloff

Random House *New York*

Statistical data in the graph and tables for American Business
Products, Armstrong World Industries, Inc., ASARCO
Incorporated, Borg-Warner Corporation, Cubic Corporation,
General Foods Corporation, P. H. Glatfelter Company,
International Multifoods, International Paper Company,
LeaRonal, Inc., Maryland Cup Corporation, Meredith Corporation,
Northwestern Steel & Wire, RCA Corporation, Republic Corporation,
Russell Corporation, Simmonds Precision Products, Inc.,
Stewart-Warner Corporation, Ti-Caro, Inc., and Trans-Lux Corporation
have been excerpted from *Standard & Poor's Stock Reports* and are
reprinted here with the permission of Standard & Poor's Corporation.

Library of Congress Cataloging in Publication Data

Clairmont, George B., 1948–
Street smart investing.

1. Investments—Handbooks, manuals, etc.
2. Stocks—Handbooks, manuals, etc.   I. Sokoloff, Kiril.
II. Title.
HG4527.C58   1983   332.63'22   82-42821
ISBN 0-394-52338-5

Manufactured in the United States of America

2   4   6   8   9   7   5   3
FIRST EDITION

*This book could not have been written
without the very valuable knowledge
and encouragement of Maurice M. Clairmont
and without the continuing support of
Catherine Miller Sokoloff*

Acknowledgments

The authors would like to thank Y. Morrow, S. Hsia and S. Fireman for their considerable efforts in putting this book together. They helped check many of the facts relating to company and stock histories. We greatly appreciate their invaluable contribution.

G.B.C and K.S.

Contents

Introduction

You can always find value and profit opportunity in the stock market. It doesn't matter whether the market is in the midst of a euphoric rally or the bleakest bear market. Nor do you have to rely on startling predictions or specific events—all that's needed is just a good appreciation of value, a healthy dose of patience, and the inclination to do a bit of elementary research. Many small investors consistently make money in the market in good or bad times because they understand that some stocks will do well wherever the market may be going, or at least will be less prone to severe loss, while other stocks may be painfully vulnerable. In any case, it is beginning to dawn on many investors that the old mundane stock market—the same one that has disappointed so many since the 1960s—just may be the place to invest for the 1980s and the 1990s.

The stock market will probably remain forever stodgy for the people addicted to the excitement of the commodities markets or the aesthetic pleasure of owning collectibles, such as art, antiques or precious stones; or for those others who prefer the solidity and comfort of owning real estate or other "hard assets," such as gold or oil wells. But many of those same people have begun to think about equities again, having become disenchanted with investments that have lately proven to be wildly volatile, difficult to understand and often hard to get out of. After the social upheaval of the 1960s and the economic excesses of the 1970s, during which time people plunged into all sorts of esoteric new investments, it appears that investors are now looking for a safe place to put their money and are once again considering the stock market. Naturally, we are prejudiced about stocks, but there are some genuinely compelling reasons why investing in stocks makes sense.

For one thing, uncertain times make diversification into stocks a wise strategy, Indeed, many new clients, or friends who were out of the stock market for years and are now coming back, tell us that the diversification factor is the major reason for their renewed interest in stocks. Also, after the wild fluctuations of prices of other investments, people are so shell-shocked that even the once feared volatility of the stock market is beginning to look sedate. "Since all other investments act crazily, why don't I put some of my savings into something I can read about and understand, something backed by physical assets and something that I can get out of quickly?" says a friend who had been whipsawed in the commodity markets.

For another thing, information *is* readily available on almost every stock listed, and after some rudimentary study such information is understandable to anyone with only a smattering of financial and accounting knowledge. Most people can teach themselves to read and interpret an annual report if they are sufficiently motivated (usually by owning the stock of a company). Also, graduates of high schools and colleges have increasingly come to understand that a comprehension of the financial markets helps them to survive in the world of business. It is also well understood that a person's financial savvy usually rises in direct proportion to the amount of money he has to invest—and now that the baby-boom generation is entering the peak earning years, this group may start saving (and investing) more money. In short, there is a growing realization that the stock market is comprehensible, that the necessary facts and figures are easily obtained and, in fact, are required by accountants and the Securities and Exchange Commission to conform to certain standards. Therefore, value and price history can be checked if investors are inclined to do so. The intrinsic value of real estate, art, collectibles, oil, commodities, et cetera, cannot be easily checked and may not be understandable to a layman. This is perhaps one reason why tax shelters are often the vehicles for these kinds of investments, the theory being, "Well, I would have paid the money to Uncle Sam anyway."

In addition, liquidity has become of much greater concern for most investors. The sudden reversals of business conditions, violent interest rate swings and the pace of economic and political and social change have, in our opinion, so traumatized people that there is now a decided bias toward having large amounts of cash available at all times. Liquidity is another positive factor offered by the stock market. You can enter and exit at will, since it takes only five business days for the execution of a trade to settle and the money to change hands. You may not get out at a price you like, but you can liquidate the stocks quickly and easily—all it takes is a phone call to your broker. Real estate tax shelters and some of the other illiquid investments discussed above obviously cannot get you cash in a hurry.

There now seems to be recognition that a stock is not just a financial asset but actually a tangible asset that is supported by brick and mortar, natural resources, real estate and the "means of production" of physical goods and physical services. In effect, when you buy a share of stock you are acquiring indirect ownership of assets, earnings capability of those assets and the acumen of the business managers.

Finally, as we'll show later, there have been some excellent returns realized in the market doldrums of 1969–82, a period when many pundits labeled the stock market as an investment medium of no return, one in stagnation or actual decline. In short, we believe that the stock market is and always has been an excellent investment medium and that by approaching it with a certain philosophy and psychology, as well as with some understanding of how to find and screen stocks, most investors can make money or at least preserve what they have against inflation, severe recessions and other economic dislocations. So our book's purpose is not to elicit fear or greed but, rather, to allay fears and give our readers some confidence as they select and buy stocks.

This is also a book for those who think it is a good idea to invest in American companies. And it is for those who have some capital and savings and who are unsure where to invest that money for the long term. The book assumes you have some financial and accounting knowledge, though not of a very sophisticated sort. In our view, the prevailing sentiment among most investors today is confusion. Because of the turbulent markets of the past several years, most investment goals revolve less around large increases in wealth than around capital preservation, which, as far as we're concerned, is prudent and wise.

Price Anarchy

It is a fact that many sophisticated investors, even experts, were fooled by the volatile markets of the late 1970s and early 1980s, much to their financial chagrin. Recent fluctuations in all investment markets—real estate, bonds, commodities, equities, currencies and collectibles—have been so wide that the traditional benchmarks of value, both on the high and the low sides, have been rendered meaningless. What was cheap or expensive—a value—could generally be agreed upon in the 1950s and 1960s. But in the 1970s, these bands of value, these trading ranges, were broken and price swings became so wide that only price anarchy reigned.

Gold in one year rose to $875 an ounce and within two years fell to $300. Silver went as high as $50 an ounce and two years later was selling at $6. In the cattle markets, the price of a hundredweight could fluctuate from $55 to $75 in the space of as little as three months. Treasury bills fluctuated 5 percent, or 500 basis points, in six months, and the prime rate could climb from 8 percent to 20 percent in the course of a year. Meanwhile the stock market could lose 20 percent of its market value in a year, and individual stock prices could rise 300 percent and then fall back to their original level, also within a year. Real estate values, traditionally a more illiquid investment, could rise and fall by 25–50 percent in a year.

Price turmoil, in short, has bred a certain degree of confusion and insecurity and has led many to speculate for the quick kill. And often, speculative orgies so engendered have led to market reigns of terror—for instance, when the silver bubble burst in the crisis of March 1980. Another example was the bond market collapse of 1979–80 that lingered into the following year.

The new speculative investment media, such as treasury bill and bond futures, real estate funds, and oil partnerships, also created more chaotic markets, as amateurs and novices in these markets distorted the fundamental values. The advent of stock market index futures in the spring of 1982 has also fed more risk into the stock market system.

Essentially, in all markets, the present emphasis has been placed on market timing. This approach is not value investing but outright speculation based on a hope of catching the swings in market rhythms. The difficulty, of course, is that for all the charts and computer systems and other more occult methods used for this purpose, no allowance can be made for the unexpected. Some totally improbable event makes the headlines and scuttles the rhythm of the markets that many technicians and believers in cycles depend upon. Ask any beleaguered grains or metals trader what kind of havoc the unexpected 1982 Falkland war or the 1979 Soviet invasion of Afghanistan played with the direction of their markets. For that matter, even weekly money-supply figures that deviate from what is expected can cause reactions of 3–5 percent in the stock or bond market values in a matter of days. Thus, speculating on the direction of a market involves a financial ability to sustain wrenching losses if necessary and also requires an element of luck if you are to succeed. Investing intelligently should involve neither.

Street Smart Investing

This brings us back to the subject of commonsense investing— understanding value and finding and buying a bargain. Your definition of a bargain may be different from ours because your past experience and risk tolerance are not the same as ours. Right away we will confess that our risk tolerance is probably lower than that of most investors. Most important, a bargain by our definition is one where the downside—the loss factor—is small, simply because we have a healthy respect for the kind of financial carnage that can occur in the stock market.

We have all heard of people who suffer major financial setbacks from their market investments. Many times we've gotten calls from friends numbed by the free fall of one of their cherished "glamour" holdings. Usually this is a result of a selling panic occasioned by terror among institutional investors after there has been some sort of disappointment in expectations for the stock. Often a panic develops into a severe and unjustified overreaction that feeds on itself, hurting both serious investors and speculators alike. It has happened to anybody who has ever been in the market, and it is extremely unpleasant.

While many people will spend a lot of time shopping around for a car or a refrigerator, they can impulsively make an investment, perhaps in the thousands of dollars, on the strength of a phone call from a broker or a tip from a friend. Yet we've all done this and almost always have lived to rue it.

It was precisely because of our fear of such financial suffering that we sought a way to insulate ourselves from the political and financial storms that can roil the markets with such terrible effect. Growing up in New York in the 1950s and 1960s, we were taught to be "street smart," a term that does not mean the same as "clever." It means, instead, that we were prudent enough to stay away from certain areas of the city at certain times because we knew we might get hurt there. Being street smart means you know how to stay out of trouble.

This book is about being "Wall Street smart." We can't guarantee you against losses with our system, but any losses you do have probably won't turn out to be big ones even if a major catastrophe strikes the market. Our investment system is a strategy set out especially for investors, not speculators, and it will only work over the long term—that is, a minimum of two years. We cannot shield you from volatility in the market, nor do we promise fantastic gains based on our predictions. If you can apply our guidelines, you should receive returns of more than double, or even triple, that of short-term interest rates in a normal market and stay in the black even in periods of great market distress. A decent return in the stock market can be made in the best and worst of times. The way to do this is to try to account for the worst that can happen and not be mesmerized by the prospects for enormous gains. We like any stock, whatever its business, as long as it is cheap and as long as the markets are not under immediate stress.

In an article that appeared in *The Wall Street Journal* in the fall of 1980, George B. Clairmont was described as a "doomsday investor whose approach produced a Noah's Ark of survival issues." This is not entirely true, since we do not expect the Apocalypse, but we always try to act as if a major market downtrend could occur at any time. Accordingly, we try to pick stocks that have intrinsic value, earnings power and valuable assets.

The Financial Markets:
The Nervous System of the Economy

While an end to Western civilization and capitalism may not yet be upon us, it should be evident to nearly everyone that the financial markets are in a profound period of chaos. These markets, after all, are the nervous system of our political and economic society. In the financial gloom of early 1982, certain stocks in real, uninflated terms stood at levels not reached since the Great Depression, while others sold at levels not seen since World War II. At the same time, interest rates in the bond market were at historically high levels, with the real interest rate—the effective rate after inflation—at more than 8 percent. Fernand Braudel, the eminent French historian, insists that "we are going to be in crisis until the year 2000 or more because we are undergoing a crisis of structures." His implication is that situations take care of themselves if given time and that no government or great leader can expect to achieve a lasting cure if "quick fix schemes" are pursued. Though painful, there exist, says Braudel, built-in historical checks and balances out of which new structures eventually evolve.

In any case, the past fifteen years have produced a grand and wild brawl in the United States. The nation, its companies and most of its populace are now suffering from the hangover of the bender that has produced absurdly high interest rates, high unemployment, recession and bankruptcy. And this is a world-wide phenomenon. One needs only to look at the situation in Poland, Rumania, Mexico or Argentina to see what easy credit, corruption and waste can do to once prosperous countries.

In today's world, however, governments do not go bankrupt; they just print more money, worsening inflation. Why is this done if it is apparent that so many citizens will be indirectly taxed and, in fact, be made poorer, rather than richer? The new paper money, of course, goes to pay for things people want, and each of the many programs and transfers of money that make up national budgets has its own constituencies, voting bloc and lobbies. The government doesn't go bankrupt, since it can't shut down, and so instead we, or our companies, bankrupt ourselves and our system by not paying for what we need to keep up and by not saving for the future. Huge deficits have been forecast not just in the United

States but in many countries, leaving financial markets suspended in uncertainty. There is fear that money for the private sector cannot be borrowed if the government must wrest all available credit for itself to pay its bills. Business, therefore, suffers a psychological loss of confidence—in effect, a nervous collapse.

Crisis as Opportunity

This book was written in late 1981 and early 1982, and at this writing we do not want to attempt to predict when and if a recovery will occur. Still, we do believe in cyclicality, and historically all markets eventually do come back. Like most market-oriented people, we almost have to believe that as a raison d'être. In fact, it is the collapses, dislocations and market anomalies that give us our buying opportunities. One of the most practical and usable aspects of many Eastern religions is the belief that every crisis creates an opportunity. Perhaps this is why Westerners find it so difficult to understand what appears to be stoicism on the part of Asians. Basically, winning in the market requires that attitude of stoicism, and buying stocks and making money from what you buy is a discipline based on capitalizing on crises, real or perceived.

Markets, one must remember, are not perfectly rational systems but merely a crucible of expectations, beliefs and hopes. They are moved by human perceptions and human interpretation of "facts" and "information," which may be true, exaggerated, understated or even false. Therein lies the chance for a profitable investment, especially when people almost always overreact to what appears in the media. What motivates markets is human belief and action. A market system has the same foibles that we have as individuals. It may go to extremes, be inefficient at times, overreact, be shortsighted, and grossly overvalue or undervalue itself. It may even lie. Still, it is the best system for providing reasonably accurate information about the economic needs of any society.

As a well-known economist, Paul Johnson, said in an address to the *Bank Credit Analyst* Conference in May 1981: "The market is a system for the speedy conveyance of cheap, accurate and objective information. It is speedy because the market is functioning around the clock all over the world. It is cheap because it is the free by-product of the buying and selling function. It is accurate because it is based on an endless multiplicity of real transactions. And, it is objective because the market is not an institution with a purpose and an ideology but a mirror of human desires in all their nakedness."

The stock market provides an instant reading of what people are believing and expecting and how they are acting on these emotions. That does not mean that these perceptions are rational, practical or even meaningful for the long term. But they are an accurate and objective snapshot of fear and greed. Consequently, markets must be respected. After years of observation and participation we've developed our own private beliefs about market behavior. Among them:

1. It is hard to make money in the markets, and when it becomes too easy, as it did in 1929, 1966–68, 1978, 1979 and 1980, the game is about to end. If you don't know much about the stock market and you are suddenly a financial genius, something is wrong.

2. Market moves never occur when they are expected to. They usually happen later than expected, and they go farther than anyone predicted at the time.

3. The market always does what it has to in order to confound the greatest number of participants. The unexpected is what usually occurs. But because no one expects it to happen, the thought may not have even occurred to the participants.

4. A trend is in force until firm evidence to the contrary surfaces. A bull market will get as high as possible with as few people as possible knowing about it. Likewise a bear market will try to slip as far down as it can before people catch on.

5. Widespread predictions in the financial press about a forthcoming event should be disregarded. In fact, you should probably take an opposite position if the din is loud enough.

6. No system exists for predicting any market. What works in one stock market environment, may fail in the next one. As soon as a certain forecasting method becomes widely used *and followed*, it invariably gives off misleading signals.

7. Markets are dominated by fear and greed. You should sell into greed and buy during fear.

8. Big market moves are few and far between. Most of the time, the market is consolidating as it prepares for a big up or down move. The process may take years and will occur, as noted, when least expected.

9. A market trend that appears to be irrational should be taken

seriously. In other words, if a market goes up when the news says it should be going down, the market may be looking across the valley.

10. The markets bring out the best and worst in everyone. If you are greedy, the market can turn you into a pauper. If you are arrogant, the market can humble you. If you are obstinate, the market can break you.

11. The markets should not be fought. They know more than you do, and the greatest mistake you can ever make is to value your own opinion higher than the market's message.

So it should be obvious to you by now that we are intense believers in the irrationality of markets, their cyclicality, but most of all their volatility, which could continue at higher levels in the 1980s. Assuming you have the courage to invest in the stock market, we are going to take you on a survival outing. The market environment is undoubtedly treacherous, no question about it, but it still can be entered if you're provided with the knowledge to cope with its dangers.

In this book, we'll first discuss what we believe is the right philosophical attitude if you are to invest sensibly. Next we'll try to encourage you by telling you why we think there's an excellent case for investing in equities, particularly in the 1980s. Then we'll come to the core of this book, a set of guidelines for finding and screening undervalued stocks and an explanation of where to find clues to good investments. Next we'll set out three approaches to value, which include buying neglected stocks, buying stocks that are distressed, and buying special situations. In each instance, we will provide concrete examples. Finally, we'll talk about how to use certain techniques to insulate yourself, at least partially, from market turbulence.

STREET SMART INVESTING

Chapter 1

The Philosophy of
Bargain Hunting

AMONG THE MANY CHALLENGES that now confront capitalist economies are the frequency and scope of change. This acceleration of change has so buffeted nations, communities and individuals that time-honored traditions, accepted modes of behavior, and previously successful economic policies are in danger of being swept away. Increasingly, people are possessed by feelings of helplessness as to how they should lead their lives, with volatility forcing most of us to react to events rather than to take control of them.

The ravages of a structural inflation in the 1960s and 1970s, the declining supplies of resources, escalating competition in a more interdependent world economic system, and the threat of political upheavals between "have" and "have not" nations and groups have contributed to our economic insecurity. One psychological outcome of our recent past is an increased emphasis on instant gratification, which contributes greatly to the volatility of all markets because it leads to purely speculative decisions and extremely short-term commitments in all investment markets.

During the last several years, many investors became so fearful of missing the latest opportunity to capitalize on market volatility that they were overcome by the avaricious desire to achieve financial security through a spectacular investment success. The insecurity that breeds this speculative mania will not subside until confidence returns to the world economies and financial markets, an event that does not seem probable for some time.

But wide price swings in any market have always provided tremendous opportunities to canny investors armed with the knowledge and objectivity to capitalize on them. Throughout history, many fortunes have been made by those who had the confidence and expertise to recognize underlying value and who bought and sold on the basis of value and not emotion. The key point is that these successful investors knew what price represented value. Most of them were bargain hunters with enough confidence in themselves to avoid the manic depression of the market. They operated on the vital premise that well bought is half sold, no matter how much doom and gloom might exist at the time. The shrewd investors who made killings in the past often bought assets that were driven down to bargain prices because of fear and economic distress. Indeed, Bernard Baruch once said that the time to buy commodities is when the business outlook is so bad that their price has fallen far below the cost of production.

We intend to provide you with some basic procedures for making and keeping money in what we consider to be the most promising market around, the equity stock market. Basically, we shall present an approach that tries to mitigate the volatility of the market so that investors can achieve a consistent rate of return that is superior to the level of short-term interest rates. Our strategy is not at all complex. Our techniques will require only a few hours a week, which should not prove a burden on the busy executive or professional person. But this is not an academic investment exercise but an eminently practical one. We have demonstrated over an extended period of time that it is possible to invest in common stocks with a limited amount of risk and a good potential for profit, certainly sufficient to preserve and enhance capital. Furthermore, we have achieved these results consistently no matter how turbulent the financial markets.

We asked Touche Ross, one of the eight big accounting firms, to review and audit the investment performance of two companies controlled by George B. Clairmont. The auditors summarized the combined results for these two companies for the years 1976–80, including the profits realized in each year and for the whole period, as well as the unrealized profit in the portfolios at the end of 1980. Realized gains were 22 percent a year, and unrealized gains amounted to the equivalent of 17½ percent, representing capital appreciation of 39½ percent a year. This figure was supplemented by an average yearly dividend income of 7¾ percent, which, when added to realized and unrealized gains, indicates a total return on average investment of just over 47¼ percent each year for the five-year period.

The annual capital appreciation performance record of the portfolio is set forth in Table 1. The yearly capital appreciation or loss for the Dow Jones Industrial Average, S&P 400 Index and Value Line Index are also listed in Table 1.

Our strategy worked even during the bad years in the stock market. In 1977, for example, the Dow declined by 17 percent, the S&P 400 by 12 percent and the Value Line was about even, but Clairmont's portfolio actually rose by close to 14 percent. The same thing happened in 1981, although the performance was not audited in time for this book. However, several of Clairmont's clients have corroborated that their capital appreciation was on the order of 12.6 percent as audited by their accountants. This result compares favorably with the declines of 9.2 percent in the Dow, 11.2 percent in the S&P and 5 percent in the Value Line.

A more important feature of the historical record is the defensive nature of the portfolio. At year end 1980, the portfolio consisted of eighty stocks, only ten of which were selling below the original purchase price. The total losses of those ten stocks amounted to less than 1 percent of the entire portfolio's value.

The auditors also calculated that the average holding period for stocks during the six years under examination was thirty months. This illustrates another important discipline of the strategy—patience to hold on to the stock until one's self-imposed rate of return is achieved.

Many people would consider Clairmont's investment results exceptional. But, in reality, stocks have turned in a good performance

TABLE I

ANNUAL CAPITAL APPRECIATION, 1976–81

	CLAIRMONT'S INVESTMENT COMPANIES	DOW JONES INDUSTRIALS	S & P 400 INDEX	VALUE LINE INDEX
1976	42.30	17.00	17.53	31.25
1977	13.88	(16.86)	(11.95)	(.23)
1978	23.98	(1.57)	3.87	7.15
1979	33.82	3.37	12.15	25.34
1980	36.40	17.61	30.44	21.71
1981*	12.60	(9.20)	(11.20)	(5.00)

*Unaudited and based on client reports

since the major bear market low in the fall of 1974. The Institute of Economic Research has calculated that between the 1974 low and the end of 1982, the total appreciation (including dividends) of all stocks listed on the New York Stock Exchange was 572 percent, and for all the stocks on the American Stock Exchange, 1,188 percent. In theory, by simply buying equal amounts of every stock on both exchanges, a completely naïve investor could have achieved a return of better than 100 percent a year for this eight-year period. But as a practical matter, one cannot buy every stock listed on the exchanges, and the frequent market drops make a buy-and-hold strategy difficult.

The key factor in any investment strategy, and the cornerstone of our decision-making process in selecting stocks, is to avoid losses by buying stocks that are cheap. In other words, we believe that price is everything. *The main precepts of our bargain-hunting philosophy are conservatism in price, judgment, consistency in price objectives, the patience and discipline to hold for the return required and the common sense and/or objectivity not to be guided by temporary emotional changes of perception in the market.*

Safety Nets

When we focus on price, we use various analytical techniques to arrive at what we consider a floor for the stock—in effect, a safety net for the investor. What we want to know is how much we could lose if the stock market collapsed or if the company's fortunes deteriorated in bad times. We also want to know the trade-off between the downside risk and the potential for the stock on the upside. In other words, we want to quantify the risk/reward ratio of every stock we buy.

For instance, suppose we determine that the worst case for a stock is a decline of 10–15 percent, because it should be cushioned by substantial asset value, earnings stability, dividend yield or price history, or a combination of these factors. Suppose, further, that the stock offers the potential of a 40–50 percent gain in price in a normal economic or stock market environment. These odds, of better than 4 to 1 on the upside, are what we look for in an investment.

As a case in point, consider a stock that sold at a price/earnings (p/e) ratio of 5 to 11 over the last six years—a good period to use because it encompassed a doubling in the price of oil, double-digit inflation, a collapse in the bond market, several money crunches, the worst recession in forty years and unprecedentedly high interest rates. The median p/e ratio here is 8, and barring an abnormal event that could alter historical parameters of value, we would try to buy the stock between its median and low p/e of the period.

Another safety-net strategy is to try to establish the liquidation value of the company—in other words, if the company were to go out of business tomorrow, its assets sold and its liabilities paid off, what price would the shareholders receive? Although few companies ever do liquidate, attempting to estimate the break-up price can help you to determine value. If you find that the company is really worth a lot more than the going stock price, others may eventually reach a similar conclusion. Another corporation may launch a take-over at a price close to the company's liquidation value. Alternatively, other investors may start to see the stock's hidden assets and gradually move the price up to a more realistic valuation.

There are other safety-net tip-offs as well. If a company repurchases its own stock, that means management, knowing the inside story, probably considers the stock to be an excellent value in comparison to other capital investment opportunities. The repurchase of stock will shrink the number of shares outstanding and, all other things being equal, produce more favorable earnings comparisons in the future. Of course, this is a general comment and there are caveats. Sometimes managements of companies are so threatened by a takeover by an unappealing (to them) corporate raider that they have actually impaired their companies' growth by using sorely needed cash to buy back stock, thereby increasing debt or decreasing competitiveness in order to perpetuate their control.

By the same token, if another company is acquiring the stock or has accumulated a big block of stock at a certain price, that could also be a tip-off of value. In all probability, the company has done its homework and spotted an underlying value that was not apparent to the investment community. While corporate executives are capable of making mistakes just like other investors, they tend to invest intelligently because they are looking at the company as managers —what is the entire company worth, what do its operating units earn in a normal year, and is the stock market correctly valuing the underlying assets and earning power? The sale of an asset or a division at a huge profit might also be a signal that the company is holding other valuable assets at greatly undervalued prices.

There are caveats to each one of these safety nets, which we will deal with later. But our major point is the importance of using objective techniques to quantify a price that represents a good value.

One well-known cliché about investing in stocks is to "buy low and sell dear." In order to follow that maxim, you must be philosophically inclined to quantify your risk in an investment. If you have done that, you can sleep well at night, knowing that you haven't overpaid for a stock. If you have correctly determined the amount of risk in an investment, the payoff will almost surely come.

Percentages

One of the major reasons for investor disappointment is the desire by some to achieve fast and spectacular results. One could make a sports analogy, where the most exciting plays are the home run or the fifty-yard touchdown pass. The desire to be a sports hero or a financial wizard is widespread among us. But while Reggie Jackson may get the loudest applause when he hits a home run, he also gets the loudest boos if he strikes out.

The same thing happens in the stock market, which also has its share of home-run hitters, like the "gunslingers" of the late 1960s. Supremely confident of their invulnerability in picking stocks, these "go-go" boys bought stocks regardless of price or value or risk. Often the mere rumor that a gunslinger had bought a certain stock would cause its price to rise as thousands of disciples leaped on the bandwagon. Sometimes the stock picks engendered self-fulfilling prophecies, because a buying panic developed. However, when the speculative orgy ended, as it always does, and profits turned to hideous losses, these heroes slumped from sight.

The point here is to exercise restraint. Seek a modest, consistent return and perhaps an occasional big win. But don't expect to make and keep money if you always pursue enormous gains.

The Opportunity Cost

In order to achieve consistent results, define your investment goal or the annual return that is acceptable in light of what should be your primary objective: preservation of capital and risk reduction. At a minimum, the serious investor should seek to beat the rate of inflation on an after-tax basis. Assuming, say, a 10 percent rate of inflation, a 20 percent capital gains tax and 5 percent state and local taxes, you would need at least a 12–15 percent return on capital. With a 5 percent inflation rate you would need about an 8 percent return. Of course, this figure would vary according to your income tax bracket, the dollar amount of the capital gains, the level of inflation and the tax rate in your state and community.

Many stocks offer a good dividend yield, which can be included as part of the desired investment return. But we prefer to look at dividend income as a pocket allowance rather than an integral part of the investment objective. Dividend income is taxed as ordinary income and is therefore subject to the 50 percent maximum tax as well as state and local taxes.

Any investment in the stock market must also be compared to alternative investment opportunities, or what's sometimes referred to as the opportunity cost of capital. What would you forgo by tying up your money in the stock market instead of other investment vehicles, such as real estate or money market funds?

In a market environment where money market funds yield, say, 10 percent, most people would probably consider the opportunity cost to be around 6 percent if their tax bracket was 40 percent. Money market funds are liquid but are not totally riskless, since up to 40 percent of the assets of many funds are invested in commercial paper. A financial environment of high real interest rates, credit squeezes and leveraged corporate balance sheets could pose the threat of corporate bankruptcies and defaults on commercial paper.

For this reason the conservative investor may prefer to use treasury bills as the benchmark for comparing opportunity cost. Treasury bills have virtually no principal risk and are generally considered the safest investment vehicle available. If you assume that treasury bills are yielding, say, 10 percent, and you are in the 30 percent tax bracket, your after-tax yield is slightly over 7 percent. If you don't achieve a much better after-tax return than 7 percent from the more risky stock market, you should feel short-changed.

In any case, we believe that commonsense investing in the stock market should garner at least 15–25 percent in appreciation a year before tax, no matter what the stock market does. Such a return should overcome the recession, inflation and the opportunity cost hurdle.

Once your financial goal is clearly defined, it is easier to evaluate the attractiveness of a particular investment. For example, in the beginning of 1981 we became interested in Colgate-Palmolive, which at the time was selling for $14 a share. Colgate's earnings had been more or less static since the mid-1970s, rising from $1.95 in 1976 to $2.40 in 1980, mostly because of price increases and inflation rather than internal growth. Several unprofitable divisions, particularly Helena Rubinstein, a cosmetics division, had penalized earnings progress.

At 14 a share, Colgate appeared undervalued to us. The stock fell as low as 10–11 in 1980 from 13¾ in 1979, but had sold above 25 during every year since 1972, except 1979 and 1980, when it got only as high as 19⅝ and 17⅝, respectively. Its book value, at $14.50 when we made our purchase, was below the price of the stock, and its price/earnings ratio was 5½, or, as historical analysis showed, the lowest p/e in ten years.

Another plus was the fact that the earnings momentum of the company seemed likely to increase, as the company had finally divested itself of all its losing operations. A dividend increase seemed possible, and the company appeared poised for a return to the respectability it had enjoyed in the mid-1970s, when its p/e averaged around 10.

But there was another very real attraction. The lowest high for the year in the last ten years was 17⅝. Thus, it appeared reasonable that the stock might once again reach 17⅝ within the next twelve months. To the investor who concentrates on percentages, this meant that the upside target for the next twelve months was an appreciation of $3.25 after commissions, or about a 22 percent gain.

The company also yielded more than 7.5 percent at a price of 14, so assuming one held the stock for twelve months, the total pre-tax return might be on the order of 30 percent. Even after adjusting for taxes, the return would have exceeded 20 percent. Obviously, though, with the prospects of improving earnings, the real goal was a price rise to the low 20s, which would result in an approximate capital gain of 50 percent or better.

The point here is that you don't have to look for stocks that will double or triple. With a little homework, you have a reasonably good chance of achieving a rate of return of 25 percent annually. Even stocks of laggards and maligned companies can provide handsome returns if bought at the right price and with an eye to the downside risk.

It's important to think of any investment in terms of percentage price appreciation. A rise in the price of a stock from 10 to 14 represents a 40 percent pre-tax return. But to achieve 40 percent for a higher-priced stock—say, one bought at 50—the price objective would have to be 70. Take the case of IBM, which we bought at around 50 in 1980. At 50, the p/e ratio was 8, the lowest in over ten years. Furthermore, IBM had traded above 70 in each of the last five years, so we believed there was a reasonable chance that the stock would rise back to 70 within the next twelve months. As it turned out, the stock did rebound to above 70 a share before the end of 1980, and we sold out at 68 in that year. Thus, even the most visible companies can offer an opportunity for a capital gain if you choose to go for the percentages, not for the spectacular results. One final quality is necessary to complete the mental attitude of the successful investor: patience. It makes little sense to spend time searching for a low-risk investment and then sell just because the value of the stock is not recognized immediately, either because the company's underlying assets are not yet appreciated or the general market environment is unfavorable. Yet investors frequently do this.

Impatience is partly a function of the social conditioning that we have all undergone—the desire for instant gratification, action, quick results. It is also partly caused by a lack of confidence, which is most pronounced in the amateur investor, who may have purchased the stock at a good price but lacks the knowledge, fortitude or time to review the investment and its underlying value. How many times have you heard investors lament selling a stock just before it soars in price?

What amateur investors often forget in the pursuit of an instant killing in the market is the importance of long-term performance. If a stock is mired at the same price for two years, but spurts 50 percent at the beginning of the third year, the investment will have returned 25 percent per year. No one likes to accept a loss or a static investment month after month. As the world becomes more changeable and unpredictable, most of us have a predisposition to see things happen, even if they result in a mistake. We have come to expect and are perhaps too sensitive to fluctuation and, therefore, react impulsively instead of with determination.

We have also sold stocks in times of market stress but have always been chagrined when the stocks we dumped because of a gloomy market outlook staged a tremendous comeback. Finally, realizing that picking bottoms (or tops) was an exercise in futility, we forced ourselves to accept periods where the stocks that we bought would show no movement or unpleasant, unrealized losses. Eventually, we were almost always vindicated.

One way of looking at the problem is to compare the nomad and the farmer. The stock market nomads are forever wandering from one popular investment or faddish industry group to another. They are always caught up in the vagaries of market timing and new concepts that are so often prevalent in markets. But the investor who takes a stand and says to himself that his investment is planted despite market swings or market favor or disfavor is like a farmer who sows knowing there will be a year of drought or bad crops from time to time but that, over a period of time, he will most probably reap his profits. Especially in the case of buying asset-oriented companies that come under earnings pressure and thus receive market contempt, the time horizon can be long. Buying undervalued assets and waiting for profits can be, and often is, frustrating in a society that demands instant results.

Thus, the need for patience cannot be overestimated. Often the stocks we buy for our portfolio do nothing (even perhaps decline a bit) for long periods of time. However, if they were bought at the right price, the value invariably appears either because of some event, such as earnings progress and a takeover, or recognition of undervalued assets, as was the case with the Real Estate Investment Trusts that held equity in potentially valuable property and with natural-resource companies in the late 1970s.

The Opportunists

The people most envied, even at times greatly resented for their successful investing, are the bargain hunters: Henry Singleton, chairman of Teledyne; Victor Posner of NVF and Sharon Steel; Saul Steinberg of Reliance; and other savvy but less public figures such as Warren Buffett, David Murdock, Carl Icahn, the Bass brothers, the Belzbergs, the Pritzkers, Laurence and Preston Tisch, Robert Wilson, Sol Goldman, Harry Weinberg, Charles and Herbert Allen, Carl H. Lindner II, Ivan Boesky, Irwin Jacobs and Seth Glickenhaus. Kiril Sokoloff publishes a privately circulated bi-weekly newsletter, *Street Smart Investing* (see appendix for address), which closely monitors the buying and selling activities of these bargain hunters, as well as of forty to fifty others.

Regardless of short-term earnings swings, these investors hold for the long run, confident that the company will eventually reward them with significant gains because of its underlying asset potential and intrinsic earnings power. If plagiarism is the sincerest form of flattery, then the investment community pays the bargain hunters the highest compliments. Whenever word gets out that one of these investors has bought a stake in a company, the stock price of the "target company" is invariably run up.

A case in point was the gradual accumulation by Teledyne of nearly one-third interest in the shares of Curtiss-Wright at an average price of around $17 a share. Curtiss-Wright had produced an indifferent earnings record, and under the aggressive leadership of its chairman, T. R. Berner, had embroiled itself in a long-drawn-out takeover conflict with the Kennecott Corporation, the largest U.S. copper producer. In what amounted to a stand-off for both companies, Curtiss-Wright traded 4.8 million of Kennecott's own shares and Curtiss-Wright's Dorr-Oliver subsidiary, which Kennecott coveted, to Kennecott in return for $168 million in cash and 2.8 million of its own shares. The exchange gave Teledyne and the wily Singleton 57 percent of the now reduced capitalization of Curtiss-Wright, which retired the 2.8 million shares it received from Kennecott. Also, because of the huge cash payment, Curtiss-Wright now had cash per share of $35. This was not lost on the investment community, and the shares of Curtiss-Wright jumped as high as $50 a share in 1981, up from $19 a year earlier, giving Teledyne a substantial investment appreciation.

Playing on his perhaps undeserved reputation as a ruthless raider of companies, Victor Posner sometimes frightens management into buying him out at a substantial profit. This happened in the case of Marley and Foremost-McKesson, two instances where Posner doubled his money by selling out to a "white knight"—in the case of Marley—and to the company itself in the case of Foremost-McKesson.

The term "white knight" is used by Wall Streeters to denote an acceptable rescuer who will save the "victimized" target company from the clutches of an unwanted buyer. The top executives of Marley, a producer of cooling towers, electrical generators and heating and refrigeration equipment, preferred to be bought out by a private investor group, thus keeping their jobs, rather than be "at the mercy" of Posner and face insecurity about their own and the company's future. Posner capitalized on the fears and sold his position at a nice profit. Because of similar disquiet, top management of Foremost-McKesson, a distributor and producer of drugs, liquor and animal feed, felt compelled to use corporate cash flow and borrowings to repurchase Posner's position to fend him off.

Carl Icahn made a good profit on Hammermill Paper, which is listed on the New York Stock Exchange. Icahn gradually accumulated around 11 percent of Hammermill in the low 20s, believing that the stock was undervalued. His judgment was borne out when Hammermill's management decided to purchase his holdings at $36 a share, rather than run the risk of a hostile takeover.

Then, in early 1982, Icahn, as leader of an investment syndicate, went after Marshall Field, the old-line Chicago retailer. Marshall Field had two years previously been prey to a hostile bid from Carter Hawley, the California retailer, which had been rebuffed by Marshall Field's tactics of buying a retail chain in Carter Hawley's territory and then claiming antitrust. Icahn and his co-investors were probably most attracted to some of Marshall Field's real estate holdings, particularly the 50 percent-owned Water Tower, one of the most valuable properties in Chicago, since Marshall Field's earnings record was dismal. But this time Marshall Field decided to surrender its independence. Fearful of a successful effort by the Icahn group, which it regarded as asset strippers and corporate plunderers, Marshall Field agreed to be bought by British American Tobacco's retail group, which already owned Gimbels and Saks in New York, at double the average purchase price of Icahn's group.

In the late 1970s, David Murdock, another astute financier, built up a large position in Iowa Beef, the largest meat packer in the United States. Murdock held this investment for three years before Armand Hammer, chairman of Occidental Petroleum and a friend and business associate of Murdock's, agreed to purchase the company at nearly $75 a share, or twice Murdock's own price.

The investment successes of the late Charles Bluhdorn of Gulf & Western are legion, since he traded blocks of stocks as if he were a sugar trader, which he once was. Having accumulated large holdings in Cluett, Peabody and Collins & Aikman, Gulf & Western eventually sold its position back to the respective companies at a nearly 40 percent profit. Bluhdorn was known for making undervalued investments based on his own homework and had no problem holding on to an investment for a long time, regardless of the ups and downs of the market or the problems of the company. In an article in *The Wall Street Journal* in the fall of 1981, it was revealed that Gulf & Western had bought positions in nearly fifty stocks, representing a total market value equal to 25 percent of that of Gulf & Western. It was further reported that Gulf & Western held more than 20 percent of the stock of five companies and owned more than 5 percent of a dozen companies.

The one general investment tenet motivating all the big-name investors here was a *bargain*, a stock selling below a price justified by underlying assets and/or future earnings prospects.

The Bargain Basement on Wall Street

Bargain hunters generally find opportunities in three types of investment situations. The first kind is what we call "Sleeping Beauties," companies with excellent earnings records and with valuable assets but which, for a variety of reasons, have gone unrecognized and unloved. The stock market has simply neglected them or has not yet discovered their investment merits. Such stocks, therefore, sell at undeservedly low levels.

One little-known company fitting this mold was Sonoco Products, which made such paper conversion products as cones, spools and bobbins, among other items, mostly for the packaging, textile and chemical industries. Basically, it made commonplace value-added products that were in short supply and needed by a wide number of industries. We first noticed Sonoco by reviewing earnings reports in the newspaper and got intrigued by the more than 7 percent return on sales that this apparently ordinary manufacturer seemed to make consistently. The business was clearly not interesting to the Wall Street glamour seekers intent on "concepts" or new technological gimmicks, which was why Sonoco was trading at $14 or $15 a share, or around five times 1979 earnings of $2.38, despite average earnings growth of over 15 percent for ten successive years.

What attracted us to the stock was a price around book value, little long-term debt (only 10 percent of total capitalization) and a return on shareholders' equity of over 15 percent for more than five years, including the 1974–75 recession. In short, Sonoco was a solid company ignored by the financial community. It took smart sponsorship by some savvy fund managers and an earnings gain to $2.90 a share in 1980 before Sonoco finally caught Wall Street's attention. But in early 1981 the stock jumped up to 30, and even in the depths of the 1981 and 1982 stock market debacle, it never dipped below 22.

The second buying opportunity comes when large, well-known companies fall temporarily out of favor. Institutional investors dominate the stock market these days and they often have little patience with unexpected surprises in corporate performance. Frequently, if a company has a temporary earnings decline or a problem with an important new product, many institutions simultaneously dump their holdings. Their selling often drives the stock price below the intrinsic value of the company and offers us a way to buy the stock with little risk.

An example is Cessna Aircraft, which we bought in April 1980 at 13½. The company was under a cloud at the time because of technical and earnings problems with a new jet. On the positive side, the company was a leader in the private-aircraft industry (controlling more than half the market), had an excellent long-term earnings record and was respected for its technical capability, despite the problems with the new jet.

After the bad earnings announcement, the stock dropped from

29 to 13½ in only two months. At 13½, the stock was selling at six times earnings, the low end of the p/e range for the previous four years. Another plus was that Cessna's closest competitor, Beech Aircraft, had been acquired in 1979 by Raytheon at about twelve times earnings, thereby giving us a valuable benchmark of value. Finally, Cessna was selling under book value, which was unusual for a sophisticated high-brand-image company.

We were confident that the company would overcome its problems with the new jet and resume its standing as the leader in its industry. And we felt that the money managers' reaction to what we sized up as a temporary setback after years of success was decidedly overdone and so took advantage of the opportunity offered to us. One year later, in April 1981, the stock reached 30, where we sold our position, realizing an annual return on our investment of 122 percent.

The third area of bargain hunting is somewhat more complex, involving various categories that we lump together as "special situations." The underlying idea is that a company is involved in some unusual development that will change investor perception from negative to positive. Such a development may take the form of a change in top management, a profitable sale of some of the company's assets (redeployment), a write-off of a highly unprofitable business or division, the repurchase of the company's own stock or a change in management policy, such as stressing profits instead of volume. Another possibility is that the company could become the target of a corporate takeover. We will discuss this investing strategy later, but we might mention that an integral part of it involves riding the coattails of the bargain hunters mentioned earlier. For example, Mario Gabelli, whom *Barron's* has called one of the best stock pickers around, has categorically stated that "following big investors into stocks can be very attractive." Gabelli made money on Curtiss-Wright, taking Teledyne's lead. He also invested in General Tire after Bluhdorn started purchasing the stock in the mid-teens in 1980. The idea here is that if an investment is good enough for the opportunist's large amount of money, it's good enough for a small investor's limited funds.

Often, a signal for a real bargain is a build-up of an investment by a well-known opportunist. This does not mean one should throw caution to the winds and blindly follow the opportunists into a target company, but, in all probability, such a company was purchased at distress value. The payoff may be quite a long time in coming, but even a two-year holding period is worthwhile if the gain is in excess of 100 percent, which has been our experience in riding the coattails of these bargain hunters. Pride of authorship is fulfilling, but why not follow the experts, when their choices often offer such large profits?

Chapter 2

Crisis as Opportunity:
The Case for Investing
in Common Stocks

ALTHOUGH THIS BOOK studiously avoids making predictions, there is one forecast that we feel confident of. Just as the decade of the 1970s was the era of inflation hedges, so the 1980s will be the decade of common stocks. To be sure, a number of factors are working together to favor stocks as the preferred investment medium over the rest of this decade and possibly beyond. For one thing, common stocks are enormously undervalued. In the summer of 1982, the Standard & Poor's 500 Index of common stocks, adjusted for inflation, was actually selling below the peak prices reached in 1929. While the price of everything else soared in the 1970s, common stocks lagged way behind; eventually a catch-up will occur. One well-known investment adviser has said that in early 1982, on a valuation basis, stocks were actually selling below the levels reached at what was up until recently the greatest buying opportunity of this century—the 1932 bottom. History suggests that extreme undervaluation is eventually followed by proper valuation and, in due course, overvaluation.

Many professional and individual investors are leery of stocks at this writing because of the obvious economic and financial problems in both the U.S. and world economies. We, too, have been concerned about these problems and we do not wish to downplay their significance. But our rebuttal to the doomsayers is this: stocks would not be so undervalued if the economic condition of the world were not so precarious. Indeed, it is the very crisis atmosphere of today that has created these enormous values. Stock prices would certainly be significantly higher if the federal budget was balanced, interest rates were at levels prevailing in the 1960s, inflation was clearly vanquished, OPEC was dismembered, corporate liquidity was restored to respectable levels, the Social Security system was soundly financed, and the time bomb of international debt was permanently defused. As they say in the financial community, a bull market climbs a wall of worry.

Just for the record, let's review some of the financial problems facing the world today, but keeping in mind all the while that crisis is opportunity. To begin with, the financial condition of the world economy is in the worst shape since World War II. Debt to equity ratios for U.S. businesses increased from .85 in the mid-1970s to 1.05 in 1981—as total corporate debt nearly doubled to $1.2 trillion. Henry Kaufman, chief economist of Salomon Brothers, recently estimated that world debt outside of the communist bloc jumped from $3.6 trillion in 1971 to $14.3 trillion in 1981, an annual rate of increase of 15 percent. The well-publicized loans to less developed countries presently amount to $525 billion, up from $90 billion a decade ago. Many of these countries are seeking moratoriums on principal and interest.

The current world-wide recession exacerbates the debt situation because profits slump, exports slow, corporate cash flow worsens, yet the crushing burden of interest payments on that debt remains. Indeed, the burden of debt has affected the profitability of many corporations, both here and abroad. Prior to the mid-1970s, interest expense as a percent of corporate pre-tax profits fluctuated between 5 percent and 15 percent. But by 1981, interest expense as a percentage of corporate profits rose to 45 percent. In recent years corporations increasingly relied on short-term borrowing, and the ratio of short-term to long-term debt in the nonfinancial corporate sector rose from approximately 40 percent in the mid-1960s to about 70 percent in the early 1980s. The interest on short-term debt fluctuates with short-term interest rates, and thus the cost of borrowing soars during periods of high short-term interest rates. The difference to corporations between a 10 percent and a 20 percent prime rate in 1981 was around $42 billion.

Put another way, in the early 1980s corporate free cash flow (what a company can keep after paying dividends and making the necessary expenditures to maintain its existing capital investment) dropped to 18 percent of profits from what was traditionally over 30 percent in the 1960s and 1970s. Consequently, less money is

available for growth and investment in technology that would enhance future productivity.

The heavy reliance of corporations on short-term debt has omi-
nous implications. If a financial crisis were to develop, the growth
in short-term credit might slow or even reverse. In the aftermath
of the Penn Central bankruptcy, the size of the commercial-paper
market shrank by 21 percent. At this writing, the size of the
commercial-paper market is nearly four times as great as it was in
1970, and thus any crisis of confidence could have potentially a
larger impact.

Also, as interest rates reached historically high levels in 1980
and 1981, an enormous volume of outstanding debt in the economy
was being refinanced at increasingly higher interest rates. This
created a situation that some analysts call negative compounding.
Just as high compound-interest rates can increase wealth at phenomenal rates, so crushing debt burdens during a period of high
interest rates can increase debts by record amounts.

The Bane of Inflation

Much of the reason for the huge increase in debt during the 1970s
was inflation and the expectation of more inflation, due in large
part to OPEC price shocks. Borrowers could pay back in cheaper
dollars and invest the proceeds of the loan in a rapidly appreciat-
ing inflation hedge, such as real estate. But a tight monetary policy
and the highest real-interest rates in many years pose enormous
problems for heavily leveraged individuals and corporations, especially if their assets, such as real estate or precious metals, decline
in price.

The attempt to end forty years of inflation is a difficult task and
full of risks. Overextended borrowers or those positioned heavily
to benefit from more inflation are finding themselves in desperate
financial straits in the current period of disinflation. The risk is a
financial crisis and a wave of bankruptcies. But even if we can
escape a serious financial dislocation, the transition to permanent
disinflation or a lower rate of inflation will be difficult.

At this writing, the wages of nearly 10 million employees, 6 million wage earners covered by collective bargaining and close to
35 million Social Security recipients are tied to changes in the

Consumer Price Index, which amounts to de facto indexing. In effect, wage indexing builds inflation into the system. Moderating wage demands is a critical factor in any successful battle against inflation because some 75 percent of total business costs are labor-related. While the current recession is forcing many wage concessions, deeply ingrained attitudes about steadily increasing salaries are hard to change.

A recent survey by A. Gary Shilling & Co., economic consultants, found that more than 50 percent of the American population—a voting majority—depend on government for part of their income. Here are Shilling's figures on the number of people who depend on government spending for part of their income: government-pension beneficiaries, 4.4 million persons; veterans' pensions and compensation, 4.6 million persons; Social Security, 35.5 million persons; welfare, 12.9 million persons; unemployment insurance, 2 million persons; federal and state employees, 18 million persons; private employment based on government spending, 9.5 million persons; miscellaneous, 6.2 million persons; and dependents of the above, 23.1 million persons. That amounts to 50.2 percent of the total population. As the hue and cry over the Reagan budget cuts illustrated, it will be difficult to alter these political realities of government spending.

Inflation has, of course, made money management a very complex task. On the one hand, volatility increased because of fear of inflation and the desire by investors to seek a refuge. In effect, inflation encouraged widespread speculation. People who under normal circumstances were extremely conservative justified all sorts of crazy speculations under the guise of beating inflation.

But excessive speculation and inflation invariably breed a response by the government and the Federal Reserve Board in the form of tight monetary policies. Credit stringency in an over-leveraged economy raises the specter of a price decline in all types of assets and makes liquidity the best investment, as was the case in 1981 through mid-1982. Often the fiscal and monetary authorities—in attempting to control inflation—may go too far or sometimes act at cross-purposes. If these policies lead to too severe an economic slump, politics forces the authorities to reflate. This has happened at least three times in the past fifteen to twenty years, and 1983–84 may see a repeat performance. Of course, each time the system becomes more fragile and overextended. If the Administration relents on its anti-inflation policies and aggressively reflates, inflation will eventually accelerate and holding liquidity will be less attractive. This is the quandary that investors face in today's volatile world. While many people use this list of financial problems as a reason to avoid equities, we think significant opportunities have been created by today's crisis environment. Investors who wait to buy stocks until the problems are solved will end up paying much higher prices.

Have Inflation Hedges Lost Their Luster?

Another reason we favor stocks is that they are likely to outperform the investment alternatives. Take real estate, perhaps the most popular inflation haven of the last decade. People wanted equity in a hard asset, so houses came to be viewed as a prime investment, and both residential and commercial real estate prices rose to unheard-of heights. Speculators competed with users to buy real estate, farms, condominiums, office buildings, apartment houses, shopping centers and houses. Even raw land was viewed as attractive because, as Mark Twain once said, "they're not making any more of it." A major inducement for a real estate investment was the ability to borrow money for twenty to thirty years at a fixed rate, pay the loan back in depreciated dollars, and profit handsomely if the real estate asset increased in value. Those who bought real estate with borrowed funds in the early 1970s or before could hardly fail to make money.

In fact, the appreciation was such that many homeowners took out second mortgages on their houses in order to realize some of the profits, using the proceeds to invest in more real estate or purchase other inflation-hedge assets. Thus, much of the mortgage financing of the late 1970s was used not for new construction, but rather to finance the inflation in existing buildings. As evidence, consider that the annual ratio of total mortgage financing to the total cost of new-home construction jumped from 90 percent in the 1960s to 145 percent in the 1975–78 period.

But it would appear that now all this has changed. Long-term, fixed-rate debt may have become a dinosaur—and, if so, its extinction is an event worth noting. New borrowers are now asked to pay interest rates well above the current inflation rate and their long free ride on fixed, low and long-term interest rates is over. Because of the enormous borrowing needs of the government and businesses, the burden of debt and increasing public awareness, savers are demanding and getting the best real rate of return ever. Financial deregulation, whereby banks and savings institutions can offer current market interest rates, is also benefiting the saver at the expense of the borrower. This has the potential of bringing to a close one of the most successful business and investment strategies in years. Fluctuating and high real-interest rates make the cost structure of operating real estate more expensive, which in turn reduces cash flow.

This new interest rate environment is forcing many real estate speculators to sell their real estate investments. In many cases, the purchasers of this real estate are the large institutions, a classic sign if there ever was one that real estate has seen its peak. Institutional investors seem invariably to buy most heavily at tops and sell most heavily at bottoms.

Other popular inflation hedges have also lost some of their allure. High interest rates during 1980–81 deflated the speculative bubble in the markets for commodity futures and collectibles. Apart from those few who got some aesthetic pleasure out of holding art, most people found that these investments provided poor returns in comparison with the high interest rates on money market instruments available in the early 1980s.

It is probable that in periods of increasing economic activity, commodity prices will rise again, but it will be a far more orderly market than was the case in the late 1970s and early 1980s. For the next few years, commodity price trends will once again be largely dictated by the real users of the commodity, not the speculative community. Gold, however, is a different case and will continue to be perceived as a psychological haven in times of political and financial stress.

Amateur speculators have found that commodity trading is not a freewheeling way to make money, but rather the riskiest of all financial speculations. As so often happens to amateurs speculating without expertise, experience or sufficient capital to weather unexpected reversals and margin calls, the public got in late and was taken advantage of by the professionals. For the many small investors who were least able to absorb a capital loss, the experience with commodities, whether in futures or the actual commodity, was emotionally exhausting and financially devastating.

The same thing happened in the art and collectibles markets, where prices were bid up to ridiculous heights. Once prices started to weaken and the fond dreams of unending appreciation died, many speculators did not know how to get rid of their esoterica. They discovered to their horror that there was often no market for the collectible except the dealer from whom they bought it. As a result, many professional dealers made fortunes buying back items at a fraction of the price they had sold them for. We know a doctor who put two thirds of his savings into rare coins in the late 1970s. In the negative economic environment of 1981, the doctor needed some cash and tried to sell the coins. To his dismay, he found that he could only sell the coins back to the dealer he had bought them from—at a 40 percent discount from his purchase price.

A similar fate overcame those who wanted to speculate in the bond market, traditionally the most conservative investment medium. However, volatility struck the bond market, too, and bond investors incurred huge losses in 1979, 1980 and early 1981 when interest rates rose to record levels. Certainly, some investors made money speculating on interest rates, if their timing was precise, but all too many were whipsawed by interest-rate volatility. No longer the conservative investment they used to be, bonds can now be considered as speculative as the stock market.

Many high- and middle-income investors sought tax shelter in the 1970s through syndicated limited partnerships. These investors put money into real estate, oil exploration or other well-known shelters, such as movies or coal. For the most part, the results of these tax shelter programs were indifferent, if not terrible, depending on the amount of cash invested, the honesty of the promoter and the fees paid to the general partner. The problem with many of these shelters was that the investor bought in at already inflated prices, and in many cases the investment did not make economic sense.

Speculative losses and shattered confidence caused much of the public to turn to money market funds or new savings accounts. These are useful vehicles for a small investor, but they are not without risk, as so many people seem to think. Since money funds don't have a capital base, any bad paper will be offset against shareholders' capital. Loan losses cannot be ruled out, especially in the area of commercial paper, where there is considerable investment by aggressive funds. While some funds claim to be "government-only," many invest in government "repos" and government agency paper, which are not as safe as a direct obligation of the U.S. government. In the case of the savings accounts, it is widely known that many savings institutions are locked into unprofitable, long-term, fixed-rate mortgages.

In a period of deteriorating financial condition of corporations and financial institutions, the quality of loans becomes an increasing concern. By putting money in a money market fund or a savings bank, an investor is actually in the lending business, hardly the safest strategy for preservation of capital.

Many have called the 1980s the decade of the entrepreneur, and indeed, there is a great underlying interest in owning or starting a business. But there are several pitfalls. The current economic environment is proving very difficult for small businesses, as high interest rates and a poor economic environment are causing more bankruptcies than at any time since the 1930s. In tough economic times, it is the strong, well-financed company that survives. Also, the inflation of recent years has made the start-up of a business an expensive proposition. Where $100,000 might have been sufficient to launch, say, a small business a decade ago, up to $1 million might be needed now. In times of tight and expensive money, it is hard to raise the money for a new business venture, no matter how attractive the concept.

Other popular money havens of the late 1970s and early 1980s are perhaps more risky than currently perceived or unattractive in comparison with common stocks. Tax-exempt securities, for example, have become increasingly popular, despite massive principal losses suffered in the 1970s. Individuals reportedly bought 74 percent of all newly issued tax-exempt bonds in 1981, compared with 19 percent in 1980.

But the underlying credit quality of many tax-exempt issuers must be questioned. A slowing in economic activity and reduced federal grants-in-aid have cut into state and local government revenues. Meanwhile, the cost of borrowing has increased for municipalities because the credit ratings of many state and local governments have deteriorated, and the traditional buyers of these issues (the commercial banks and fire and casualty insurance companies) have dramatically slowed their purchases because they don't need tax-free income or have heavy loan demand. Also the drop in the top tax bracket from 70 percent to 50 perecent put further upward pressure on municipal bond yields in 1981.

One danger in the municipal market is its growing dependency on the individual investor. Back in the 1960s and 1970s, commercial banks often bought between 60 percent and 100 percent of the net new issues. In 1981, commercial banks bought only about 15 percent. If, for some reason, the individual investor stops buying municipals, the municipal market could find itself in trouble, with the liquidity of new or old issues sharply reduced. The New York City fiscal problems in 1975 put a damper on investor interest in municipal bonds, and any municipal bankruptcy would likely have a similar effect this time around.

Bank certificates of deposit must also be evaluated in light of the increasing number of banks with major delinquent loans. The banks with an international exposure are particularly vulnerable in this regard. According to recent estimates, the nine largest U.S. banks have lent almost twice their capital and reserves to six of the largest developing countries—Brazil, Mexico, Korea, Argentina, Taiwan and the Philippines.

It is truly amazing how the debts of many foreign nations have increased in recent years, as we pointed out earlier. The Soviet bloc owes nearly $90 billion to the West, including Poland's $27 billion, Rumania's $10 billion and Yugoslavia's $10.5 billion. Mexico now has private and public debts estimated at over $80 billion, the largest of any developing country. Debt "rescheduling" among these countries is becoming commonplace. Mexico, Argentina, Brazil, Poland, Rumania, Bolivia, Costa Rica, Liberia, Madagascar, Nicaragua, Senegal, the Sudan, Turkey and Zaïre are only a few of the countries that have recently been unable to make their debt-service payments on time. And in several cases, some countries have actually declared unilateral moratoriums on debt service.

The burden of servicing all this debt is crushing many developing countries. Amex Bank recently completed a survey which indicated that debt service in 1981 for all developing countries amounted to $175 billion, or roughly half the current account balance of payments of these countries. What has happened is that many of these countries are actually borrowing money to meet interest payments. One can only ask whether these loans will ever be repaid and question the underlying financial stability of the many banks that have part of their assets tied up in such loans.

Government bonds and notes were also popular in the early 1980s. While these are safe securities in terms of principal repayment, one cannot rule out short- to intermediate-term market fluctuations in their prices. Several experts worry that federal spending is out of control and that the U.S. Treasury needs to raise enormous sums of money in coming years, possibly more than the bond market can handle. It will be hard to reduce the budget deficit, and consequently, yields (and prices) of government securities could fluctuate sharply as the political battle is fought.

It is important to recognize that an investment in the bond or money market is a bet on the direction of interest rates. While a number of traders have made fortunes doing that in recent years, we believe that predicting interest rates is one of the most difficult tasks in the investment world, particularly for the nonprofessional investor.

One cannot rule out a big and extended drop in long-term interest rates, especially if the fight against inflation is successful, as it appeared to be as this book was written. But a forty-year bear market does not end quickly, and cautious investors may want to see how the bond market performs in an economic recovery before committing funds to this market.

Foreign stocks were also popular in the 1970s. As the U.S. dollar declined against the Japanese yen, the German mark and the Swiss franc, assets denominated in these currencies rose against the dollar. So, even if the stock markets in these countries remained flat, an investment in these markets paid off for U.S. investors, who were able to hedge against the depreciation of the dollar. But, in many cases, the stock markets of certain foreign countries outperformed those in the United States, irrespective of any currency adjustment. For instance, between late 1974 and 1977, the British equity market was the top performer in the world and in 1978, the French market was number one, rising 78 percent.

Of course, if one had been smart enough to shift back and forth between various foreign stock markets at the right time, one's return could have been exceptional. If one had bought the British stock market in February 1960, switched to the U.S. market in November 1960, then to Spain in February 1962, to Canada in February 1963, to Italy in July 1965, to Australia in April 1966, to Japan in September 1968, back to Italy in February 1973, to the British market in January 1974, to Japan in January 1975, and to Australia in March 1980, one could have achieved a 4,300 percent increase in assets over the twenty-year period. By contrast, if one had bought Standard & Poor's 500 Composite in 1960 and held on, one would have only doubled one's money by 1980.

But it appears as if foreign stocks may not fare so well in the 1980s. First, the U.S. dollar showed remarkable strength in 1981 and 1982, as high U.S. interest rates increased the attractiveness of holding dollars. Second, relative political stability and more opportunity for economic growth and technological innovation have caused a lot of foreign money to come to the United States. Also, it is difficult to get accurate information about foreign companies and foreign stock markets, which makes an investment in these markets difficult for U.S. investors. The amount of information available in the U.S. markets is vastly superior to that found anywhere else in the world. Many professionals would argue that the U.S. market is complex enough without having to spend a lot of time trying to find information about various foreign markets, economies and the local outlook for corporate profits, inflation and currency value. Finally there is the ever-present risk of currency fluctuations that could severely reduce returns in U.S. dollar terms.

It is interesting to note that one expert who has spent a good portion of his professional career investing in foreign stock markets is now putting a majority of his funds in the U.S. markets. John Templeton, the manager of the Templeton World Fund and the Templeton Growth Fund, and holder of probably the best long-term record among investment advisers, considers U.S. stocks to offer good relative value. In an interview published in the New York *Times* of February 10, 1982, Templeton was quoted as saying that the U.S. stock market, as represented by the Dow Industrials, offers the best bargain in his forty-five years of managing money.

The 1980s: The Decade of Common Stocks

This brings us to an investment vehicle and a strategy that offer a good chance of preserving one's wealth: buying selected, undervalued U.S. stocks during major market declines. In a general sense, stocks combine many of the attractive features of the popular investments of the 1970s, but have few of their limitations. One reason for this is that an investment in the stock of a company that owns the means of production, natural resources, real estate or industrial and consumer products is an indirect way to invest in many of these same assets at wholesale rather than retail prices.

Of course, this argument became too popular in the rampaging inflation of 1979 and 1980, when portfolio managers, stock market investors and the public bid up energy and natural-resource stocks in a buying semipanic. A year later the rapid decline in the inflation rate caused some painful losses to many of those who had bought these stocks as they became disenchanted with the inflation-hedge credo.

The stock market also offers liquidity, which is essential during the turbulent economic times we are facing. No one can be sure that a sudden financial accident won't make liquidity important. Even Bunker Hunt had to scramble desperately to raise cash when the value of his huge silver position plummeted in early 1980.

Also, the vast amount of information on individual stocks offers a good way to get a perspective on the distortions of economic value. Before buying a stock, one can look at its ten-year history of earnings, price performance, p/e ratios, return on investment ratios, trend of dividend payment and so on. One can make comparisons between p/e's of various industries or the companies within an industry. One can see at what price a stock sold during a bear market or credit crunch and what was its lowest p/e ratio at the time. Although these historical measurements are far from foolproof, they can give you perspective and thus reduce the possibility, at least, of paying too much for a stock. Historical data on prices and on what constitutes economic value are not so easy to come by in other types of investments.

However, common sense must prevail when looking at investments from a historical perspective. Despite the fact that International Harvester was selling at historically low values in relation to its assets in early 1982, it is evident that its earnings power has been seriously impaired by intense competition, lack of responsiveness to changing markets, and declining productivity. Its very survival may even be at stake. Thus, while historical perspective may be valuable, it should not be the only benchmark for making an investment in a company's stock.

Another plus for equity investors is that the underlying assets of certain stocks have risen in value because of inflation. Higher prices for real estate, timberland, minerals, plant and equipment mean a greater value for the companies that own them. But in many cases this underlying asset value has not been reflected in stock prices, which is one reason why so many companies have been acquired in recent years.

One might ask why the increase in underlying asset value is not more fully recognized in these stocks. To begin with, the appreciation of corporate assets isn't reflected on corporate balance sheets because companies are not allowed to "write up" an increase in asset value under current accounting practices. This is another way of saying that the undervaluation of a company may not be immediately perceived.

In many cases, investors are aware of the undervaluation of a company's assets but expect no liquidation or merger and are, therefore, reluctant to bid up its price. However, over time, this attitude could change. The much publicized takeovers of such old stock market favorites as Pullman, Conoco, Marathon Oil, Santa Fe International, St. Joe Minerals, Kennecott and Cities Service indicate a continued interest in acquiring undervalued financial assets.

Stocks have some other advantages in the battle for capital preservation. Business in general is learning to live with volatility, and even such regulated industries as the railroads and utilities are getting sizable rate increases to reflect the higher cost of capital. Also, stocks offer a way of participating in the new technologies that, to a certain extent, are replacing the old, mature industries, such as autos, steels and other manufactured goods that grew up in the first half of the twentieth century. Alternatively, some previously slow-growing corporations are redeploying their resources away from stagnant businesses into high-growth areas, such as factory electronics, robots, office automation, video products and the electronic accumulation, storage and dissemination of information, so-called sunrise industries.

For instance, certain newspaper chains are expanding aggressively into the electronic delivery of information into the home, as well as electronic purchasing. Certain film companies are gearing up for the projected huge demand for filmed entertainment, which could occur if the estimate of 75 million video-cassette and video-disc recorders in the home by 1990 proves accurate. Large companies, such as Gould, General Electric and General Motors, are putting resources into the development of factory automation systems. Particularly interesting was a recent announcement by General Electric that it planned to sell its huge natural-resource subsidiary, Utah International, for $2.4 billion. John F. Welch, GE's chairman, said that his company was "determined to become firmly positioned at the leading edge of the high technology products and the high-growth services segments of industry." Those companies that aggressively move into growing businesses or successfully exploit the new technologies should be able to increase earnings and, therefore, offer a good return to their shareholders.

Another reason we favor stocks is their favorable tax treatment. Income from a bond or money market fund can be taxed at the federal rate at up to 50 percent, while the maximum tax on any capital gains for a stock held longer than a year is 20 percent. Assuming stocks are bought at the right time and price, and capital gains tax rates are possible, stocks should be able to provide a greater after-tax return than the money markets.

Finally, if the transition to disinflation is successful, investors will begin to switch their funds into financial assets, such as stocks, from tangible assets like real estate and collectibles. It is estimated that in 1975, some 70 percent of individual savings went into stocks, bonds or other financial assets, and 30 percent into tangibles. By 1979, however, 80 percent of savings were going into tangibles and only 20 percent into financial assets.

The pension provisions of the new tax law could also encourage individuals' flow of funds into the equity market. Starting in 1982, an estimated 80 million working people were able to put $2,000 a year into an individual retirement account (IRA). But even before the new tax law significantly increased the number of people eligible to join an IRA, more people were putting money into IRAs and Keoghs. For instance, in 1978, $5 billion was contributed to IRAs and Keogh Plans on behalf of 3 million tax returns. By 1979, the figure had jumped to $25 billion. Of course, 1981 figures suggest that only 6 percent of those eligible to participate in an IRA did so. But we suspect the publicity about increased eligibility for

IRAs could increase the percentage. In Canada, where tax-sheltered retirement plans have been around for a long time, public participation is estimated to run as high as 80 percent of the working population. As the number of IRAs increases, so will the amount of money directed toward equity investment.

If one assumes that eventually 40 million people contribute $2,000 yearly to an IRA and half of that goes into equities, the stock market would get an infusion of $40 billion a year. And consider also the corporate pension money that might be invested in stocks. Estimates suggest that total pension funds might increase from $700 billion at present to as much as $5 trillion by the mid-1990s. At this writing, the market value of all stocks on the New York Stock Exchange and American Stock Exchange and those traded actively over the counter was $1.3 trillion. It is not hard to see that the infusion of such vast amounts of new money could push equity prices much higher.

Even if the long-awaited, extended bull market of the 1980s does not arrive, there will still be a way to make money in stocks. For instance, during 1978–79, many market analysts concluded we were in a bear market, but, while many stocks declined, the energy and technology stocks enjoyed big bull markets. Then, after the averages topped out in late 1980 and early 1981, many believed that we were again in a major bear market, which was only partially true. Between November 1980 and the spring of 1982, most utilities, consumer and food stocks and many financial stocks had their own bull market, even while the rest of the market declined sharply.

Also, as we will discuss in a later chapter, one time-proven strategy is to wait for a major crash in the stock market and then hold on for the inevitable recovery. In bear markets, stocks invariably fall to an excessively low level during the final capitulation by investors. Buying stocks at such a time can prove profitable, even if the cyclical recovery proves weak by historical standards.

While the equity markets have many appealing characteristics, we should also emphasize that stocks can be fraught with danger. Indeed, the almost chronic and compulsive volatility of the stock market has been the bane of many small investors. The markets of the 1970s and early 1980s often flustered and frustrated many of the most adept professionals in the game. Despite the fact that we believe stocks represent a very undervalued investment arena, we want to remind you that investors can get badly hurt in one of the perverse downdrafts that periodically affect any market. Markets are a composite of investor expectations about the future, and political or economic events can drastically alter those expectations, as occurred in 1969–70, 1973–74, 1977–78 and 1981–82. Let us reiterate: the aim of the book is not just to describe techniques for winning in the stock market, but also to describe ways to mitigate losses when the market drops suddenly and unexpectedly.

In the next chapter, we will present what we believe to be a practical approach to buying value in the stock market. We believe this strategy will limit some of the risks of stocks and result in a more than satisfactory rate of return.

Chapter 3

A Checklist of Analytical Tools

DESPITE THE LONG-TERM ATTRACTIONS discussed in the previous chapter, most individual investors are still negative on the stock market. Many people think getting involved in the stock market is too complicated, and takes too much time. Many of these same people feel the small investor can't make money in the market because he doesn't have access to the "inside information" of the big institutions. Or they avoid stocks because they think the market is a huge gambling casino, an irrational arena manipulated by speculators. Or they once paid too much for a stock and lost money when its price dropped and have shunned the market since.

While there are no magic formulas for selecting value in the stock market, there is a way to reduce and offset the inherent risks involved. We attempt to do this by using a series of empirical rules of thumb to evaluate whether an investment candidate is undervalued. Our objective is to establish a target price for companies that interest us, without having to wade through an enormous amount of statistical material, which is what most security analysts do by profession. We take no issue with the profession of security analysis, but this book does not pretend to be a textbook on that discipline. We are simply trying to teach you how to look for a cheap stock with low risk, and here we want to provide you with some of the quantitative parameters that we think represent value and the mechanical applications that are necessary to identify it.

The rank-and-file investor, occupied by his own profession or business, probably does not have the time or knowledge, and most definitely not the inclination, to use his spare time to absorb the enormous accumulation of data spewed out by brokerage houses, statistical services, advisory services and the companies themselves. Many investors have opted to avoid that responsibility and have placed their reliance on the judgment of mutual fund managers, brokers, bank trust departments and investment advisers.

Some people even go so far as to follow blindly the advice of financial gurus. In early 1981, after Joe Granville issued his famous warning to sell everything, his followers responded with an avalanche of sell orders that carried volume on the New York Stock Exchange to an all-time record at that time. But, at first, the market confounded Granville's forecast, and the Dow rallied to a new high in the spring of 1981, before topping out in June. By October, with the Dow down nearly 200 points, Granville was temporarily vindicated, but the long waiting process was probably difficult to endure for his many followers. The year 1982 proved even more traumatic for Granville's followers. He maintained a staunchly bearish position (as well as short sale recommendations) during the greatest market advance in some fifty years, arguing all the way up that it was nothing but a sucker's rally.

It is common knowledge that the investment fraternity, with some notable exceptions, has been notoriously unsuccessful at making money. Often, the so-called market professionals follow the latest investment fad or so-called concepts with herdlike precision. The community of investment managers is really a very small network, easily infected by moods, rumors and, in many cases, false and superficial prophecies.

Many investment management companies use sophisticated computer models to predict stock price movement or corporate sales and earnings, apparently believing that this is a highly scientific and precise endeavor. In our opinion, there is nothing precise at all about it, because companies are run by individuals and thus are subject to the decisions of management, which may change quickly. For example, the decision to sell a division or to buy another company can alter the very nature of a company. Since investment managers do not have inside information on a company's plans, their earnings forecasts are highly vulnerable to error.

Another weakness of many investment managers is their emphasis on quarterly performance, which is exacerbated by the competition for investor funds and often blurs the objective judgment that they are supposed to exercise. The quarterly performance dead-lines force many professionals to take a short-sighted view of investments in the hope of achieving a quick and impressive gain. It is no wonder that the casual investor loses confidence in the market when he sees the huge price gyrations of stocks that advance or retreat as the institutions and funds accumulate positions and then bail out.

We believe history is an important guide to the future. This is not to say that we ignore an earnings forecast or the business prospects of a particular industry or company. Quite the contrary, it is important to respect the consensus about a particular stock, even though such a view may be in gross error. The institutions have too much power over the market to be ignored. But in the long run, because of their very size, the institutions are often hurt when they try to sell a bad investment.

Since time and a disinclination to do a thorough study are constraints on the layman, we intend to provide a checklist—in effect, a short guide—to evaluating stocks. If we can ascertain that a stock is a good value, we don't have to examine every piece of data or detail about it.

The mechanical techniques that we present in this checklist are obviously simplified, and we want to stress that they are not a sure-fire formula for investment success. The main purpose of the list is to provide a quick and easy process of elimination for someone who doesn't have a great deal of sophisticated accounting or financial knowledge. The checklist is predicated on the central philosophy, which we have already discussed, of buying cheap so that there is a limited risk in case things go badly, and a very good opportunity in case they go well, regardless of the vagaries of the market or the turn of economic or political events.

You can find the information you'll need in order to use the checklist from Standard & Poor's *Stock Guide, Stock Reports* or *Earnings Forecaster*, or the *Value Line Investment Survey*. (We discuss all these services, how much they cost, and how to get them in the next chapter.) These services provide easy-to-understand and reasonably accurate information on the financial history of most companies. Since it takes time to order and receive a company's annual report, we suggest that an active investor use these informational services instead.

The Checklist

1. Is there more than a 4½–5 percent return on sales per year in the case of manufacturing and service companies?

2. Is the price/earnings ratio eight times or less? In a strong stock market, the p/e can safely be as high as ten.

3. Is there a stable or increasing earnings trend over the last five years? Pay particularly close attention to the last two years. Earnings should have grown by at least 50 percent in the past five years and not declined more than twice, and not by more than 20 percent in the last ten years.

Also check that the earnings results were not heavily impacted by major reductions in the company's tax rate, which might have artificially boosted earnings. In light of continually changing tax reforms, it is now more important than ever to study a company's tax rate closely.

4. Is the stock selling at or under book value? Note that book value should be reduced to reflect any intangible assets. Also, factor in any pension liabilities or hidden inventory profits.

Discount to book value should also be evaluated on a historical basis. In fact, one way to pick a potential target price for buying a stock is to figure out at what price the stock would sell if it traded at the largest discount from book for the past ten years.

5. What is the company's net working capital per share, and how near is this figure to the current price of the stock?

6. Is shareholders' equity for the past five years at least 13 percent?

7. Is the return on assets 10 percent or more? If not, the company's assets are not being used productively.

8. Is the ratio of debt to total capitalization under 30 percent? In addition, no more than half of long-term debt should be tied to the prime rate and no more than half of the long-term debt should come due within three years, especially if the interest rate on such debt is low. This is important, since interest rates are so volatile today.

9. Is the current ratio more than 2 to 1, except in the case of a quick-turnover, high-volume business? This is a check of the company's short-term liquidity.

10. Is the stock price less than four times cash flow, if it can

be calculated reliably? Does the company have sufficient cash flow to pay dividends and fund capital expenditures?

11. How much stock is held by management or insiders? It is always better to have management's interests similar to those of the shareholders.

12. Check for hidden assets, such as land, mineral resources, oil, timber or stock in other companies, that may be carried at low values. These may not be reflected in the stock price and, if liquidated or sold, could cause a sharp run-up in the price of the stock.

13. Consider the company's business and its prospects. Is this an attractive industry and has it a future?

Before we talk about the application of this checklist and the rationale behind it, we would like to emphasize that not all items on the list have to be in evidence to make a stock attractive. If this were the case, the selection process would be purely mechanical, which it is not. Such subjective factors as the company and industry outlook must also be considered carefully.

For example, many cyclical companies experienced earnings declines of more than 20 percent in the severe recession of 1981–82. But this period was so unprecedented that the rule of rising or stable earnings could be relaxed for companies that had earnings troubles during those years.

Sometimes, one feature of a company is so attractive that it overrides the absence of other value measures. For example, the stock may sell at such a large discount from book value that one can overlook mediocre earnings or low return on shareholders' equity. Or, a particularly low price/earnings ratio and a climbing growth rate might carry a greater weight than buying the stock at or below book value. There is a certain empirical balancing process that must figure into any investment decision, most of which must be learned from experience. We almost never find a stock that passes all our tests—there are no "tens" in the stock market.

The 5 Percent Nonsolution

As a starting point for our screening process, we use an arbitrary 5 percent return on sales. Sometimes we drop this figure to 4½ percent if the company is attractive in other ways. We chose this number for practical reasons. Every day *The Wall Street Journal* or the New York *Times* publishes the quarterly and year-to-date earnings in comparison with the year-ago period of companies that released their earnings the previous day. We scrutinize these earnings as a first step in adding names to the universe of companies we follow.

If we notice that a company's net income divided by its sales has exceeded 4½–5 percent for each of the past two years, we review the company and submit it to further tests. Note that even if the 4½–5 percent return began in the present year, we would still take a close look at the company because the improved performance might indicate an earnings turnaround.

If a manufacturing company can generate close to 5 percent after-tax margins, it is probably beating inflation. For example, if a company produces a product in 90 days and collects cash for the sale in, say, 30 days, it has turned over its product in 120 days, or roughly three times a year. If the company's margin is 5 percent, it is netting that amount on a four-month production cycle.

A yearly inflation rate even as high as 12 percent, as occurred in 1980, means a four months' rate of 3 percent, considerably less than the company's after-tax margins. Naturally, if the company's production or receivable collection time lengthens, the margins would be lowered.

We should emphasize that many service-oriented and highly technical firms have much higher margins. In addition, some natural-resource businesses, such as petroleum or metal, might have soaring margins in a given year because of a big jump in their product price, thanks to a temporary scarcity or some political event. However, the same business could be saddled with negative profit margins in periods of glut and/or economic contraction. Petroleum companies are the obvious recent example.

Distributors and retailers may have a return on sales of only 1–2 percent, but that's not as bad as it seems. The turnover in these businesses is so great that 1–2 percent a year amounts to a satisfactory return. Thus, these companies should not be eliminated, since they may still provide a good return on equity and assets.

What the 5 percent rule attempts to do is single out those companies that appear on the surface to be operating efficiently on a regular basis. It is nothing more than a quick way to come up with investment ideas.

The Price/Earnings Ratio—Meaningful or Mythical?

One of the most important criteria on our checklist is that a stock should sell at no more than eight times earnings, except in boom times, when you might go to ten times. There are many schools of thought about trading stocks, but central to most theories is the concept of price/earnings ratio.

Mechanically, the p/e ratio is exactly what it sounds like—the price per share divided by earnings. But there's more to it than that. We look at the p/e ratio as the "pay-back period"—that is, the number of years required for the company's profits to equal the price of the stock, assuming that earnings remain constant through-out the period. Thus, if an investor bought a stock for $5 a share, and the company earned $1 a share for each of the next five years, the investor would theoretically get his money back in five years, if the earnings were all distributed as dividends. Naturally, the financial world does not exist in a vacuum; earnings do fluctuate, and so do stock prices.

Price/earnings ratios can also be useful in another way. They are a simple measure of Wall Street's expectations about a specific industry or stock. If the investment community believes the earnings of a particular company will grow, the price of the stock rises for two reasons: earnings will go up and the value investors put on these earnings will go up too. Conversely, the p/e will move down if earnings are expected to disappoint investors. This is why p/e multiple expansion or contraction is such an important focus on Wall Street.

For example, when Jimmy Carter was elected President, the pollution control companies spurted dramatically in price and p/e's, since investors felt that his Administration would back stricter air and water standards and thus usher in a spending boom on pollution control equipment. Four years later, in the expectation of a Reagan victory and an increase in defense spending, the defense stocks jumped. In a sense, the p/e ratio is a reflection of the business and earnings prospects for an individual company or industry, especially as compared with other industries and companies. The p/e ratio is also a barometer of major economic, political or social change, which could dramatically affect an industry, a company or the stock market as a whole, and make irrelevant the p/e experience of the recent past. In 1962, for example, the Dow sold at an average p/e of 22, and in 1974 at a p/e of 6.

We use eight times earnings as our benchmark because over the past five years that figure has generally represented the average p/e of all companies on the New York Stock Exchange. But, more important, a p/e of 8 may represent the balance between historical fact and future expectations. A p/e ratio of 8 or lower reflects the past of the company, not the promise of the future. In other words, the multiple is based on such critical elements as stability and growth of sales and earnings, the underlying asset value, credit rating and financial solvency. Our main point here is that we limit our risks by relying on historical facts, not expectations.

Buying a stock solely on the criterion of p/e, however, can be misleading for the amateur investor. That is why other items in the checklist also have to be included in any investment decision.

For example, in 1982 General Motors sold at about forty times expected earnings of $1.20 a share. Based on experience, this high p/e was apparently an aberration. General Motors is not a high multiple stock, and clearly, the price was propped up by other considerations, such as discount from book value, future recovery prospects, and so forth.

Often very low p/e's reflect poor earnings prospects that have already been discounted. For instance, Boeing made over $4 a share in 1981 and was selling between 17 and 20 in early 1982, or about four to five times 1981 earnings. But 1982 earnings were expected to be in a range of $2–$3 a share, representing a p/e of about 8, or twice the p/e on 1981's actual earnings.

The low p/e stocks obviously do not radiate glamour. For this reason, many may criticize our 8 p/e rule, arguing that a great many high-growth companies will always sell above eight times earnings. We reiterate, however, that we have made a conscious decision to avoid the highfliers in the hope that today's wallflowers may become next year's glamour stocks. Many historical studies, such as those put forth by David Dreman in *Contrarian Investment Strategy*, support our view that low p/e stocks provide much larger returns over time than the glamour stocks trading on high aspirations. The higher they fly, the farther they can fall. But if you start from a less stratospheric platform, the fall won't be as painful, nor will it prove fatal.

Price Fuel—the Concept of Earnings Growth

So far, we have chosen stocks with a 5 percent return on sales and a p/e of less than 8. Now, it is time to take a look at the most important motivator of stock prices: earnings growth. As a general rule, we want earnings to have risen steadily, and to be now 50 percent higher than they were five years ago. However, we will permit an earnings decline in two of the past ten years, so long as the drop didn't exceed 20 percent. We recognize that it is hard for a cyclical company to report earnings increases every year, especially in these unsettled times.

One of the important ways to determine trend is to consider how you expect the company's business to fare given the business environment of the times. If the company looks like it might have rough sledding in a recession, tread carefully. For example, the earnings trend of a machine tool manufacturer might intrigue you, but you must remember that the stock prices of machine tool suppliers could decline quickly if unfavorable earnings reports appear likely as capital goods orders dry up.

We once made a fundamental error in judgment about the business prospects of a company by looking over the valley. In late 1981, we bought Boeing at about 28, down from its 1981 high of 44. Thinking that air travel and defense spending would cushion the company's business prospects somewhat despite the recession, we failed to foresee both the air traffic controllers' strike of 1981, which affected the airlines' earnings, and a much longer and deeper recession than forecast, which caused cash-strained airlines to cut back orders for a new generation of planes. While we expected Boeing to have an earnings decline for 1982, we did not think it would be a significant reversal. At 28, we felt, the stock had already reflected and discounted the earnings drop, and in fact, we made the investment on that basis. When the stock dropped below 20, it became clear that we had made the wrong decision.

After evaluating business prospects, we take a quick look at Standard & Poor's *Earnings Forecaster*, which projects earnings, to see whether next year's earnings are expected to sustain the recent pattern. But earnings forecasts are subject to error, and we take what we see with a grain of salt. What we are looking for is an indication of how Wall Street views the earnings outlook.

Sometimes Wall Street sours on a stock because the company had a surprising earnings decline. Such a downturn does not necessarily mean that the positive earnings trend has ended or been reversed. It may be attributable only to a temporary reversal in the company's business. Many opportunities for superior percentage profit gains are lost because too much attention is paid to quarterly earnings comparisons.

Both research analysts and accountants are wary about earning's reports for any given quarter. Such adjustments to earnings as a sale or write-down of assets, inventory profits or losses, tax deferrals and foreign currency gains or losses can serve to mask a company's true operating results. In short, quarterly reports can be deceiving because companies use accounting gimmicks to spice up earnings.

For example, a company can raise the interest rate assumptions for the assets in its pension plan or reduce contributions, thereby showing improved earnings. Or earnings gains can come from the sale of investment tax credits. Or a corporation's minority holdings in another company can be used under equity accounting to report its share of the company's earnings. (In reality, the corporation only receives a proportionate share of dividends, if any, and thus, such accounting practices can artificially boost reported earnings.)

Of course, we're not suggesting that you should disregard a drop in earnings. You should be sure that it's not signaling a long-term deterioration of the company. But don't overreact, either. The company may very well still be a growth company, and rebounding earnings may offer a substantial profit to those who bought the stock when it was depressed because of the earnings disappointment. Thus, the basis of valuing a stock should not be limited to quarterly earnings results. The underlying assets and long-term earnings performance should also be important considerations.

To evaluate earnings correctly, make sure you study the company's tax rate. On the surface, the company may appear to have an uptrend in earnings, but upon further examination of the S&P stock reports, which show tax rates, you may discover that much of the company's earnings progress has actually come from lower tax rates.

Thanks to the Reagan tax reform of 1981, changes in the tax rate have become even more pronounced because companies have used leasing transactions, as well as accelerated depreciation, to reduce tax burdens and increase earnings and cash flow. Rather than getting into the many ways companies can manipulate their taxes to enhance earnings, suffice it to say that if the tax rate declines substantially—a year-to-year decline of 15 to 25 percent, let us say—the company's earnings power may be suspect. In that case, the company's earnings can be more clearly judged by looking at historical *pre-tax* earnings, usually found in the annual report. If unavailable in the annual, this comparison can be found in the Standard & Poor's corporate reports.

The real test of earnings is trend. If the trend has been erratic or has a definite downward bias, we would probably take no further interest in the company, unless the price of the stock is at a historical low. Of course, if the company is in an industry that has received a lot of negative publicity, don't go against the general perception. As a case in point, it would have been dangerous to buy the metals companies in late 1981, because of the enormous negative news about them. As it turned out, the loss of orders from the auto, building and capital goods sectors caused large losses in the industry as inventories built up and production had to be curtailed. In other words, things can get far worse than anyone ever thought at the time. However, if the earnings trend is steady or upward, and the stock is selling at the low end of its p/e range, and at a discount to book value, we would have a reasonable basis for assuming that the stock may be underpriced.

To sum up: We believe it is wrong to concentrate only on companies that are considered sure to grow, or to reject groups of stocks or industries because their business prospects are not imminently favorable. Institutional money managers fared poorly in the early 1970s because they concentrated on growth stocks, the so-called nifty fifty, which dropped markedly in the 1973–74 bear market. Further, we do not believe that you should avoid a company because its earnings are temporarily in the doldrums. Some companies that have shown themselves to be profitable over a long period of time will occasionally have a bad year. History suggests that so long as the company does not have irreparable problems, it can make a good investment.

Going by Book Value

Now we turn to the valuation of the company's asset structure to determine whether the stock price is undervalued relative to its assets. Our focus is book value, which can be thought of as the price the company would receive if it were liquidated tomorrow. In simple terms, what would be left for the shareholders after all liabilities, debts and obligations were paid off? Basic accounting tells us to derive book value per share by subtracting the liabilities from the assets and then dividing by the number of shares outstanding.

Most statistical services carry this number in their publications, and it is often provided in the company's annual report. But calculating a real book value, as we suggested earlier, is a little more complicated, since assets are usually carried at historical cost, which may be way out of line with the current value. For example, forest products companies might own thousands of acres of land that are carried on their books at a price prevailing in the early part of the century. Obviously, this land and the assets on and in it are now worth many more millions. Conversely, inventory may consist of products or materials that are obsolete and overvalued. Or inventory may be undervalued, if it consists of raw materials that have risen in price. Fixed assets, such as machinery or plant, may not be worth their fully depreciated value. The equipment may be technologically obsolete, and the plant may be located in an area that was once appealing but is now deteriorating and experiencing labor shortages or does not have easy access any more to a modern transportation infrastructure to get its goods to the markets cheaply.

Or perhaps the company's assets consist of brains (people), know-how, patents and the like, rather than bricks, mortar and other tangibles. It is extremely difficult to evaluate accurately what such intangible but very real assets are worth. Take the case of Tandy Corporation, the largest electronics and video retailer, which at the end of 1981 had a book value of about $6 a share and sold around $30 a share. At the other extreme was General Motors, which at the end of 1981 had a book value of $60, but sold at a price of $35. Obviously, investors were not using book value as a major factor in judging the merits of these two stocks.

Some analysts contend that book value is relatively meaningless in an inflationary economy since the cost of replacing existing assets is so high that, in some cases, it would bankrupt the company to do so. In fact, many companies include a note in their annual report outlining the effect of replacement cost on the company's balance sheet. These examples underscore how difficult it is to determine the real value of corporate assets, and therefore, how treacherous a number the stated book value really is.

Despite its limitations, a book value is a starting point and provides a quick, though imprecise, check into the intrinsic value of the company. Our goal is to buy a company selling at book value or less. Based on historical experience, we have found this level to represent value.

In fact, since 1978 it was almost axiomatic that a company selling under book value was a likely takeover candidate. The acquirer saw the opportunity of purchasing assets at a price cheaper than it would take to build them from scratch. The takeover made even more sense if the two businesses had a logical fit. (A classic example of this was Du Pont's purchase of Conoco. Du Pont was interested in Conoco because it saw the opportunity to integrate backwards and thus gain the petroleum feedstock necessary to fuel its chemical operations.)

When we decide to undertake a more careful examination of a company's assets, we use a very conservative approach. We start by subtracting from total assets any "intangibles," such as good will or trademarks. These may be properly valued, but our goal is to establish a highly conservative value for the company, and we don't want to include anything to which we can't ascribe a "hard" value.

Next, we look at the footnotes to the financial statements to determine the extent of pension liabilities. Where pension fund obligations exceed pension fund assets, we add any excess to the company's total liabilities.

We then explore the footnotes discussing the company's inventory. Undervaluation occurs if inventories are recorded on a last in, last out basis—in other words, the inventory is carried for accounting purposes at present cost, but may actually have been purchased some time ago at lower prices. The sale of this inventory would bring the company an immediate gain.

Net Working Capital per Share

By deducting the depreciated value of the plant and equipment from this reconstructed book value, we can go a step further to quantify asset value. By doing this, which arbitrarily ascribes a zero value to the company's plant and equipment, one can come up with a real fire-sale price. What is left is what we call net current working capital. By dividing this figure by the number of shares outstanding, we arrive at a figure for net current working capital per share, which can then be compared to the current stock price.

Believe it or not, there are many companies that currently sell, or have sold, at or below net current working capital per share. One might ask how this is possible. The company may have been ignored or it may have a very negative image. As a case in point, many textile and apparel companies recently sold below net current working capital per share. The industry's image was one of low productivity, tough competition from abroad, labor problems and antiquated methods of production. But in reality, many of these companies modernized their plants during the 1970s and solved or ameliorated their labor conflicts, so that by 1980 they had actually become efficient competitors. When the Wall Street community realized this, the group jumped because the stocks' discount from book value, and in some cases from net current working capital, was large.

Take the case of Cluett, Peabody, a major manufacturer of men's and women's apparel, including such well-known brands as Arrow shirts, Duofold underwear and Gold Toe socks. It also has a patent on the Sanforizing process. Cluett, Peabody's stock sold as low as 7¼ in 1980, when its net current working capital, according to our calculations, stood at $13½ and book value at $20½. As in many companies in its field, growth had been lackluster over the late 1970s, and the company's stock languished because of a poor image. But then earnings began to improve, rising from $1.78 in 1979 to $2.00 in 1980 and $2.36 in 1981. Short-term debt was cut back, and sportswear and classic shirts again became a fast-growing segment of the fashion business. By the spring of 1982, despite the recession, the stock rose to 17, as the discount from net current working capital appeared excessive in light of the company's earnings record and future prospects.

Return on Shareholders' Equity

Return on shareholders' equity is also an important determinant of value. Our rule is that return on equity over the previous five years must be at least 13 percent and preferably over 15 percent. An investment in a company with this rate of return provides a 15 percent return, whether it's paid out in dividends or reinvested in the business in order to maintain or enhance future growth.

Return on equity also provides an excellent way to compare the performance between companies in the same industry or between various industries. This is especially true in the case of companies such as retailers or distributors, which are high-volume, low-margin businesses, where a return on sales criterion is not so important.

The shareholders' return can give a useful insight into the quality of management, as well as its sensitivity to shareholders. A dismal return on equity would indicate a stodgy and uninspired management whose stewardship is possibly detrimental to the company. Perhaps management refuses to sell an unprofitable division that is draining the lifeblood out of the rest of the company. Or perhaps management has utilized too much debt trying to increase volume with unnecessary product lines or expanding into unprofitable geographic locations. Perhaps, also, the benefits of additional sales volume are being used to finance high interest costs, with lower profit margins undermining the earnings that flow down to the shareholders. While high but unnecessary debt may make money for the bankers and the rising volume may justify lofty salaries and perks for management, return on equity is the true measure of what the company is doing for its shareholders. There are also all sorts of games that management can play with selling and general and administrative expenses. One of the most obvious tactics employed in a corporate turnaround is a cost-cutting crusade. All sorts of marginal expenses and bloated corporate overhead can be hidden in the catchall of selling and administrative costs, and often a reduction of this category can be the first and most productive remedial step to improve return on equity.

A poor return on equity may indicate that the company is a poor investment since management cannot or will not take the necessary steps to revitalize it. This is especially true if the company compares unfavorably with others in its industry.

But again, do not rely solely on return on equity as a performance criterion. A 20 percent return on equity is considered excellent, and 30 percent remarkable, and there are companies that realize such levels. But the market value may be much greater than the equity on which such a percentage is calculated, and therefore the investor may not be getting a bargain. Moreover, the equity base may be small in relation to debt if the company has taken on large borrowings. Thus, return on equity can be a suspect number, especially if a slump occurs and high interest rates squeeze profit margins. This happened to many companies in the 1979–82 period.

Return on Assets

Just as important as return on equity is return on total assets. Our target here is at least a 10 percent return for the last five-year period. This ratio offers insight into how well the company is utilizing its assets—in other words, what kind of earnings are those assets generating? In a sense, return on assets gets at the core of the problem of undervaluation in the stock market. If a company has assets that it isn't using, and which aren't generating a return, why should the stock market value those assets in putting a price on the company? Like return on equity, return on assets can be used to compare the performance of various industries and companies.

As interest rates skyrocketed in the late 1970s and early 1980s, more and more managements started taking a hard look at what it cost to carry an asset or division that was not generating a positive cash flow and thus was burdening the company with even higher and more expensive interest costs. No longer was a business unit or asset safe from corporate scrutiny that could not justify itself by a return commensurate with corporate goals. Business planning and adherence to tough financial plans became paramount for all types and sizes of companies, which could no longer remain passive in the face of prime rates that could whipsaw their earnings. It is our belief that the increased vigilance on return on assets has largely been responsible for the unprecedented upswing in corporate restructurings and in the rash of corporate mergers and divestitures that began in 1978. In summary, an improving return on assets can often be a harbinger of a well-run company that will eventually be rewarded by the market.

Debt-to-Equity Ratios

The next area we focus on is the company's debt. Unfortunately, the complete necessary information cannot be found in statistical tables, and you will have to get hold of the company's annual report to calculate the figure. Generally speaking, a manufacturing company will have to take on debt to fund its capital expenditures and/or research and development and to buy new equipment. In most of the postwar period, the ability of a company to use debt to finance those cash outlays was considered good management, so long as the company could produce sufficient earnings to service the additional debt and generate a suitable rate of return for the shareholders.

Today, however, interest rates can fluctuate by as much as 6 to 8 percentage points in a year. Since many companies borrow money at fluctuating interest rates, their ability to borrow profitably is not nearly as certain as when interest rates moved 2 to 4 percentage points in a year.

In the recent era, which has seen the prime rate stay at 20 percent for extended periods of time, and where the cost of long-term borrowing can rise above 15 percent, as we saw in 1980–81, a company needs large profit margins to borrow. Accordingly, it is incumbent on investors to examine not only the ratio of debt to total capital, but also the interest rates and maturity schedule of existing debt. In light of the high cost of borrowing, we do not like a manufacturing or service company to have more than 30 percent long-term debt as a percentage of total capitalization.

In an industry that borrows heavily, such as airlines, utilities or automotive manufacturers, where a 40–50 percent ratio is common, we consider it a plus if the company has a lower debt ratio than its competitors.

A large debt at interest rates of, say, 8 percent or lower that is not scheduled to be paid off for five to ten years obviously helps the company greatly. On the other hand, if much of the debt will mature in the next few years, it may have to be refinanced at higher rates—which could sap the company's earnings growth. A red flag is also raised, in our opinion, if more than 15 percent of a company's capitalization consists of debt with high interest rates.

Current Ratio

Another classic measure of balance sheet health is the current ratio, or the total of current assets (cash, receivables, inventory, etc.) divided by current liabilities (consisting mainly of accounts payable and short-term debt). This ratio measures the short-term liquidity of the company.

The normal standard is for current assets to be two times current liabilities. (Companies with a very high asset turnover may have a lower ratio, since most of their inventories and receivables are financed.)

The logic behind looking at the current ratio is that it's important to preserve liquidity in times when interest costs are so high. In addition, those companies that need less short-term debt to finance their products and services will also have better profit margins than their competitors who rely more extensively on short-term debt.

It's important to realize that the current ratio can sometimes be misleading. Perhaps a company is using short-term financing to build up inventory in the face of what turns out to be a weakening economy. The high carrying cost and a poor business outlook could force the company to cut back on the inventories and take a loss. For this reason, one should make sure that a company's inventories have not ballooned to levels out of whack on a historical basis. Typically, the best way to satisfy oneself on this point is to see whether the company's inventory is turning over at a rate consistent with the past.

A company's ability to stay afloat can often depend on how rapidly inventory can be converted into cash. In an environment where business cycles appear to be getting more frequent, how nimble a company is in managing its inventory not only measures a prescient management and good financial controls and planning, but also shows an awareness of the need to conserve cash and limit short-term debt. Obviously, too much short-term debt can hurt earnings in a business contraction.

Inventory turnover is calculated by taking the cost of goods sold and dividing it by the average inventory (beginning inventory plus ending inventory, divided by two) for the period under consideration, whether quarterly or yearly. This can be compared to previous years or periods, especially contraction periods. If there is a decreasing turnover, this may mean that the company may have to take on short-term debt, and the interest on that debt could squeeze earnings. It is our belief that, to a large degree, debt management and cash flow are influenced by inventory control. Thus, inventory turn should be closely scrutinized in stormy economic periods.

Cash Flow per Share

Another factor that we have lately begun to pay more attention to is free cash flow per share. As conservative investors, we need to know whether the company has sufficient resources and cash from operations to pay its dividends (if any), to finance its ongoing capital expenditure plans and working capital needs, and to meet debt repayment obligations—without having to incur additional, expensive debt, which could squeeze earnings.

Free cash flow per share is a difficult figure to get a handle on because management's policies and goals, such as dividend financing and capital expenditure plans, frequently change within the course of a year. Thus, we believe the only way to try and quantify free cash flow per share is to incorporate the trends of cash flow and disbursement over the past three years.

We start by taking the average capital expenditures for the last three years and then we add that amount to the total expected dividend payments for the next twelve months and the amount of debt maturing within a year. If the projected level of earnings plus the average of depreciation for the past three years covers these cash outflows, then we assume the company may be able to fund its cash requirements without recourse to debt.

For example, let's take the case of a company that has capital expenditures of $30, $40 and $50 million for the past three years. Unless in its annual or quarterly reports management revealed other capital expenditure plans, we would use the average of the three years—$40 million. We then calculate the total dividend expense by taking the stated dividend and multiplying it by the number of shares outstanding. In this case, say, $20 million. We learn that debt maturing in a year is $40 million, which, added to $40 million of capital expenditures and $20 million of dividends, totals $100 million of estimated cash outflow for the coming year.

We then look for the most conservative earnings forecast around, which, let's assume, is $70 million. We derive this by multiplying the number of shares outstanding by the lowest forecast of earnings per share. Then we add the average depreciation for the past three years, which, let's say, averages out to $30 million. Thus, we can assume that the cash inflow for the company over the next twelve months will be approximately $100 million, which matches our estimate of cash outflow. This reassures us that the company will not find itself in a negative cash flow situation.

All the information needed to make these calculations can be obtained from the annual report, which usually has a ten-year history of every major financial statistic. However, certain stock market services, such as Value Line, provide a projection of next year's cash flow per share, as well as the actual figures for the past.

However, in today's economic environment, it is important to differentiate between free cash flow, which we calculated above, and the more imprecise calculation used by these stock market services, which usually derive regular cash flow by adding back to earnings noncash charges such as depreciation and deferred taxes. "Free cash flow" to us means the remaining cash left over after payments for dividends and capital expenditures, if there is any, on the theory that the company is adding to a healthy cash hoard while sustaining chosen "obligations" to shareholders and to internal growth. Regular cash flow is basically the cash the company took in before paying these "obligations," which of course can be lowered or suspended by corporate board action, although such actions would hurt the company's credibility and future. Alternatively, the company can add debt if regular cash flow is insufficient to meet dividends and capital expenditures.

For purposes of quick calculation, we use regular cash flow as a criterion for our process of elimination. If the share price is less than four times regular cash flow, we have generally found the stock to be undervalued, but if you want to be extra sure of undervaluation, use free cash flow. We repeat that you can use our criterion of less than four times regular cash flow or even free cash flow and its calculation as a guide but recognize that it could range from being inaccurate to wildly wrong, depending on what management and the boards of directors might decide to do in the course of a year.

Before passing on to the next item on the checklist, we would like to make a comment about one major use of cash flow—dividends. Generally speaking, the amount of a dividend depends on the earnings success of the firm. But there are some important exceptions here. Dividend payments are a management decision, and some executives of very successful companies do not believe in them. For instance, Henry Singleton, chief executive officer of Teledyne, has never declared a dividend, believing that money reinvested in the business would reap bigger profits in the long run in the form of price appreciation for the shareholders.

Conversely, some companies pay very high yields to attract investors. The regulated industries, such as utilities, which have tremendous capital needs but are regulated by local authorities, are prime examples. Since their prospects for growth are somewhat restricted by regulatory fiat, investors have been drawn to them as dividend or "yield" stocks. Obviously, in a period of rising interest rates, their attraction is reduced, and vice versa.

The important thing to remember about dividends is that a record of gradual increases implies management's concern for shareholders. If a company does pay a dividend, we want to make sure the dividend has been increased consistently over the years.

Management's Stake in the Company

Another key point is whether management has a financial stake in the company. All too often in these days of absentee ownership and professional management, top executives have no equity participation in the company. They often get huge salaries, have enormous fringe benefits, but own little, if any, stock in the enterprise managed. Alternatively, the managers of many small companies are paid low salaries, but their entire net worth is invested in their company. If management owns as much as 20 percent of the company, it will have considerable incentive to see that the company does well, which is important to shareholders looking for security in unsettled times.

There are some owner/managers, however, who regard their company as a private fiefdom, especially if they own 40 percent or more of the stock. Often, dividend payments and the reporting of real earnings might be manipulated to the owner's tax advantage and to the detriment of the public shareholder. Perhaps for personal tax reasons, the owner/manager does not want to receive a dividend, preferring to build up long-term capital gains in his estate. In fact, he may even want an excuse to lower the company's dividends for his own tax purposes and so will find ways, usually by playing inventory games, to report a "bad" year. The point here is that ownership by management is no guarantee that investing in a company is a totally safe proposition. It can cut both ways, but in general, owner/managers usually do look after the store, since the bulk of their own fortune is tied to the company's future.

Some management-ownership information can be found in Standard & Poor's sheets or the Value Line service, but for a true picture, get the proxy material the company publishes yearly. This not only depicts what management and/or directors own but also lists any holders of more than 5 percent of the company's stock, although it doesn't show the cost of the holding. For that you have to get your hands on the 13D filing with the SEC, which must be filed whenever an individual or company acquires more than 5 percent of a public company, but more about that later.

Hidden Assets

Often a company may have a hidden asset, which increases its appeal. Generally speaking, there are two major categories of hidden assets: natural resources, such as oil, minerals, timberland, etc., and real property, consisting of buildings or real estate, carried at low prices. Study the footnotes to the annual report to determine if any major assets were acquired many years ago and have thus appreciated greatly in value. Also, keep an eye out for the sale of assets by corporations, which can help one to determine how such assets are currently being valued. By the same token, if a particular commodity, such as oil or copper, has had an enormous increase in price, the companies that own large reserves will of course become more valuable.

One place to look for hidden assets is the annual report or 10K report, which is the expanded version of the annual report filed with the SEC, under a note usually entitled "Other Assets," "Minority Investments" or "Investments in Other Companies." Sometimes a hidden asset may take the form of an actual investment in another company that either holds valuable assets or finds itself in an exciting or blossoming business. We will discuss later an example of

Borg-Warner's interest in Hughes Tool, the drill-bit company, which became the catalyst for our own subsequent investment in Borg-Warner in the late 1970s. Often these companies acquired the investment in another company at low prices and in fact have a large unrealized gain in the stock price, which is not reflected on their balance sheet. Whether the stock is liquidated in the immediate future or not, that investment position remains a potential source of earnings, and cash, if and when it is realized.

Business and Industry

Even if a company has an excellent outlook and a good financial record, and enjoys a strong financial condition, you must always factor in the crucial element of expected business prospects. It is a tribute to the perversity of markets that historical benchmarks can be overturned and that prices can go higher or lower than could ever be anticipated from past events. As a corollary, the fixation on earnings is so strong on Wall Street that the market will often discount good or bad news up to two years in advance. This may appear illogical, but that is the nature of markets. Their movements are controlled by mass psychology, flocklike reactions, a short memory and a shorter attention span.

Timing is not only important with respect to the market in general, but also with respect to industry groups. If you are buying a company at a presumably depressed price, it follows that Wall Street is not excited about the near-term future of the company. Thus, even though the stock may be cheap on a statistical basis, there may still be risks. As we have said repeatedly, history sometimes does not repeat itself, and a stock selling at the low end of a price/ earnings range or at a very high discount to book value does not mean that it is immune from additional negative investor sentiment.

Yet, in the final analysis, it pays to play a sometimes painful waiting game by taking a long-term view of business prospects. This is obviously a contrarian approach, but if we buy after the bad news is apparently public knowledge, we should at the very least get a so-called technical rally in the stock, or a 25 percent advance. Indeed, in recent years, the average stock seems to fluctuate 25 to 75 percent within a year.

Of course, there will be instances where prospects change so fast that an enormous overreaction develops. An obvious example of this was the oil industry debacle in 1981, followed by that of the oil-service industry in early 1982. Back in 1980, by contrast, oils and their courtiers, the oil-service stocks, were the darlings of Wall Street, and prices of these stocks soared triumphantly. Energy was the key investment play, and energy supply seemed limited in face of the Arab-Israeli antagonism, inter-Islamic conflicts and other geopolitical considerations. Other fears, such as increasing industrialization and the reported peaking of oil production in the USSR, increased the attraction of an investment in oil companies even more. Yet, in early 1981, few investors noticed the developing oil inventory glut brought on by the combined forces of increased conservation awareness, high interest rates and recession. As 1981 unfolded, the world went from a very well publicized energy dearth to an energy surfeit, which was an exceedingly confusing turn of events for the poor Wall Street manager and broker to grasp, given so short a time span. As usual, the oil and the oil-service stocks dropped sharply as fears of an oil glut mounted. Eventually the supply and demand for oil will fall more into line because oil is only another commodity. However, it is our expectation that this area of the market will continue to be highly volatile because oil is so sensitive to political developments and political manipulation.

Thus, we cannot suggest that you can temper market losses or keep profits by carefully analyzing the business outlook for an industry or companies. Still, it is a definite element in investing, and, if you rely on it, be sure to set a target purchase price for the stock that is below historical norms, especially during periods of hard times and high interest rates.

Establishing a Target Price

The purpose of the above checklist is to come up with a large list of companies that are fundamentally undervalued. Once these companies have been identified, the next step is to wait for the stock to fall to a price that reduces risks to the bare minimum. We have a constantly changing "watch list" of companies that we monitor daily—waiting for the right price before we buy.

The best system we have found for coming up with a target price is the p/e ratio for the last five years. First, we take the median average of the five-year p/e range, and then go one step further and average the lowest p/e ratio over the last five years with the median average. We then try to buy the stock at that p/e level.

For example, if the p/e range was 6 to 12 over the last five years, the median would be 8. Since the low p/e is 6, and the median 8, we would then be prepared to buy the stock at a p/e of seven times (or less) the lowest earnings forecast we can find.

However, the stock is often nowhere near the p/e level we want, yet something about the company is so attractive that we buy the stock anyway. Perhaps the stock was very weak a year or two ago (i.e., the company took a write-off or didn't anticipate an economic downturn), and sold at an uncommonly low p/e, which is unlikely to occur again in the foreseeable future. In this case, we would adjust our rule to buy at the average low p/e ratio of the last ten years.

One of the most helpful historical cross-checks to establish a target price is to try to buy at, or close to, a price that represents the lowest possible discount to book value over the last ten years. By way of illustration, consider International Multifoods, a food processor and flour miller. Table 2 is an excerpt from Standard & Poor's stock report showing the price range, earnings, book value and price/earnings range for the company over the last ten years.

It is apparent that the earnings record for International Multifoods, as shown in the table, is very impressive. This earnings progress intrigued us and we considered buying the stock in early 1980 and tried to work up a satisfactory target price. First, we calculated the median between the lowest p/e in the last ten years and the average p/e of the last ten years and arrived at a target price/earnings

TABLE 2
INTERNATIONAL MULTIFOODS

Per Share Data ($) Yr. End Feb. 28[1]	1981	1980	1979	1978	1977	1976	1975	1974	[2]1973	[2]1972
Book Value	24.05	23.13	20.92	20.17	18.39	16.75	15.20	13.99	12.71	12.09
Earnings[5]	4.07	3.39	3.16	3.06	[3]2.83	[3]2.56	[3]2.19	[3]1.94	[3]1.63	1.39
Dividends	1.44	1.29	1.17½	1.07½	0.96⅜	0.80	0.69¾	0.66⅝	0.62½	0.61⅞
Payout Ratio	36%	38%	37%	35%	34%	31%	32%	34%	38%	45%
Prices[4]—High	23⅛	20⅞	23⅞	25½	23⅜	19½	13¾	14	17	17⅝
Low	17½	13¼	17	17	16¾	12⅜	8⅞	8⅜	10⅛	12¼
P/E Ratio—	6-4	6-4	8-5	8-6	8-6	8-5	6-4	7-4	10-6	13-9

Data as orig. reptd. Adj. for stk. div(s). of 100% Sep. 1976. 1. Of fol. cal. yr. 2. Reflects merger or acquisition. 3. Ful. dil.: 2.80 in 1977, 2.53 in 1976, 2.17 in 1975, 1.93 in 1974, 1.62 in 1973. 4. Cal .yr. 5. Bef. results of disc. opers. of +0.10 in 1980, −0.85 in 1979.

Standard NYSE Stock Reports
Vol. 49/No. 156/Sec. 9
August 13, 1982
Copyright © 1982 Standard & Poor's Corp. All Rights Reserved
Standard & Poor's Corp.
25 Broadway, NY, NY 10004

ratio of five times. We multiplied that by the most conservative earnings forecast we could find and came out with a target price of 17. Next we took the price of 17, compared it to the company's book value of $23 at the end of 1979, which represented a 26 percent discount, or a price to book of 74 percent. Looking back, we discovered that in 1975, the stock sold at 60 percent of book or a 40 percent discount to book, which implied a target price of 14, or four and a half times 1979 earnings. Accordingly, we held off buying the stock until it dropped to 14. The stock actually declined to 13 shortly thereafter, but by 1982, it had risen to over 30.

Another way to pick target prices is through the use of charts. While we are not chartists, we do recognize that looking at a stock's chart, which is really a picture of the history of its price behavior, can help in deciding where the "support" or "resistance" levels have been in the past. Frequently, a stock may continue to find support or resistance in the same areas.

Figure 1 shows the price history of Northwestern Steel & Wire from 1976 to 1982. Using our checklist, we had already concluded that Northwestern Steel & Wire was an attractive purchase at 23. The company was the leading producer of steel wire and structural rods

FIGURE I

PRICE HISTORY OF NORTHWESTERN STEEL & WIRE, 1976–82

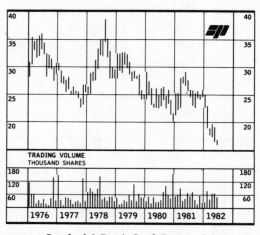

SOURCE: *Standard & Poor's Stock Reports,* July 8, 1982.

and bars, and at 23, was selling significantly below book value. The company's earnings were cyclical, but the company had no long-term debt and was highly liquid.

Most important, the stock price in each of the last ten years had reached 29, and often got as high as 35 or 36. Even more interesting was the fact that 21½ was the lowest price the stock had reached in the past ten years, despite the severe recession of 1974–75, which took the Dow down to 570. The chart shown in the figure confirmed that there was definite support at the 22–24 area, since the stock bounced off that price in 1977 and 1980, as well as in 1974.

The first level of resistance we found was in the 29–31 area, with additional resistance at 35. This corresponded well with the price history, and so we felt quite comfortable buying the stock at 23 in the spring of 1980, with the expectation of selling out at 30, for a gain of 30 percent. As it turned out, we sold the stock at 28 in the spring of 1981 because we concluded that Northwestern Steel & Wire would suffer in the forthcoming recession. We were right on this decision, and ironically, Northwestern Steel & Wire lost money for the next several quarters, and the stock declined through the 22–24 support area before hitting 16 in the 1982 recession. So you see, charts can be an excellent supplemental aid in establishing a target price, as long as they are not the sole criteria for an investment decision.

Conclusion

To become a successful stock picker, you must choose a target price based on fundamentals. Don't be overly concerned if the target price is below the current price of the stock. So long as you can find enough targets, the buying opportunities will present themselves. We have found over the years that about one stock a week hits our target price.

But again let us qualify. Using a checklist requires a final tabulation of all the investment requirements (or lack of them) combined with judgment. Normally there is usually one feature, one characteristic that sways our final decision, in effect, tipping the balance. A go or no go decision may be due to an intuitive sense that there is too much debt or that the return on assets or equity has been declining, or maybe you discovered a hidden asset that you perceive as valuable. On a macroeconomic level, the market may not be in a really negative or positive trend, which may prompt you to rein yourself in. We hope some of the examples that we'll talk about later will help clarify what the final motivation was for us in choosing a stock.

It is important to emphasize that a checklist is an imperfect tool. (To make a good investment decision one must also know where to find ideas and how to interpret their validity.) The knowledge of when to buy also plays a key role in survival investing. While a checklist may mitigate risks, it cannot eliminate the possibility that one might buy a stock at the wrong time, despite what appears to be an attractive price.

However, this checklist has saved us a lot of discomfort when we were wrong on market timing and were hurt in a sudden, surprising drop in the stock market. Even though we had to hold paper losses for some time, we had the patience to withstand temporary market declines, knowing that the market would eventually right itself and bring in a profit or at least the opportunity to get out with only a minor loss.

While a checklist is an essential ingredient of the selection process, you must also have a system for generating new investment ideas. The next chapter will enumerate some of the sources that we use to flush out potential investment candidates.

Chapter 4

Where to Find Investment Ideas

THE SECRET OF FINDING INVESTMENT IDEAS can be summarized in one word: READ. Of course, in order to spend a lot of time on business news, you must be interested in economic and financial affairs. But as you become more accustomed to accumulating and storing financial information, you will find the subject increasingly interesting, particularly if your interpretation of events leads to profits. Nothing can motivate you more than your own success.

The turbulence in the financial markets underscores the importance of becoming your own analyst. This will insulate you from other people's opinions and will give you the confidence to pursue your own ideas and goals by checking out the facts. The way to do this is with a disciplined system of reading and information gathering. Over time, you should acquire a financial file or library of companies, ideas and trends that warrant investment attention.

To sniff out opportunities from the financial news requires an understanding of what to look for. Two people might read the same article, one of whom may spot a nuance that suggests an important opportunity, while the other person sees nothing of significance. What we aim to provide in this chapter are some hints and clues on what to look for in the financial news, what to read and how to accomplish all this in the least amount of time.

Sources of Information

The building blocks of a stock market library are the annual reports; 10K's; Standard & Poor's *Stock Guide, Stock Reports* and *Earnings Forecaster*; and the *Value Line Investment Survey*. With these six sources, you can obtain a superficial profile of a company and sufficient fundamental data to perform the elimination process described in chapter 3.

If the company looks interesting after you have put it through your checklist, then order the annual report to study your prospective investment in a more thorough way. Some investors may not have the patience for more work, and in truth, we have known very successful investors who use the *Stock Guide* or the Standard & Poor's *Stock Reports* or *Value Line* as their sole source of statistical analysis and still manage to produce impressive results because they buy stocks cheaply, employing some of the precepts discussed in chapter 3. Yet always bear in mind that when you make a stock market investment, you are spending capital. If you were buying a car or refrigerator, you would certainly take some time to compare prices, performance, service and features. So even a cursory analysis of the annual report can be worthwhile and sometimes can prevent losses, if it leads to an important piece of negative information that may not be apparent from other sources.

Standard & Poor's *Stock Guide*

This monthly publication can generally be obtained free of charge from any brokerage firm or directly from Standard & Poor's (see appendix for address) for about $5.50 a month. The *Guide* contains key information on every stock listed on the exchanges, including price history for the past two years, the range for the last ten years, the price/earnings ratio based on the latest twelve months' earnings, the dividend history, the condensed financial position, a brief capitalization description (listing, for example, the number of shares outstanding) and, most important, the annual earnings per share for the past four years plus the current year's results. The *Stock Guide* also lists interim earnings for the present fiscal year, as they become available.

The *Guide* also provides the number of shares held by institutions, which, when divided by the total shares outstanding, gives you an idea of how vulnerable a stock may be to selling by institutions.

In addition, the *Stock Guide* offers a quick way to find out the level of volume in a stock over the last several months. Thus, if present volume appears to be much higher than the norm, you may have the first sign that a takeover or some other significant change in the company's life is in the wings.

The *Stock Guide* is a bible to many conservative investors. In fact, we know some people who start their stock selection process by going through the *Guide* and compiling a list of stocks that have low price/earnings ratios and a four-year uptrend in earnings. We might add that these investors do very well in the stock market.

Standard & Poor's *Stock Reports*

This service (frequently called S&P tear sheets because they are easy to tear out of their bindings) offers a great deal of historical and factual information on companies listed on the New York Stock Exchange and American Stock Exchange and those traded actively over the counter.

These reports feature a brief summary of the company's business and its product lines, an update of recent developments, a ten-year statistical table of income statement and balance sheet data, including the most recent quarterly sales and earnings reports, and a comparison of key financial ratios, including many that we look at. In short, the service offers a complete composite of the past and present.

A subscription covering the stocks in all three markets, which is updated quarterly, costs $1,704.15 a year, although discounts of 20 percent are sometimes available to first-time subscribers. Note that most local brokerage offices have a complete set, and a broker will be happy to send out any specific reports that you might need.

Standard & Poor's *Earnings Forecaster*

This publication provides a summary of all available earnings estimates generated by brokerage houses and other investment research organizations. Because earnings estimates can vary enormously, this report tells us whether a consensus exists. Prompted by our inherent desire to be conservative, we normally use the lowest earnings forecast in the service to arrive at a target price based on a low historical p/e.

The *Forecaster* costs about $300 a year and is generally published on a weekly basis. We are very much interested in the pattern and frequency of earnings revisions because that tells us what is happening to expectations about the market.

Just a word of warning based on personal experience here. George Clairmont is a director of Wayne Gossard Corporation, an apparel company listed on the NYSE. As an insider, Clairmont was bemused to learn that the *Earnings Forecaster* had security analysts projecting $2.45 for Wayne Gossard as late as the second quarter of 1982, when he knew from internal memos and projections to the board that the company would probably be lucky to make $1.20 that year. What other frightening deviations can these analysts who purport to be experts on the companies they follow come up with? So look at all earnings projections skeptically.

Value Line Investment Survey

This service is published by Arnold Bernhard & Company (see appendix for address) and contains information similar to that in Standard & Poor's *Stock Reports*. However, *Value Line* focuses more attention on stock recommendations and earnings forecasts than S&P.

The publication also offers opinions on when a stock should be bought as well as on its financial safety. *Value Line* includes information on the company's present and future growth rates, institutional and insider buying and selling of the stock, and how much debt service is covered by earnings and cash flow. The cost is about $365 per year.

Thus, for approximately $1,500 to $2,500 annually (which is tax-deductible) you can have in your own library all the basic financial and statistical information (updated on a quarterly basis) that you need. For about half this amount, you could buy the Standard & Poor's *Stock Reports* and *Value Line* on an annual basis, without the quarterly updates.

We do suggest that you have access to this material. If the cost is too much, you can ask a broker to send copies of any Standard & Poor's *Stock Reports* you are interested in, write the company requesting a copy of its annual report, or visit a local brokerage office and public library, both of which are almost certain to carry the service.

Company Annual Reports and 10K's

As we mentioned before, a complete financial profile is also available from the company's annual report. For those investors who wish to dig deeply into a company, we recommend the 10K report, a more complete version of the annual report, with supplementary financial information filed with the Securities and Exchange Commission. You can get a copy of both reports by writing to the company's shareholder relations department. Standard & Poor's *Register of Corporations, Directors and Executives*, available in most public libraries, carries the addresses and phone numbers of more than 37,000 companies, and the company's address is also listed on the bottom of the Standard & Poor's tear sheets and in the Value Line company reports.

Only a professional investor will spend long hours reading financial articles and reports. Therefore, we have devised a system that allows us to complete the necessary reading in a minimum of time. Our best sources of ideas are *The Wall Street Journal, Forbes, Business Week* and *Fortune*. Other financial magazines that run stories about companies as well as about industrial and economic trends are also helpful. To conserve time, we concentrate on certain aspects of these publications.

A Fast Way to Read The Wall Street Journal

The Wall Street Journal, the largest-circulation paper in the United States, performs a service vital to the informed investor. A wealth of investment ideas can be found in its pages, if you know what to look for.

We do the following when we read the *Journal*:

1. We scan the news summary on page 1 for major developments that could affect the stock market or the shares of the companies that are on our "watch list."

2. We read the "Abreast of the Market" column, which analyzes

the previous day's market movements and discusses the activities of the most active stocks and why they moved. Often the column highlights breaking news stories on companies or, more important, calls attention to the stock groups the institutions are moving into or out of. This may provide some hints of companies that should be on our "watch list."

3. We scan the "Heard on the Street" column, which is usually devoted to a particular stock or a particular industry group and its prospects. On occasion, it will discuss institutional holdings and what these behemoths are buying and selling. This may give you clues about undervalued stocks that short-sighted institutions have soured on.

4. We check the table that lists the percentage losers and gainers for the New York Stock Exchange. Large percentage moves may tip off an impending takeover, signal the purchase of a company's shares by another corporation, or indicate a forthcoming favorable or unfavorable development, such as an unexpectedly bad or good earnings report. In any case, you can get wind of interesting investment prospects from here.

5. We look at the daily 52-week highs and lows on the New York Stock Exchange, and we also take a quick look at the fundamentals of all companies whose stocks are hitting new lows, if we are unfamiliar with them. This often is a good place to find undervalued companies. By the same token, if a stock that we own reaches a new high, and its price is excessive, given the company's fundamentals, we may have good cause to sell out.

The new lows list can be extremely helpful when we have a large shopping list of attractive companies for which we have already established target prices and need to sift it frequently. Think of this as a kind of "tickler file" that can jog you into reexamining an already interesting investment proposition.

6. We check out the most active stocks on the New York and American stock exchanges and the over-the-counter market. Heavy volume in a "secondary" (not a glamour or blue-chip) stock might tell us that something unusual is brewing.

However, you should be extremely cautious in using this indicator because it produces many false alarms. Nevertheless, if the volume is unusually heavy, the stock is moving up, and the fundamentals are still positive, one might have an interesting investment opportunity.

7. We read the "Money Market" page, which summarizes the previous day's activities in the bond markets. It also describes the general market attitude on the direction of interest rates and what might affect them in the near future. This is a crucially important factor to follow because we believe at least two thirds of the equity price movements are directly dependent on the trend in interest rates. When interest rates rise, bonds and money market instruments offer stiff competition for stocks. Also, there's the fear that rising interest rates increase the odds of a recession or even a credit crunch, which could depress corporate earnings.

In reading the "Money Market" page, try to get a feel for the supply and demand of credit. If the debt calendar (the supply of new debt issues in a week or a month) is light and bond offerings are oversubscribed, this is a favorable sign. Conversely, if new bond offerings are repeatedly unsold at the end of the day, that's a negative sign.

8. We study the quarterly earnings reports. As discussed in the last chapter, we go through these to monitor the earnings progress of the companies that we own and to find new prospects. After we find a company with a 4½ to 5 percent return on sales, we begin to study it more closely, and if it appears interesting, we'll run it through our checklist. This analysis is especially helpful in ferreting out lesser-known and smaller companies that are often traded over the counter. However, if a company does not meet this standard, it should not be automatically discarded. Another article or source may show it to be an interesting situation, and the company may possess other favorable attributes other than simply a good return on sales.

9. We read the brief summary of stockholders' meetings, which highlights management comments at the annual meeting. These often prove informative, since management frequently divulges expectations for earnings over the next several quarters and their views about present business conditions. If things are going badly, management often provides insights into the areas of the business that are dragging down earnings. And, conversely, if the outlook is good, you can get an insight into the parts of the business that are doing well. Sometimes, you can find announcements of pending events that might affect the company's fortunes, such as a redeployment of assets, an acquisition or a merger, introduction of a new product or process, and so forth.

10. We study any major article on a company that we're interested in or that we have put on the "watch list." Often *The Wall Street Journal* reviews the history and prospect of a company in an article that yields highly useful information. For example, we once invested in a company called McDonough because we read an article in the *Journal* quoting the company's founder on his intention to sell or liquidate the company. Within two years, this actually came to pass, and the price of the stock nearly doubled.

In passing, we might also add that the New York *Times* Business Section also profiles certain companies, and the investigative nature of these articles often provides a great deal of useful information.

Business Magazines

Business weeklies can also be a source of good information. Subscriptions to *Business Week, Forbes* and *Fortune* are useful since these magazines frequently carry profiles of companies. Obviously, there are other business magazines that provide good leads, but in the interest of time, these three will most likely prove sufficient.

Forbes and *Fortune* are published every other week and *Business Week* once a week, so reading the three is not too time-consuming. You can save even more time by focusing on the index and limiting your attention to the write-ups on individual companies.

In *Business Week*, we skim the news items, which consist mainly of insights into the week's financial events. We like to read *Business Week*'s point of view on the economic and financial situation because it often provides in-depth coverage not available elsewhere. The magazine also carries interesting articles on commodities, technological breakthroughs, regulatory changes and other domestic and international trends. In fact, we have often found that *Business Week* presents one of the most succinct and informative outlooks on events in the world that may influence U.S. companies or businesses.

The magazine also carries a section called "Inside Wall Street," which deals with corporate finance or mergers and acquisitions. This column often discusses companies that are potential takeover targets or highlights those with hidden assets.

Business Week usually reports on two or three companies each week, under the heading of "Corporate Strategies," which zeroes in on management policies and the direction in which the company is headed. Again, very useful and thought-provoking investment ideas can be found here.

One of the most original business magazines and certainly a good source of ideas is *Forbes*. Its main emphasis is on highlighting companies, but with a difference. *Forbes* editorializes freely (usually correctly) and, for the most part, tries to pin down management on its policies and views. Its writers are good at highlighting management's successes and failures, and consequently what emerges is not only a thorough portrait of the company but also insights into management's thinking and ability.

Moreover, *Forbes* is extremely stock market–oriented and has a flair for coming up with what will appeal to professional traders and market watchers. Reporters at *Forbes* are taught to keep an eye out for value, and we often learn about companies with hidden assets from reading their articles. On the other hand, *Forbes* is never reluctant to torpedo overblown stocks when the market price has raced ahead of intrinsic value.

One of the most useful tools in the magazine is a section called "Statistical Spotlight," which can often generate candidates for your "watch list." This is nothing more than lists of stocks that are apparently cheap for various reasons, such as low price/earnings ratios, discount from book value, high dividend yields or any other factor that may cause undervaluation.

In a nutshell, *Forbes* has a definite interest in undervalued companies and goes out of its way to focus on them. If we wanted a single source for ideas, we would have to pick *Forbes*. Its company analyses are clear, profound and usually accurate, and its discussions of market psychology are illuminating, amusing and controversial.

Forbes is also the champion of the equity markets and deserves the nickname used by one of our friends, a professional trader, who calls it the "stock market's referee." When *Business Week* wrote a cover story in 1979 suggesting that the equity markets were dead, *Forbes* countered within several weeks with a cover article arguing that stocks were alive and well in a telling tongue-in-cheek rebuttal.

If you can find the time, and are interested in further scouting for ideas, *Dun's Business Month* or *Institutional Investor* can prove useful. All of these magazines carry excellent articles that may give you insight into a certain company or industry. You need not inundate yourself with information, since *Forbes* and *Business Week* will probably provide sufficient investment ideas to follow up on.

One other source that we find provides an excellent market summary is *Barron's*, the de facto trade paper of the stock market. It is published weekly and appears in the New York City area on Saturday, carrying the past week's prices and a summary of the week's action in the markets. *Barron's* is one of our favorite places for finding new ideas.

One of the first things we do with *Barron's* is to check off those companies selling at or near their 52-week lows. We also study a section at the end of the magazine called "Market Laboratory," which recaps weekly percentage gainers or losers and highs and lows on the New York Stock Exchange, the American Stock Exchange and the over-the-counter market. We pay particular attention to new weekly lows, as this is a fast way to pick up stocks that may be unduly depressed because of a market overreaction.

Barron's includes several other features that are short and highly relevant. For instance, "The Trader" column summarizes major technical and fundamental moves in the market over the past week, providing unusually perceptive reasons for these moves. There are also sections on dividends, yields, the money markets and commodities. In addition, *Barron's* carries three or four company profiles, which you should read to get a more specific look at a firm.

Finally, there is Alan Abelson's famous "Up and Down Wall Street" column, which begins with some of the funniest and most biting satire in America and ends with serious comments about particular stocks, either questioning highfliers or pointing out good values. In fact, Abelson's pen is so powerful that there was a flap years ago about people who tried to bribe *Barron's* employees for advance copies of the newspaper in order to take advantage of price moves they felt would occur because of his column. One should also look for special feature articles in *Barron's*, such as interviews, round-table discussions or articles on companies or industries that one might want to add to one's "watch list."

It may be useful to say a few words about brokerage house reports and stock market letters. We get research from a number of brokers, and their factual data, in general, are excellent. The problem with brokerage house recommendations is that the horse is often out of the barn by the time the recommendation appears.

The stock may have already advanced or declined sharply, depending on whether the advice is to buy or sell. Thus, take research conclusions with considerable skepticism.

In a revealing and witty book called *Confessions of a Wall Street Insider*, C. C. Hazard tells us how brokers' securities reports are often used to generate commission sales activity. Obviously, a broker's meal ticket depends on volume, and buy or sell recommendations offer good excuses to "churn" customers' accounts. We suggest caution in following brokerage recommendations, but we do think it is a good idea to retain, for future reference, some of the information that brokerage houses produce. Almost all research departments in brokerage houses produce a weekly summary of the full-length reports published the prior week. It is a good practice to ask for this summary and single out reports on companies or industries that may interest you, rather than plodding through a lot of superfluous data. Finally, ask your broker for a summary sheet of industry rankings and earnings per share projections for all industries and companies that his research department follows. It might also be a good idea to request from your broker any value screens, such as a compilation of undervalued securities.

We also find useful such weekly market letters as Standard & Poor's *The Outlook,* which often gives sound but conservative advice, and the *Speculator,* which covers low-priced stocks. (*The Outlook* costs $160 yearly and the *Speculator* $157.50.) Neither is vital nor foolproof, but both are good supplemental information resources. Two other good market letters are Stan Weinstein's *Professional Tape Reader* and Richard Russell's *Dow Theory Letters,* which can be very useful in stock selection and market timing. Addresses for these newsletters are given in the appendix.

Remember that the point of using these sources is to make up a target list of companies. Once an article on a company, a 52-week low in a stock or a news item has provoked your interest, you still must analyze the fundamentals and put the company through the gauntlet of your checklist.

The Fast Way to Read an Annual Report

Most people, unless they have a way with numbers, regard analyzing an annual report as a daunting experience. A company may present so many figures and other information that it seems impossible to distinguish what is important from what is irrelevant. Because our system is predicated on risk avoidance, we are specifically looking for certain financial information relevant to our philosophy: hard book value, good cash flow, a reasonable chance for improving earnings, a good or recovering business with desirable products or services and perhaps a hint of hidden assets.

An annual report provides a snapshot of the present, but it also provides a history of the company, which after all is an insight into management's success or failure in controlling the company's destiny. When you look at the annual report, don't be lured into complacency by an outstanding record. A good record is only that. Economic or political shocks or a corporate miscalculation could ruin that record, perhaps irreparably.

Here's how we look at an annual report.

1. Check the auditor's opinion. Is it qualified or not? A qualified opinion usually means a major current or potential problem exists, which the auditors can't or won't quantify. If the report is qualified, it might be best to avoid the company.

2. Check the company's accounting policies, which usually are discussed in the first footnote. It's important to know how conservative management is about accounting. Are the research and development costs charged as incurred or capitalized? Are inventories last-in-first-out or first-in-first-out? If last-in-first-out, management is accounting for inflation and is not relying on inventory profits to prop up earnings. Is management contributing enough to pension funds or are there unfunded pension costs? Do pension liabilities exceed pension fund assets? Are interest costs for major projects expensed or capitalized? This may also be a way for management to manipulate earnings.

For example, in a difficult year, management can bury expenses by underfunding pensions. Actuarial tables are based on subjective assumptions about the company's employees, how long they will remain with the company, how many of them will be vested (eligible to receive benefits) and for how long.

Until fairly recently, companies that were building plants, warehouses or other projects shifted their accounting of interest and other so-called soft costs (architectural, legal, permits, etc.) incurred in construction to suit their objectives. If the company was enjoying a profitable year, these costs would be immediately expensed on the profit-and-loss statement. Conversely, in a bad year, management might decide to "capitalize" them (that is, include these costs on the balance sheet as part of fixed assets without expensing them at all). Accountants now frown on this type of inconsistent bookkeeping, and the rules are far more stringent, disallowing a year-to-year switch of expensing or capitalizing for a single project. Nevertheless, management often does employ the straight capitalization method on some or all projects, which can distort depreciation levels in later years, and cause fluctuations in earnings.

3. Try to calculate a hard book value. We have already explained the procedure but let's repeat it. Take net worth as shown on the balance sheet, deduct intangibles and pension liabilities in excess of pension fund assets (if any) and add back any inventory profits. Also take a closer look at fixed assets and "investment" assets to see if these are broken down. It is important to determine whether the company has valuable holdings in real estate, in resources or in other companies that are carried on the books at much lower prices.

4. Check the footnote about the company's debt. Is debt at relatively low interest rates and due over the long term or short term? In the debt footnote, the company usually lists its debt obligations with their respective rates and maturities. What we are looking for is to determine how much long-term money the company has borrowed at low rates. In another footnote, or in the debt footnote, there is also detailed information on the company's lease obligations. Again it helps to know whether lease payments are high relative to the total obligations of the company and certainly relative to the sales of the company.

During recessionary times, it is even more important to notice whether debt repayments and lease payments are also bunched up in one year, so that a company might be forced to refinance at high rates. Smart managers will try to smooth out repayment schedules to avoid a cash drain in a particular year that could affect earnings and undermine cash flow for future years to come.

5. Check for potential litigation or contingent liabilities that could materially hurt the company. If there are a lot of contingencies—let's say more than three—don't take the company's word that these matters are immaterial.

Several companies involved in asbestos production, such as Manville, Raymark, Eagle-Picher and Jim Walter, have been and still are affected by thousands of claims from previous employees engaged in asbestos manufacturing. Despite the fact that these companies have made many statements to offset negative publicity, their image and stock price have suffered.

A. H. Robins, a drug company known for its cold remedies, used to produce a contraceptive called Dalkon Shield in the early 1970s. This product apparently caused some deaths and serious infirmities among its users, and litigation against the company took close to ten years to settle. To this day, A. H. Robins is saddled with a negative image. During the period that A. H. Robins was negotiating the settlement of its many lawsuits, the stock sold at multiples substantially below those of other drug companies because of the contingent liabilities from Dalkon Shield.

6. Study the source and use of changes in working capital. How were the funds derived? Mostly from earnings, debt or equity? How much cash came from the sales of assets? Where did the cash go? Was it spent on dividends, on new plant and equipment or for the repayment of debt? If debt was added to maintain dividends or at the sacrifice of research and development, the company might be undermining its long-term future. Or if all the funds went to pay off debt, and hardly anything was spent on corporate expansion, the company's long-term growth would be inhibited. In general, one should try to understand management's priorities and policies, their aggressiveness or passivity.

8. Read the management's discussion and analysis of results of operations and financial conditions. This often gives an idea of what went right or wrong with the company over the past year and the outlook for the future.

9. Read the president's message to stockholders, which sometimes deals with management's concerns and future policies.

10. Familiarize yourself with the company's products and services by scanning the sections on each division or product, especially in the case of a company that's involved in technology. We have often found that if we can't understand the company's business from reading the annual reports, we're better off not buying the stock. If you are able to understand the company's business, how visible are the company's prospects? Are the company's products or services appealing, and will they be in demand in the future?

Analysts may blanch at this superficial way of analyzing a company report, but it is a fast way to learn where the company has been, where it is now and what pitfalls it may face. Our review may not satisfy the purist, but it is a practical way of acquiring a profile of the company in a short period of time.

The Proxy Statement and Other Takeover Tips

In conjunction with the annual report, you will also receive a proxy statement, whose importance is discussed in more detail later. Included in this report are details of management compensation, including perquisites, stock holdings and any side agreements between directors, managers or officers and the company, such as employment contracts, option agreements or consulting agreements. This helps us to measure the largesse of the board. Most especially it exhibits the extent to which management and its directors hold control, if any, over the company. Any insider (defined as manager, officer, director or outside investor with holdings of more than 5 percent of the stock) must disclose his investment in the proxy. That information can help someone who wants to speculate in takeover plays or to get an idea if the company is ripe to be sold by its controlling interests (see the discussion of Norris Industries, in chapter 5). Used in concert with *SEC Today, Weekly Insider Report, The Insiders,* and *Insiders' Chronicle,* they can provide valuable insights as to possible takeover or merger candidates. Incidentally, *Insiders' Chronicle,* a weekly, gives extensive reports, with excellent descriptive highlights, on companies that are controlled or have a large investor position. It also furnishes insider trade reports, including the price at which bought or sold, the number of shares involved, and which insider did the selling and buying. (See appendix for addresses and prices of these publications.)

Industries We Avoid

In an effort to save time, you might narrow your investigations by avoiding a number of industry groups. While some of these industries may offer very attractive trading opportunities from time to time, we think they are uninteresting investments. For instance, we usually avoid the following:

1. Utilities. These companies are overly regulated and are heavily in debt, most of which must eventually be refinanced at usually higher interest rates. In addition, they have very little free cash flow, their accounting method often inflates earnings, and they are subject to a host of environmental and government regulations.

2. International money center banks and savings and loan companies. Most of the assets of these companies are invested in paper money, in which we do not have much confidence. In addition, they are often thinly capitalized, and in the case of banks with large international operations, their loan loss exposure may be high.

We shudder to think of the disruption in the international banking system, indeed the whole economic order, if Poland, Rumania or one of the Central American or South American countries had to default on their debt repayments. Thanks to high oil prices, a rapidly growing population and urbanization and a great deal of corruption and mismanagement, many Third World countries are staggering under impossible debt loads and are given constant transfusions by large international banks, as well as by government loans and foreign aid. In our minds, these loans and grants will never be repaid. In short, a redistribution of wealth on the government level and so-called "evergreen" loans on the banking level are now almost an accepted fact in the world economic order. This situation makes us very queasy.

We do, however, think there is some merit to investing in small, regional banks, preferably in high-growth areas, such as the South and Southwest and Far West. We are interested in banks that sell at about five times earnings and at one half of book value. Normally these banks only make loans to customers in their general geographic area and are very cautious about extending credit, unless they know the company's management well. Generally, it is rare for these banks to suffer significant loan losses. Also, they generally have secure and growing deposit bases.

As for savings and loan institutions, the late 1970s and early 1980s brought about enormous losses for most S&L's. Mergers and some liquidations have become endemic, and we believe it will be a long time, if ever, before this industry is viable again.

3. Airline and trucking companies. Truckers must cope with fierce competition and poor labor relations. A shakeout is under way, and only the stronger truckers and some independents will survive. Meanwhile, the railroads, revitalized through mergers and

more efficient handling and marketing techniques, are giving the truckers severe competition.

Airlines must also modernize their fleets because of changing market conditions, the need to achieve greater fuel economy and availability of more fuel-efficient planes. Finally, recent deregulation has also spurred price wars and vicious competition in both industries, which does not help earnings and puts pressure on debt service.

4. Steels. The large steel companies in the United States are backward in their modernization programs in comparison with much of their international competition. In the past, they have not been able to raise prices enough in boom times to earn sufficient profits to tide them over during poor times. They are also saddled with heavy pension obligations. Finally, new and lighter alloys and substitute substances such as carbon compounds have cut into consumption of steel, and as technological advances are made, it is possible that steel will become less competitive as a manufacturing material.

5. Automotive companies. The American auto companies are highly dependent on consumer discretionary income, which is not good in a time of declining standards of living, such as the late 1970s and early 1980s. In Europe, for instance, a car is kept two or three times longer than in the United States, where the average American, through powerful advertising and planned obsolescence, is accustomed to trading in his car every three or four years, or less.

The enormous penetration of foreign auto companies into our economy is largely the fault of our own producers. They were shortsighted and resisted building the small cars the American consumers wanted. As a result, it is hard to have confidence in the U.S. auto industry. In the next five years, these companies must try to catch up, but the cost will be tremendous, and the net worth of the automobile companies is much impaired. It is an open question whether they can succeed, and we prefer to wait on the sidelines until the outcome is clearer.

6. Leisure stocks and toy companies. These companies, which are too seasonal, also depend too much on prosperity and discretionary income. Too many toy companies are subject to rollercoaster swings in price because of a fad that catches the public's fancy. However, certain movie stocks do have enormous hidden assets in the form of their film libraries, which will become more

valuable as the video revolution unfolds. Software, in the form of old movies and new productions, is in great demand for the emerging cable industry, which is why Coca-Cola bought Columbia Pictures in early 1982 and a private investor group bought Twentieth Century-Fox in 1981.

The gambling or casino stocks were also a popular investment group in the late 1970s, but with the several exceptions of those that hold valuable land, this is an industry group we feel should be avoided.

7. Small high-technology companies. Prices of these small "hi-tech" companies usually sell at price/earnings multiples that are way beyond our permissible parameters. Also, technology changes rapidly, and the industry is fraught with competition—which makes it difficult for the amateur investor to stay current.

In our minds, high-technology stocks are for venture capitalists and entrepreneurial-minded people who invest in them after careful on-the-spot discovery and detailed understanding of production and marketing problems. Wall Street analysts who do study these companies often have only a superficial view of the company, derived from a quick visit or from an equity-hungry management's public relations presentation. They just simply do not foresee the competition and potential production snafus or the feast-and-famine side to these esoteric endeavors. Many times these highfliers have been easy to get into but, sadly, the exit often occurs only after the paper profits have turned to real losses, when the earnings progress of the high p/e stocks evaporates.

The older, well-established technological companies, which, on occasion, get depressed because of market conditions, recession or competition, get our vote—so long as the price, price/earnings ratio and financial fundamentals warrant it. They are more seasoned and should have the financial strength to weather recessions and to fight competition.

This still leaves us with a large universe of stocks to choose from: companies engaged in the production of either consumer or industrial products, resource companies or those directly or indirectly involved in the ownership of valuable, underpriced real estate, and a series of "smokestack America" type companies, many of them cyclical, such as paper, cement and chemical operations, as well as well-known technological and defense companies.

These companies are interesting just because they are cyclical.

They are fundamentally sound companies whose products are always in demand. Because of recessions, excess capacity, or over-building in good periods, a temporary oversupply for their products sometimes develops, which encourages price wars and, therefore, lower earnings—until supply and demand eventually come back into balance.

In the early 1980s, those basic industries that relied too heavily on housing and automobiles faced a traumatic period in their cor-porate histories because their basic markets were contracting or even dying. Some of the more complacent companies fell by the wayside, were forced into bankruptcy, merged or partially liqui-dated themselves, closing factories and firing much of their work force. The changes were painful, but at this writing, it appears the survivors will emerge much stronger. The shakeout will lessen com-petition, and many of these companies will benefit from new markets in young and growing industries or in new geographic areas. For example, rubber companies have developed compounds that revolutionized roofing repairs (see Carlisle Corporation in chapter 7). And the metal fabrication industry has come up with powdered metals, which are tougher and more economical.

Common sense indicates that the best way to buy these com-panies is when they are out of favor. At such times, they sell at prices that provide a sufficiently large return to compensate for the lengthy holding period.

How to Find Investment Clues

When reading about possible investment opportunities, the most important thing to look for is anything that will affect the earnings and/or assets of a company. The following list of clues may help you find investment ideas:

1. Earnings forecasts or reports on results by company officials. These often give an indication of what is to come in the future and what the outlook is for the various parts of the company's business.

2. Changes in management. This might signal a rejuvenation of a company that was saddled with uninspired management. Of course, it could also be a bad sign, since the company may now be without direction.

3. Purchases of blocks of stock in the open market of one com-

pany by another. Is this for investment or eventual takeover? Is the target company undervalued?

4. Redeployment of assets. This usually occurs when a company sells off a division or certain assets that have hindered earnings growth. Often a profitable sale of an asset can produce a big cash reserve for a company, making it susceptible to a takeover. Or, alternatively, the money could be reinvested in a growing area of the economy.

5. Indication of hidden assets. Has the company sold off an asset that was carried on the books at a much lower price? If so, are there other such assets?

6. The introduction of new products or manufacturing processes that seem to be well received in the market.

7. Increases or decreases in commodity prices, if the company is a producer or user of that commodity. For instance, a dramatic increase in sugar prices will obviously be a windfall for a sugar-refining company since this is its dominant raw material. However, remember that one could get whipsawed if the commodity suddenly falls precipitously, as all commodities did in the 1980–82 period.

8. Dividend increases, decreases or omission. This often presages management confidence or worries about the company's future earnings picture and cash position.

9. Interest rate trends. If interest rates decline, earnings of interest-rate-sensitive stocks, such as banks and insurance companies, should benefit.

10. Labor negotiations. Strikes will often depress earnings temporarily and cause downward pressure on the stocks of companies in that industry. Good buying opportunities may be available at attractive prices in such situations, provided that the strike does not irreparably damage the company. Labor "givebacks" in the early 1980s were also a harbinger of recovery for cash-stripped companies or industries that had fallen on hard times mainly due to excessive labor contracts. The survivors do well.

11. Repurchase by the company of its own stock. This could lead to higher earnings, since the company has fewer shares outstanding. However, if the company was short of cash in the first place, and was forced to buy back its stock from an opportunist, this could prove a strain on its finances. And if the company had to borrow money to fund the stock purchase, earnings could be squeezed.

12. "Coattail effect": merger or acquisition by one company in an industry often has a complementary effect on the stocks of companies in the same industry. Likewise, a sale of a division or asset can cause a reassessment in the stock market of stocks that have similar assets or divisions.

13. Announcement by management that it is looking to merge or sell out.

14. Purchase of more than 5 percent of the stock of a company by a financially strong company or individuals. This might presage a takeover or at least prep up the price of the stock.

Any one of these developments could cause the price of a stock to advance sharply, as investors rush to get on the bandwagon. Obviously, that is not the most ideal time to buy. No matter how good the company looks, one should wait for a downward reaction. While the stock may not drop to the level it sold at before the announcement, it still may react to a more attractive price after the initial excitement subsides.

The next three chapters will illustrate specific examples of how we found, analyzed and bought the three types of bargains we talked about in chapter 1. We will explain why we bought what we did, what prompted the decision and how we bought the stock.

First, we will talk about "Sleeping Beauty" stocks—the neglected, fundamentally sound companies. Then, we will illustrate how to buy the large, well-known companies that have fallen out of favor. Finally, we will demonstrate how to take advantage of special situations, such as takeovers, earnings turnarounds and companies that are undergoing radical and fundamental changes.

Chapter 5

The Art of Discovering "Sleeping Beauty" and "Cinderella" Stocks

ONE OF OUR GREAT JOYS comes from finding what we call "Sleeping Beauty" and "Cinderella" stocks. Such stocks can be defined as those with a long record of good earnings progress and/or undervalued assets supporting them, neither of which are reflected in the current price of the stock. Why do Sleeping Beauties remain unrecognized? Why, in a world of instant communication, computerized investment services and apparently close scrutiny of investments, do some quality companies with good fundamentals go begging?

Many Wall Street professionals and academics argue that the stock market is "efficient" and that stocks will find a natural and rational price level based on supply and demand. But if this were always the case, then there would be no undervalued investments. The real truth is that the market is not always efficient.

One reason is that many companies have no visibility or sponsorship—they aren't in the public eye. Another reason is that many companies don't have a large enough floating supply of stock to interest the institutions, which are the dominant factor in the stock market. Institutions are not interested in stocks with a capitalization of less than 5 million shares, which probably account for a majority of those on the New York Stock Exchange, those on the American Stock Exchange and those traded actively over the counter.

On an average day, the banks, insurance companies, mutual funds, pension funds and others that invest large sums of money in the market account for an estimated 75 percent of all stock market volume. So, if they neglect a stock, it can often languish for years, despite good earnings growth.

Institutions as a group may often own 25 to 75 percent of a company's stock and, thus, are very concerned about liquidity or the amount of "float" of a stock. For our purposes, float can be defined as the supply of actively traded stock. Shares held by management, directors or the family of the founders are not likely to be traded, although such shares are issued, registered and outstanding for purposes of calculating earnings per share or book value. Thus, closely held stock should be excluded from calculations of float.

Stocks with big capitalizations lend themselves more easily to institutional portfolio management. Investment policy committees at some institutions set quotas on the percentage of an industry or even a company that must be represented in each portfolio. For example, in the heyday of so-called one-decision stocks in the early 1970s, Citibank required its portfolio managers to place 10 percent of any portfolio in the stock of IBM and 5 percent in Xerox, with small commitments to other companies like Avon, Burroughs, and so forth. Although this type of investment decision-making has proven unsatisfactory, it still goes on because it is easy to administer, monitor and execute.

Portfolio concentration by institutions often centers on stocks or industries considered glamorous or exciting. Portfolio managers and research analysts cannot cover every type of investment, and they frequently stick to those areas where their interest is subliminally titillated: state of the art technology, new products and services, gimmickry and gadgetry. As a result, many mundane but profitable businesses are ignored. The company that manufactures storm windows or paper cups and plates does not have the same glamour as a company that is involved in advanced microprocessors, laser guns or biogenetics.

"Concepts" and fads also have a heavy influence on institutional portfolio strategy. As soon as an exciting new story comes along, fund managers rush to participate, neglecting considerations of price as well as the steady, plodding companies in unglamorous businesses. Fund managers generally prefer to go along with the crowd, rather than take a contrary stance. It is this herd mentality that causes so many good companies with good records to be ignored.

One way to find Sleeping Beauties is to review a large number of corporate proxy reports, the notice announcing the forthcoming annual shareholders' meeting and the matters to be voted upon. (We try to get on as many shareholder mailing lists as possible, and whenever a proxy statement comes in we study it closely.) One interesting feature of the proxy report is that it lists the amount of stock held by the directors. Such information could provide a hint as to whether the company is vulnerable to a takeover or a buy-out. If a large percentage of the company is owned by a family or founder (with no heirs actively involved in the business), the company may decide to sell out to another corporation, particularly if the principals are elderly and eager to do some estate planning.

The proxy statement of Norris Industries alerted us to exactly this kind of possibility. Norris was a manufacturer of automotive parts, plumbing hardware and household products, and was controlled by Kenneth Norris, the son of the founder. The Norris family members owned some 24 percent of the outstanding stock of the company, and they had indicated in 1979 that they might consider selling out. Kenneth Norris was fifty and it appeared he, too, might go along with a buy-out, if the price was right.

When we contemplated buying Norris in October 1979, the stock was selling at 21. The company had a hard book value of 22, practically no long-term debt and a current ratio of 3 to 1. Earnings had been in an uptrend since the recession year of 1974, and the company's return on shareholders' equity had exceeded 15 percent in every year since 1975.

On the other hand, 1979 and 1980 were projected to be down years in earnings because of sluggishness in the automotive and housing industries, which were important to the company's business. Yet, despite this, Norris was still generating a fair profit. All in all, we thought the stock's undervaluation and the prospects of a takeover outweighed the negatives, and we bought the stock.

But by December 1980, predictions of an even worse year in 1981 for housing and autos made us nervous about holding Norris. At the time, the stock was trading at 25½, so we were able to sell our position at a small profit. As it turned out, we would have done well to hold on. Ten months later, a private investor group offered to buy Norris at 43 a share. The group that purchased Norris was put together by Kohlberg, Kravis, Roberts & Company, one of the most successful practitioners of leveraged buy-outs. In what was a typical arrangement, the purchase was financed through a combination of equity capital and debt. While the debt load was heavy, the buyers hoped the cash flow from Norris's business would cover the interest and principal payments. Leveraged buy-outs offer a way for wealthy individuals to participate in the purchase of an undervalued company. However, the volatility of interest rates in recent years has reduced the attractions of leveraged buy-outs. We don't expect the trend to resume until interest rate fluctuations have calmed down, but it is interesting to note that the neglected company with solid fundamentals is the most frequent target of leveraged buy-outs.

Finding small, profitable and growing companies is sometimes tedious, but it can be quite rewarding. The method that has been most fruitful for us is to look for companies that have after-tax margins of 5 percent or better. We also receive good ideas from value screens published by *Forbes* magazine or brokerage houses such as Oppenheimer & Company. Our goal is to find companies that earn money even though they may be somewhat cyclical.

These stocks often have price moves of 25 to 50 percent a year, since the float is small, and a limited amount of additional buying or a minuscule increase in sponsorship can produce a large price jump. Therefore, one should try to buy these stocks when the market has dropped significantly.

However, a small float can work against you, too. If a holder of 1,000–2,000 shares decides to sell because of a piece of bad news, the stock price could decline sharply. On the other hand, such selling is usually over within a matter of days or weeks, and the stock can rebound. In the case of the large capitalization stocks, an institutional selling program can depress prices for even a year or two.

The Sifting Process—Finding the Shiny Pebbles That Can Turn into Gems

There is always a weighing and balancing thought process in calculating a set of criteria such as we have devised in our checklist. This process is especially crucial in making investment decisions about unknown or neglected stocks. So in order to clarify how to find and decide on these investments, we will give some examples. Before that, though, let's examine conceptually our recipe for investing in this type of company, what's important to us and how we go about this process of search and investment.

Most often, our starting point is the earnings reports published in the newspaper and our return on sales hurdle. As a starter, we mark off all those companies that we are unfamiliar with and have one or preferably two years of at least 5 percent return on sales. Having selected these companies, we then go to the S&P guide and look at the stock's p/e ratio. Generally, if the stock of the company is selling over ten times last year's earnings, we will discard it unless we really like the business it's in. Next, we'll go over the earnings trend and determine whether earnings have grown 50 percent in the past five years. It's important to remember that this type of analysis is superficial, because it doesn't take into account the quality of those earnings, since at this point we are only examining the S&P statistical guide.

We'll also try to ascertain what kind of consistency earnings have had, whether or not annual earnings have declined more than twice and by how much in the past ten years. To do that we have to switch to the S&P sheet or Value Line historical tables. If we see that earnings have taken some real dives on a year-to-year basis over the past ten years, we have to start thinking about the business the company is in and how the prospects of that business appear to us now and over the next two years. Obviously, if it seems that the business will be in the doldrums and the company under continuing earnings pressure in the depths of recession with no quick chance of recovering, it might be best to pass on the company.

If the company's products and/or services in our opinion are in stable demand and not too dependent on capital spending or on consumer discretion, we'll continue our evaluation process. Or if we find a company that has quality products or provides a necessary recession-resistant service or has a bright future owing to some proprietary technique or product or a state of the art product or technique, our interest may be spurred on, especially if the barriers to getting into its business are difficult to overcome and if the company has proved over the years that it has fended off competition well. Clues to this can be found in looking at return on assets and equity. Before we do that, though, we still have to make a subjective, intuitive and commonsense decision about the company's business. In the 1981–82 recession, you could have bought companies in capital goods that were the leaders in their field with sparkling returns in good periods, but if you were concerned about timing, the economic environment was not yet in place for these companies' stocks to rise because bad or indifferent earnings would weigh them down. That does not mean that an investor with patience and guts should not invest, because history proves that in most cases when the recovery finally occurs, the price gains are dramatic.

On the other hand, there may be many other undervalued stocks that have a better and faster prospect of moving up. And human nature dictates that most investors want fast results. For instance, we know many contrarians who made a lot of money biding their time and picking up small, unknown companies that were in commodity businesses such as textiles or metal fabricators, or multiline manufacturers that were under some margin pressure. But these companies had declined to such low price levels in tandem with market declines that they came roaring back as their resilience became apparent to Wall Street.

One check on resilience is to examine the S&P sheet and/or *Value Line* and see how return on assets and return on equity fared in good times and bad. In fact, that's our next step, to see if our hurdle rates of 10 percent and 13 percent were achieved on a consistent basis. This test can give you some idea of the historic productivity of the company's assets. Are they getting full returns in bad times, or are there significant dips that may indicate problem children in their portfolio of assets that can develop into a continued drag on earnings?

A check on historic returns on equity can prove to be an incisive measure of how well managed a company is. Is management making good investment decisions by reinvesting profits cleverly either in capital spending or in research and development? Is it judicious in its balancing of debt or are its acquisitions and investments too heavily leveraged with too great a usage of debt so that when there is a downturn in business, the interest costs cut into profits despite the fact that return on assets is high? In short, how well does management spend the cash available to it, either through using its earnings or its credit availability. Perhaps too much of its earnings was paid out in dividends, and the company had to borrow to pay for it. A strong and consistent return on equity performance can help spot such problems.

The next step in our calculation is to analyze debt. Most smaller companies in our experience seem to manage debt quite well. Often they are controlled by families or groups that are inherently conservative. There also doesn't generally seem to be a need among small companies for corporate machismo, incurring debt to finance grandiose growth. It is particularly important for small companies to nurse their growth and avoid overleverage, no matter how successful their record, since in a recession they might not be able to cope with high debt if sales and earnings margins plummet. Cash flow is king for a smaller company trying to expand, and so we think it's important to investigate thoroughly the company's debt structure. In order to do this, you'll need the annual report, although you can get an idea of the debt to capitalization by perusing the S&P sheets. If at first glance debt is too high—that is, over our 30 percent ratio—refer to the brief description on the S&P sheet called "Finances," which gives a general summary of the major components of debt, including interest rates and maturities. If rates are low (under 8 percent) and maturities long, perhaps you should reconsider elimination of the company even if debt is over 30 percent. If not, pass the company by.

The S&P sheet also shows a current ratio number, and this figure ought to be considered next. You want to be careful of a small company that is using a lot of short-term debt to finance inventories and receivables. If the current ratio is less than our 2 to 1 hurdle, don't go any further, especially if the economy is under stress, unless you are so intrigued by other pluses that you will wait to obtain the latest quarterly report on the company (which can be requested by mail) to check that inventory build-up is not getting out of hand.

Finally, we check Value Line for a quick reference to book value per share, which that service carries for some 1,700 companies. Is the stock price below book value or even close or below net current working capital? This will tell us nothing about the earnings momentum of the company, which if rising will ultimately cause a "sleeper" to come alive, but it may provide a downside cushion. Surprisingly, many of these companies sell below book or even at a price where they are better dead than alive—that is, what you would realize from asset sales after paying off all debt.

Since cash flow is so important to this kind of company, use the annual report to try to get a handle on cash flow per share, as we've described earlier. You can usually get some insight into management dividend and capital expenditure policy from the section called "Management Discussion of Results" or from the president's message to shareholders. Since earnings forecasts are not readily available on small companies—because few, if any, analysts follow them (which is why they are unrecognized)—use the quarterly reports of results (10Q reports) for clues as to how the company is doing this year as opposed to last, and try to guess at future earnings. As a quick and rough exercise, we take first-quarter earnings, multiply that by four, and then adjust up or down 20 percent, depending on our own private opinion of how we expect business conditions to progress for the rest of the year. Then we use last year's depreciation figure to derive our simple regular cash flow. (Free cash flow per share is not absolutely a mandatory check that you have to go through, but if you want to be thorough, you should do it.)

Two last items to look for: management stake in the company (since often these companies are founder- or family-controlled and thus generally managed conservatively) and hidden assets (that have some real value but are not reflected in the book value of the company).

Trans-Lux Corporation

Let's recap with a live example: in early 1980, we came upon Trans-Lux, listed on the American Stock Exchange. Trans-Lux had always conjured up images of movie theaters to us until we started to take a good look at the company. We noticed in the earnings results in *The Wall Street Journal* that in 1979 the company had a 10.7 percent return on sales, up from 9.5 percent in 1978, which we considered quite remarkable. Next we scanned the S&P guide and discovered that at its 5½ price, the company was selling at about five times the $1.05 per share it had earned in 1979. More intriguing was the fact the earnings had rapidly expanded from losses in the 1975 recession (due to inventory problems and write-offs of obsolete inventory) to $.14 in 1976, $.45 in 1977, $.80 in 1978 and $1.05 in 1979. We were somewhat put off by the battered earnings in 1973 and 1975, when the company had losses, but after looking at its annual report were able to overcome our doubts.

Virtually 80 percent of income came from teleprinters and

stock tickers, a product line we were familiar with. The financial markets' activity was sure to grow. Trans-Lux had an established reputation, and, in our view, anyone in the video communications business, especially in the financial markets, was in a growth market. As an additional lure, the company had a stable theater operation and a special entertainment presentation called the "New York Experience" that had proved profitable over the years. All in all, the business appeared healthy even during recessions. The company had excellent products and other growth prospects in multi-

TABLE 3
TRANS-LUX CORPORATION

Per Share Data ($)

Yr. End Dec. 31	1981	1980	1979	1978	1977	1976	1975	1974	1973	1972
Book Value	10.53	9.29	8.50	7.37	6.07	5.57	5.37	5.32	5.49	6.62
Earnings[1]	1.27	1.24	1.05	0.80	0.45	0.14	d0.25	0.07	d0.45	0.36
Dividends	0.10	0.10	0.10	Nil	Nil	Nil	Nil	Nil	0.35	0.35
Payout Ratio	8%	8%	9%	Nil	Nil	Nil	Nil	Nil	NM	97%
Prices—High	12¾	11	8½	7¼	3¼	3⅜	3⅜	3¾	10⅜	12⅞
Low	7⅛	4¾	4½	2¼	2	1⅝	1¼	1	2¼	7½
P/E Ratio—	10–6	9–4	8–4	9–3	7–4	24–12	NM	54–14	NM	36–21

Data as orig. reptd. 1. Bef. results of disc. ops. of +0.47 in 1973 and spec. items of +0.05 in 1979, +0.04 in 1977, +0.04 in 1976, +0.08 in 1974, −0.80 in 1973. d-Deficit. NM-Not Meaningful.

Income Data (Million $)

Year Ended Dec. 31	Gross Oper. Revs.	Oper. Inc.	% Oper. Inc. of Revs.	Cap. Exp.	Depr.	Int. Exp.	[3]Net Bef. Taxes	Eff. Tax Rate	[4]Net Inc.	% Net Inc. of Revs.
1981	25.5	5.91	23.2%	[5]4.49	2.82	0.22	3.28	29.6%	2.31	9.1%
1980	20.5	4.62	22.5%	4.31	2.56	0.23	2.60	12.9%	2.22	10.9%
1979	17.6	4.33	24.7%	3.44	2.20	0.22	2.28	17.4%	1.87	10.7%
1978	15.7	3.82	24.4%	3.54	1.96	0.18	1.90	20.9%	1.49	9.5%
1977	13.2	3.32	25.2%	2.36	1.97	0.22	1.15	20.3%	0.90	6.9%
1976	11.0	2.86	25.9%	1.76	2.46	[2]0.22	0.32	11.1%	0.29	2.6%
1975	9.9	2.92	29.6%	2.57	3.16	[2]0.28	d0.49	NM	d0.48	NM
1974	9.6	3.30	34.3%	1.57	3.09	[2]0.46	0.17	24.1%	0.13	1.3%
[1]1973	10.2	3.22	31.7%	0.85	2.98	[2]0.45	d1.03	NM	d0.90	NM
1972	11.9	4.20	35.2%	2.17	2.71	[2]0.44	1.23	40.4%	0.73	6.1%

Balance Sheet Data (Million $)

Dec. 31	Cash	—Current— Assets	—Current— Liab.	Ratio	Total Assets	Ret. on Assets	Long Term Debt	Common Equity	Total Cap.	% LT Debt of Cap.	Ret. on Equity
1981	1.89	3.59	2.12	1.8	24.1	10.3%	2.70	18.2	22.0	12.3%	13.3%
1980	1.37	2.92	1.53	1.9	21.1	10.8%	2.77	16.4	19.6	14.2%	14.1%
1979	1.64	3.20	1.79	1.8	19.4	10.2%	2.80	14.5	17.6	16.1%	13.8%
1978	1.47	2.53	1.83	1.4	17.9	9.2%	2.90	13.0	16.0	17.8%	12.5%
1977	1.98	2.76	1.35	2.0	16.6	5.5%	2.74	12.3	15.2	18.0%	7.6%
1976	1.43	2.30	0.95	2.4	16.1	1.8%	3.75	11.3	15.1	24.8%	2.6%
1975	1.00	2.04	1.01	2.0	16.7	NM	4.60	11.0	15.7	29.4%	NM
1974	1.89	3.13	2.10	1.5	18.5	0.7%	4.64	11.5	16.3	28.5%	1.1%
1973	1.02	1.95	1.92	1.0	19.5	NM	5.78	11.5	17.5	33.1%	NM
1972	1.76	2.52	1.18	2.1	22.9	3.1%	7.89	13.8	21.7	36.3%	5.3%

Data as orig. reptd. 1. Excl. disc. ops. 2. Net of int. inc. 3. Incl. equity in earns. of nonconsol. subs. 4. Bef. spec. items. 5. Net of curr. yr. retirement and disposals. d-Deficit. NM-Not Meaningful.

Standard ASE Stock Reports
Vol. 17/No. 72/Sec. 23

September 9, 1982
Copyright © 1982 Standard & Poor's Corp. All Rights Reserved

Standard & Poor's Corp.
25 Broadway, NY, NY 10004

media entertainment, according to the president's message in the annual report. Reviewing the S&P sheets again, we noticed return on assets had been improved and had reached our benchmark of 10 percent in 1978, as earnings had escalated, while return on equity finally achieved our hurdle of 13 percent in 1979.

The next step was a review of long-term debt, which, according to S&P, was only about 15 percent of total capitalization at the end of 1979. When we looked at the annual report, we found that half of it was 5 percent convertible debentures. What did trouble us was a current ratio of only 1.8, since the company financed most of its inventory and receivables by using short-term bank debt. We overcame this prejudice, reasoning that the company's product lines were vibrant and viable and that the cheap long-term debt and its small size allowed for financing capability. Moreover, a check of the annual report revealed a book value of $8.50 and, by our reckoning, close to $2 in net current working capital; so at a purchase price of 5½, there was some degree of comfort in asset cushions, since the company also owned valuable and marketable land in Connecticut under its movie houses. Finally, following our formula, described earlier, cash flow per share was about $2 and was covering both capital expenditures and dividends, leaving about $.30 left over to reduce debt in 1979. So we bought the stock at 5½. As earnings rose from $1.05 in 1979 to $1.24 in 1980 and $1.27 in 1981, the company eventually generated a small following that got the stock price up to 12¾, at the top of the market in June 1981, and kept it mainly hovering around 9–10 even in 1982's bear market.

There are other sources for finding neglected stocks. Periodically, many brokerage houses publish pamphlets on their choices of emerging growth stocks, some of which have merit if they haven't been touted yet. And as we've said before, *Forbes* devotes a section on "Up and Comers" in each issue and *Barron's* profiles one or two smaller companies every week. If you are really set on finding the next sleeper, you can subscribe to the *OTC Review* (see appendix for address), which also highlights over-the-counter companies, with their yields and current, rather complete statistical information.

If you become an active devotee of the art of discovering these backwater stocks, the best time to buy them is in a real downturn in the market, when most stocks sell at depressed levels. As the selling waves wash ashore, you can find a lot of shiny pebbles that can quickly turn into gems. Now let's take a look at some other examples to show why and how we bought some of these gems.

LeaRonal, Inc.

One day in 1977, when we were looking at *Forbes'* "Loaded Laggards" valuation screen, we came upon a company that immediately caught our interest. The company was called LeaRonal, and it was engaged in the business of electroplating, principally with gold, to be used in semiconductors and electronic devices for the communications, defense and consumer-appliance industries.

The company had competitors, but it also had patents on several key processes that were opening up new applications over the next couple of years. We thought new and existing customers might order more products than the company could supply. Meanwhile, the company continued to develop new applications for its principal and existing customers.

At the time, the stock was selling at about 4, which was close to our estimate of the company's hard book value. LeaRonal's return on sales was a low 3.5 percent, but that didn't bother us too much because the business had rapid turnover. Furthermore, the return on equity had not dipped below 14 percent even during the 1974–75 recession, and typically averaged about 20 percent. Debt was only 0.8 percent of the total capitalization, and the current ratio was more than four times current liabilities, indicating the financial strength of the company and its ability to function without resorting to debt. The officers and directors of the company controlled more than 30 percent of the stock and obviously were running the company very well.

Since 1971, LeaRonal had never sold above 6 and had traded between 1½ and 3¾ for the previous three years. The company had sufficient cash flow to finance its future growth in what we concluded was a good and growing business. The only down year in recent history was the recession year of 1975. A final plus: LeaRonal's inventories consisted mainly of gold and silver, which we felt were attractive investments and very marketable at the time. All in all, we felt that at $4 a share, LeaRonal was a good addition to our portfolio, mainly because of its record of high returns on equity without using a lot of debt.

LeaRonal required a lot of patience, but it paid off in the end.

TABLE 4
LeaRonal, Inc.

Per Share Data ($)

Yr. End Feb. 28 [1]	1981	1980	1979	1978	1977	1976	1975	1974	1973	1972
Book Value	NA	6.06	4.77	3.82	3.17	2.74	2.39	2.14	1.84	1.49
Earnings	1.64	1.66	1.24	0.88	0.57	0.47	0.32	0.39	0.43	0.31
Dividends	[3]0.50	0.30	0.24½	0.23¾	0.09	0.10½	0.12⅝	0.05½	0.06⅝	0.05½
Payout Ratio	30%	18%	20%	27%	16%	23%	40%	14%	15%	18%
Prices[2]—High	24½	23⅝	9	6½	3⅝	3⅛	2⅞	3¾	5¾	6⅛
Low	15⅜	7⅛	5½	3⅜	2⅝	2	1¾	1½	2¾	4¼
P/E Ratio—	15–9	14–4	7–4	7–4	6–5	7–4	9–5	10–4	13–6	20–14

Data as orig. reptd. Adj. for stk. divs. of 100% Feb. 1981, 33% Mar. 1980, 25% Feb. 1979, 10% May 1974, 50% Jun. 1972. 1. Of fol. cal. yr. 2. Cal. yr. 3. Five payments. NA-Not Available.

Income Data (Million $)

Year Ended Feb. 28 [1]	Oper. Revs.	Oper. Inc.	% Oper. Inc. of Revs.	Cap. Exp.	Depr.	Int. Exp.	Net Bef. Taxes	Eff. Tax Rate	Net Inc.	% Net Inc. of Revs.
1980	234	16.1	6.9%	2.10	0.80	0.37	[2]16.1	49.6%	8.04	3.4%
1979	199	12.2	6.1%	1.40	0.59	0.25	[2]12.3	49.7%	[3]6.06	3.0%
1978	114	8.1	7.1%	0.83	0.47	0.07	[2] 8.5	48.3%	4.31	3.8%
1977	77	4.9	6.4%	0.67	0.42	0.01	[2] 5.5	46.6%	2.85	3.7%
1976	61	4.9	7.9%	1.08	0.28	0.01	4.9	51.5%	2.36	3.8%
1975	55	3.6	6.4%	0.49	0.31	0.01	3.5	52.0%	1.63	3.0%
1974	67	3.7	5.6%	0.85	0.27	0.03	3.9	47.9%	1.98	3.0%
1973	84	4.5	5.4%	0.62	0.22	0.08	4.5	49.7%	2.17	2.6%
1972	45	3.2	7.1%	0.20	0.18	Nil	3.1	48.2%	1.57	3.5%
1971	31	2.2	7.3%	0.10	0.15	Nil	2.2	45.7%	1.15	3.8%

Balance Sheet Data (Million $)

Feb. 28 [1]	Cash	Current— Assets	Current— Liab.	Ratio	Total Assets	Ret. on Assets	Long Term Debt	Common Equity	Total Cap.	% LT Debt of Cap.	Ret. on Equity
1980	8.64	35.0	9.2	3.8	41.4	20.9%	0.54	29.4	32.2	1.7%	30.5%
1979	2.62	30.8	11.2	2.7	35.9	19.6%	0.11	23.4	24.7	0.5%	28.8%
1978	3.86	22.0	6.2	3.5	26.1	18.1%	0.12	18.9	19.9	0.6%	25.0%
1977	3.60	17.7	4.9	3.6	21.5	14.6%	0.14	15.7	16.6	0.8%	19.5%
1976	2.57	14.7	3.2	4.6	18.0	14.5%	0.15	14.0	14.8	1.0%	18.1%
1975	1.83	12.3	1.6	7.6	14.7	10.6%	0.16	12.3	13.1	1.2%	14.0%
1974	3.21	14.0	4.4	3.2	16.1	12.6%	0.17	11.1	11.7	1.4%	19.1%
1973	2.44	14.0	5.4	2.6	15.4	17.1%	0.18	9.7	10.0	1.8%	24.8%
1972	1.64	9.0	2.0	4.4	10.1	17.9%	Nil	8.0	8.1	Nil	22.2%
1971	1.32	6.3	1.2	5.2	7.2	17.9%	Nil	5.9	6.0	Nil	21.1%

Data as orig. reptd. 1. Of fol. cal. yr. 2. Incl. equity in earns. of nonconsol. subs. 3. Refl. acctg. change.

Standard NYSE Stock Reports
Vol. 49/No. 131/Sec. 18
July 9, 1982
Copyright © 1982 Standard & Poor's Corp. All Rights Reserved
Standard & Poor's Corp.
25 Broadway, NY, NY 10004

Despite a lackluster performance throughout 1977 and a good part of 1978, we held on to the stock because we believed it was a conservatively managed company with proprietary processes operating in a burgeoning market.

We actually owned the stock until 1980, at which time we sold it at 18. Thus, our holding period was four years, but our return was close to 600 percent, or 150 percent a year. The return was exceptional, and it can be partially attributed to the phenomenal rise of gold and silver prices in late 1979 and early 1980, which boosted the value of the company's inventories. But it also shows that if you stick with a good choice and have the patience to wait for the rise, the percentage rise can be huge and come all at once.

In fact, we sold too early. By mid-1981 the stock reached 24½, having earned $1.66 in 1980, up from $.47 in 1976. Meanwhile, over the same period, the company's price/earnings multiple increased from 6 to 12, a typical example of multiple expansion brought about by a good earnings record that was ultimately recognized.

Meredith Corporation

A small article in *Forbes* magazine in 1975 on Meredith Corporation was the catalyst for one of our most successful investments. Meredith was best known as the publisher of *Better Homes and Gardens*, but it also did printing work for others and published trade magazines and newspapers that had carved out rapidly growing markets. What caught our attention in the *Forbes* article was the company's ownership of five TV and six radio stations in major markets, which we knew to be unusually profitable businesses.

At the time, the stock was selling for $10 a share, which we considered an undervalued price because of the broadcasting properties. The stated book value of the company was $15 a share, but after talking to some Wall Street analysts, we determined that the broadcasting properties were carried on the books at a substantial discount from market value and were probably worth at least $30 a share. That meant the real equity per share was closer to $45, or four and a half times the price of the stock, and that's what propelled us to buy.

Meredith's long-term debt was 17 percent of total capitalization, and its current ratio was 2.2 to 1, indicating a strong financial situation. At $10, the stock was selling at five times earnings per share, 70 percent of stated book value and only 22 percent of real book value. Meredith was also controlled by two families and offered the prospect of a buy-out at some future point. All in all, we concluded the downside risk was minimal, and the upside potential was good.

By 1981, the stock had soared nearly five and a half times, as advertising revenues increased and investors discovered the hidden

TABLE 5
MEREDITH CORPORATION

Per Share Data ($)

Yr. End June 30	1982	1981	1980	1979	1978	1977	1976	1975	1974	1973
Book Value	41.41	34.85	27.97	26.05	23.78	22.34	19.00	14.60	14.30	13.40
Earnings[2]	8.57	[1]8.13	[1]6.87	[1]5.28	4.77	3.97	4.33	2.03	2.47	2.22
Dividends	1.70	1.46	1.26	1.10	0.90	0.75	0.70	0.70	0.70	0.70
Payout Ratio	20%	18%	19%	21%	19%	19%	16%	35%	29%	32%
Prices[3]—High	79⅝	66½	54¾	36½	40¼	29¼	19	13½	11⅜	20½
Low	52¾	47⅜	32	27	24⅜	17¼	10¼	8⅜	7	8⅛
P/E Ratio—	9–6	8–6	8–5	7–5	8–5	7–4	4–2	7–4	5–3	9–4

Data as orig. reptd. **1.** Ful. dil.: 7.92 in 1981, 6.71 in 1980, 5.17 in 1979. **2.** Bef. results of disc. opers. of +0.07 in 1974, −0.35 in 1973, and spec. item(s) of −0.63 in 1981, +0.09 in 1977, +0.27 in 1976, +0.05 in 1975, −4.87 in 1973. **3.** Cal. yr. NA-Not Available.

Income Data (Million $)

Year Ended June 30	Revs.	Oper. Inc.	% Oper. Inc. of Revs.	Cap. Exp.	Depr.	Int. Exp.	Net Bef. Taxes	Eff. Tax Rate	[4]Net Inc.	% Net Inc. of Revs.
1982	449	59.4	13.2%	15.5	10.6	3.75	[3]50.4	46.6%	26.9	6.0%
1981	403	50.8	12.6%	21.9	9.4	3.61	[3]43.4	41.1%	25.6	6.3%
1980	349	46.9	13.5%	15.0	10.3	3.15	[3]38.4	44.3%	21.4	6.1%
1979	318	38.9	12.2%	21.5	8.9	3.14	[3]29.8	45.3%	[2]16.3	5.1%
1978	287	31.9	11.1%	19.4	7.9	1.85	[3]25.3	41.9%	14.7	5.1%
1977	236	25.1	10.7%	18.1	4.9	1.86	[3]21.7	43.7%	12.2	5.2%
1976	191	22.1	11.6%	9.4	4.2	1.96	[3]24.1	45.0%	13.3	7.0%
1975	160	16.9	10.5%	4.7	4.2	1.89	[3]11.7	47.8%	6.1	3.8%
[1]1974	150	19.5	13.1%	7.3	4.0	2.39	[3]13.7	47.3%	7.2	4.8%
[1]1973	140	17.9	12.8%	4.5	3.5	2.48	[3]12.1	47.9%	6.3	4.5%

Balance Sheet Data (Million $)

June 30	Cash	—Current— Assets	Liab.	Ratio	Total Assets	Ret. on Assets	Long Term Debt	Common Equity	Total Cap.	% LT Debt of Cap.	Ret. on Equity
1982	45.3	154	73.6	2.1	354	8.1%	32.4	167	227	14.2%	17.1%
1981	22.5	126	56.1	2.2	316	8.6%	33.8	151	209	16.2%	18.1%
1980	15.8	106	52.3	2.0	277	8.2%	29.5	131	182	16.2%	17.5%
1979	18.5	104	44.5	2.3	246	7.2%	29.6	113	163	18.1%	15.3%
1978	12.3	94	40.7	2.3	208	7.5%	18.9	100	136	13.9%	15.6%
1977	32.6	92	31.7	2.9	181	7.1%	16.8	88	124	13.5%	14.8%
1976	37.9	88	29.7	3.0	161	8.9%	17.8	77	112	15.9%	18.5%
1975	11.7	57	26.3	2.2	136	4.6%	16.4	65	96	17.2%	9.6%
1974	6.9	54	29.2	1.8	127	5.2%	10.2	60	82	12.4%	12.4%
1973	15.7	74	25.1	2.9	145	4.0%	28.8	54	94	30.7%	10.5%

Data as orig. reptd. **1.** Excludes discontinued operations. **2.** Reflects accounting change. **3.** Incl. equity in earns. of nonconsol. subs. **4.** Bef. results of disc. opers. and spec. item(s) in 1974, 1973, and 1981, 1977, 1976, 1975, 1973.

Standard NYSE Stock Reports
Vol. 49/No. 216/Sec. 16

November 9, 1982
Copyright © 1982 Standard & Poor's Corp. All Rights Reserved

Standard & Poor's Corp.
25 Broadway, NY, NY 10004

value of the broadcasting properties. We sold out in December 1981 at 62¾ because we became concerned that advertising revenues might suffer in the ongoing recession.

Borg-Warner Corporation

In 1979, we were looking through *Value Line* and came upon a profile of Borg-Warner. Well known for its York air conditioners, the company was also involved in auto equipment (transmissions, clutches, pumps), chemicals and plastics. But what really intrigued us was Borg-Warner's 18 percent interest in Hughes Tool, a leading oil-service company with a dominant position in hard drill bits. The oil-service industry was expanding rapidly because the high price of oil had launched the greatest drilling boom in decades.

At the time, Borg-Warner's stock sold for around $14 a share, which was significantly below the company's stated book value of $23 a share. But even that figure was understated, because the Hughes Tool holdings, which were carried at cost, had subsequently doubled in market value. We calculated that by ascribing the current market value to the Hughes Tool investment, Borg-Warner's book value was something on the order of $27 a share.

Borg-Warner had other attractions as well. Earnings had jumped from $1.16 in the recession year of 1975, to $2.11 in 1976, to $2.47 in 1977 and to $3.12 by 1978. Long-term debt was only 12.4 percent of capitalization and in 1979 return on shareholders' equity was 15.4 percent.

Despite these positive factors, the stock had been a laggard for years because investors perceived Borg-Warner's business as highly dependent on the auto and housing industries, which were in a slump because of high interest rates. On the positive side, we noted that dividends from Hughes Tool might partially offset this dependence on cyclical markets. And, as it turned out, despite the downturn in its major markets, the company made $3.63 in 1979, up from $3.12 in 1978.

At $14 a share, where we bought the stock in 1979, the company was selling at five times 1978 earnings (slightly above its lowest p/e of the last ten years) and at around 57 percent of book value per share. We also noted that the price history of the stock showed considerable buying support at around $13, and, in fact, the stock had never sold below that price during the previous four years. Thus, we concluded that even if the market tumbled, the worst case for the stock was $13, or some 16 percent below the stock price at the time. In sum, we concluded the downside risk was manageable.

By 1980, the stock hit 22, and by late 1982, it rose to over 40. Interestingly, institutional holdings of Borg-Warner doubled between 1978 and 1981. As so often happens, once the company's fundamentals became appreciated, the company won sponsorship and the stock broke out of its undervalued range.

TABLE 6
BORG-WARNER CORPORATION

Per Share Data ($)

Yr. End Dec. 31	1982	¹1981	1980	1979	1978	1977	1976	1975	1974	1973
Book Value	NA	29.51	27.26	25.41	22.73	20.45	19.08	17.65	16.97	16.45
Earnings	NA	4.00	2.93	3.63	3.12	2.47	2.11	1.16	1.33	1.85
Dividends	1.43	1.28	1.17³/₈	1.03⁷/₈	0.92¹/₂	0.82¹/₂	0.70⁵/₈	0.67¹/₂	0.67¹/₂	0.67⁵/₈
Payout Ratio	NA	31%	39%	28%	29%	33%	33%	58%	50%	35%
Prices—High	40³/₄	28³/₄	22³/₄	18⁵/₈	17¹/₄	16⁷/₈	15³/₈	10³/₄	11¹/₄	18³/₈
Low	22	18⁵/₈	14⁷/₈	13¹/₂	12³/₄	12⁵/₈	9⁷/₈	6⁵/₈	6³/₈	8³/₈
P/E Ratio—	NA	7-5	8-5	5-4	6-4	7-5	7-5	9-6	8-5	10-4

Data as orig. reptd. Adj. for stk. div(s). of 100% Nov. 1981. 1. Reflects acctg. change. 2. Incl. service revenues after 1981. NA-Not Available.

Income Data (Million $)

Year Ended Dec. 31	Revs.	Oper. Inc.	% Oper. Inc. of Revs.	Cap. Exp.	Depr.	Int. Exp.	Net Bef. Taxes	Eff. Tax Rate	⁴Net Inc.	% Net Inc. of Revs.
¹1981	2,761	207	7.5%	176	73.8	²52.1	³234	24.2%	172	6.2%
1980	2,673	204	7.6%	134	64.4	49.0	³178	26.5%	126	4.7%
1979	2,717	273	10.1%	131	59.6	33.1	³226	30.1%	156	5.7%
1978	2,326	270	11.6%	115	55.2	26.7	³225	39.1%	134	5.8%
1977	2,032	225	11.0%	77	50.9	25.8	³178	40.1%	104	5.1%
1976	1,862	191	10.3%	36	43.4	26.0	³151	44.2%	82	4.4%
1975	1,639	124	7.6%	56	42.8	36.4	³ 68	31.1%	¹ 45	2.7%
1974	1,763	142	8.0%	83	43.1	38.1	³ 75	29.3%	51	2.9%
1973	1,547	185	11.9%	70	40.5	21.7	³135	45.7%	71	4.6%
1972	1,283	157	12.2%	63	37.3	17.1	³113	46.6%	59	4.6%

Balance Sheet Data (Million $)

Dec. 31	Cash	Current Assets	Current Liab.	Ratio	Total Assets	Ret. on Assets	Long Term Debt	Common Equity	Total Cap.	% LT Debt of Cap.	Ret. on Equity
1981	94	827	560	1.5	2,191	8.4%	156	1,231	1,460	10.7%	14.5%
1980	46	751	432	1.7	1,902	6.8%	166	1,142	1,365	12.1%	11.4%
1979	41	845	451	1.9	1,817	8.9%	156	1,061	1,262	12.4%	15.4%
1978	90	789	388	2.0	1,652	8.6%	164	945	1,182	13.9%	14.8%
1977	25	649	316	2.1	1,450	7.2%	148	844	1,067	13.8%	12.6%
1976	117	689	316	2.2	1,293	6.6%	128	713	922	13.9%	11.7%
1975	39	590	244	2.4	1,193	3.6%	163	659	900	18.1%	6.6%
1974	22	688	264	2.6	1,285	4.1%	247	639	957	25.8%	7.9%
1973	25	642	308	2.1	1,171	6.6%	135	611	812	16.7%	11.9%
1972	25	528	202	2.6	1,021	5.9%	141	579	781	18.1%	10.2%

Data as orig. reptd. 1. Reflects accounting change. 2. Reflects acctg. change. 3. Incl. equity in earns. of nonconsol. subs. 4. Bef. spec. item(s) in 1972.

Standard NYSE Stock Reports
Vol. 49/No. 231/Sec. 6

December 2, 1982
Copyright © 1982 Standard & Poor's Corp. All Rights Reserved

Standard & Poor's Corp.
25 Broadway, NY, NY 10004

Russell Corporation

In 1980, we became interested in Russel Corporation because of an outstanding quarterly earnings report. On further examination, we learned that Russell had averaged more than a 6 percent return on sales for the previous five years, a very good performance for an apparel company. Russell had created a niche for itself as the largest manufacturer of athletic uniforms and sportswear, a market that exploded in the 1970s because of the growing interest in outdoor sports, jogging and health. Long-term debt was under 25 percent of capitalization, the current ratio was 4.1 to 1, and over the previous five years, the company had consistently averaged a return on equity of better than 15 percent. Earnings had grown consistently from $.60 in 1976 to $1.37 by 1979. The company was closely held, but the owners were not involved in management.

The fundamentals appeared persuasive, and with an $8 book value, the stock appeared undervalued at 7¼. The company had more or less languished in a range between 4 and 8 for the previous

TABLE 7
RUSSELL CORPORATION

Per Share Data ($)

Yr. End Dec. 31	1981	1980	1979	1978	1977	1976	1975	1974	1973	1972
Book Value	**10.61**	8.91	7.42	6.44	5.41	4.67	4.50	3.88	3.39	3.12
Earnings[1]	**2.04**	1.78	1.37	1.21	0.89	0.60	[2]0.62	0.59	0.36	0.28
Dividends	**0.37**	0.31	0.26	0.22	0.15	0.13	0.10½	0.09¼	0.08½	0.06¾
Payout Ratio	**18%**	17%	19%	18%	16%	22%	17%	16%	23%	24%
Prices—High	**16¾**	12½	8⅛	9½	5⅜	3¾	2½	1¾	2⅝	2½
Low	**10¼**	5½	5	4⅝	2⅝	2¼	1¼	1	1⅛	1⅞
P/E Ratio—	**8-5**	7-3	6-4	8-4	6-3	6-4	4-2	3-2	7-3	9-7

Data as orig. reptd. Adj. for stk. divs. of 100% in Jun. 1981, 50% Jul. 1978, 100% May 1976. 1. Bef. spec. items of +0.09 in 1975. 2. Ful. dil.: 0.61.

Income Data (Million $)

Year Ended Dec. 31[1]	Oper. Revs.	Oper. Inc.	% Oper. Inc. of Revs.	Cap. Exp.	Depr.	Int. Exp.	Net Bef. Taxes	Eff. Tax Rate	[2]Net Inc.	% Net Inc. of Revs.
1981	**270**	**54.8**	**20.3%**	**[3]31.9**	**9.46**	**5.22**	**41.2**	**41.6%**	**24.0**	**8.9%**
1980	238	45.6	19.1%	20.4	7.36	3.10	36.3	42.6%	20.8	8.7%
1979	191	35.6	18.7%	19.0	5.88	3.12	28.0	43.0%	16.0	8.4%
1978	176	32.6	18.5%	12.4	4.78	2.90	25.5	45.0%	14.0	8.0%
1977	146	24.4	16.7%	17.5	3.66	2.41	18.9	45.7%	10.3	7.0%
1976	125	15.9	12.8%	18.9	2.75	2.47	11.3	41.1%	6.7	5.3%
1975	103	16.3	15.9%	10.6	2.65	2.26	11.7	45.8%	6.4	6.2%
1974	107	16.1	15.0%	2.7	2.70	2.27	11.4	48.3%	5.9	5.5%
1973	91	10.8	11.9%	4.6	2.38	2.23	6.5	44.8%	3.6	3.9%
1972	75	9.0	12.0%	3.7	2.39	1.77	5.1	44.4%	2.8	3.8%

Balance Sheet Data (Million $)

Dec. 31[1]	Cash	—Current— Assets	Liab.	Ratio	Total Assets	Ret. on Assets	Long Term Debt	Common Equity	Total Cap.	% LT Debt of Cap.	Ret. on Equity
1981	**1.09**	**98.7**	**32.2**	**3.1**	**201**	**13.0%**	**30.6**	**123**	**167**	**18.3%**	**21.3%**
1980	3.98	88.5	21.6	4.1	168	13.3%	30.5	103	144	21.1%	22.1%
1979	9.48	80.1	17.5	4.6	144	11.7%	30.2	86	125	24.1%	19.9%
1978	2.14	72.1	21.1	3.4	125	12.2%	21.7	73	102	21.3%	21.1%
1977	1.75	61.1	16.4	3.7	105	10.5%	20.1	61	87	22.9%	18.2%
1976	1.84	52.5	10.0	5.3	91	7.3%	21.0	53	80	26.3%	12.8%
1975	5.21	48.1	7.2	6.7	80	8.4%	22.3	45	72	31.0%	15.1%
1974	1.01	42.9	10.7	4.0	70	8.6%	15.3	39	58	26.3%	16.1%
1973	1.58	39.3	11.8	3.3	67	5.6%	16.2	34	54	30.0%	11.0%
1972	0.83	36.0	12.0	3.0	61	5.0%	13.7	31	48	28.4%	9.4%

Data as orig. reptd. 1. Prior to 1971 fis. yr. ended Jun. 2. Bef. spec. items. 3. Net of curr. yr. retirement & disposls.

Standard ASE Stock Reports
Vol. 17/No. 93/Sec. 27

November 23, 1982
Copyright © 1982 Standard & Poor's Corp. All Rights Reserved

Standard & Poor's Corp.
25 Broadway, NY, NY 10004

three years because it had little sponsorship and was tainted with the label of a garment manufacturer, a notoriously unpopular industry on Wall Street.

For the previous ten years, as noted earlier, the apparel industry had been viewed as subject to foreign competition, low labor productivity, poor labor relations and outmoded production facilities. But in reality, the industry had taken some important steps to better its position. As an example, it had met the challenge of foreign competition by buying new and sophisticated machinery, which helped reduce the labor content of its finished product. Consequently, the United States had actually become one of the world's low-cost producers of apparel.

These changes were largely ignored by investors, who had made up their minds in the mid-1970s that apparel companies were unattractive investments. Once investor sentiment about an industry turns negative, it takes a lot of fundamental improvement before opinion changes. Finally, by mid-1980, the financial community realized that earnings of apparel makers were rising and that the stocks were undervalued. Changing investor sentiment pushed Russell's stock as high as 16¾ in 1981 and 24⅝ in 1982.

Maryland Cup Corporation

A profile in *Barron's* alerted us to the undervaluation of Maryland Cup, a producer of disposable cups, bowls, plates and cutlery that were mostly sold to fast-food outlets, institutions and retail supermarkets. Maryland Cup was also the world's largest manufacturer of ice-cream cones and was a major producer of drinking straws. We concluded that the company was a major beneficiary of the trend toward eating away from home or in the backyard and of the desire for more leisure time. Thus, it was not hard to project continued growth in sales and earnings.

In 1978, when we first looked at the stock, it traded in the low 20s, at about seven times earnings, or around the level of the previous three years. The company's return on equity was 13.5 percent and return on assets only about 7 percent, not necessarily within our parameters, but we felt continued earnings growth would improve these percentages over time. The current ratio was 2.6 to 1 and the long-term debt was 30 percent of total capitalization, about average for a manufacturing company of this kind. Another plus was that most of the debt was at low interest rates, maturing between the mid-1980s and the mid-1990s. Finally, book value was about $22 a share, and the family management controlled 55 percent of the stock. The institutions had largely ignored the company, probably because of insufficient float. All in all, we concluded the stock was a good percentage play.

In 1980, Kraft—later to become Dart & Kraft—made an offer to buy the company, and the stock price shot up to 37½, clearly

TABLE 8
MARYLAND CUP CORPORATION

Per Share Data ($)

Yr. End Sep. 30	1982	1981	1980	1979	1978	1977	[1]1976	1975	1974	1973
Book Value	NA	32.92	29.22	25.96	22.30	19.94	17.76	15.97	14.76	13.73
Earnings[4]	[2]4.66	[2]4.52	[2]3.89	[2]3.33	[2]2.86	[2]2.61	[2]2.18	[2]1.56	[2]1.39	[2]1.50
Dividends	0.85	0.73	0.62	0.54⅜	0.48	0.42¾	0.37⅞	0.35	0.34⅜	0.32½
Payout Ratio	18%	16%	16%	16%	17%	16%	17%	22%	25%	22%
Prices[3]—High	47¾	43¾	37½	31⅞	28½	20⅝	18¾	12⅛	13⅛	23⅞
Low	31⅝	27¼	19¼	17⅞	18¾	15⅜	11	7½	6⅝	8⅛
P/E Ratio—	10-7	10-6	10-5	10-5	10-7	8-6	9-5	8-5	10-5	16-5

Data as orig. reptd. Adj. for stk. div(s). of 50% Nov. 1978, 3% Jan. 1977. 1. Reflects accounting change. 2. Ful. dil.: 4.43 in 1982, 4.28 in 1981, 3.67 in 1980, 3.14 in 1979, 2.69 in 1978, 2.47 in 1977, 2.07 in 1976, 1.50 in 1975, 1.34 in 1974, 1.44 in 1973. 3. Cal. yr. 4. Bef. spec. item(s) of +0.90 in 1979. 5. Rate based on initial quarterly payment after 3-for-2 split. NA-Not Available.

Income Data (Million $)

Year Ended Sep. 30	Revs.	Oper. Inc.	% Oper. Inc. of Revs.	Cap. Exp.	Depr.	Int. Exp.	Net Bef. Taxes	Eff. Tax Rate	[4]Net Inc.	% Net Inc. of Revs.
1981	647	80.6	12.5%	32.7	20.1	[3]5.52	55.5	45.1%	30.5	4.7%
1980	579	72.9	12.6%	25.4	19.1	9.98	44.9	41.7%	26.1	4.5%
1979	491	59.4	12.1%	37.6	17.4	8.60	34.3	34.7%	22.4	4.6%
1978	423	57.0	13.5%	29.1	15.6	6.45	35.9	46.7%	19.2	4.5%
1977	374	51.9	13.9%	27.5	14.3	5.90	[2]32.3	45.7%	17.5	4.7%
[1]1976	310	44.1	14.2%	22.6	12.7	5.09	[2]27.3	46.3%	14.6	4.7%
1975	265	35.2	13.3%	19.1	11.5	4.67	[2]19.6	46.7%	10.5	4.0%
1974	228	30.7	13.4%	14.8	10.9	3.82	[2]16.9	44.8%	9.3	4.1%
1973	189	32.0	16.9%	16.3	10.1	2.90	[2]19.2	47.5%	[3]10.1	5.3%
1972	169	29.5	17.4%	9.1	9.5	2.98	17.4	47.9%	9.0	5.3%

Balance Sheet Data (Million $)

Sep. 30	Cash	Current Assets	Current Liab.	Ratio	Total Assets	Ret. on Assets	Long Term Debt	Common Equity	Total Cap.	% LT Debt of Cap.	Ret. on Equity
1981	23.6	187	70.6	2.6	377	8.2%	57.8	223	302	19.2%	14.5%
1980	25.4	181	61.5	2.9	360	7.5%	83.9	196	297	28.3%	14.1%
1979	5.2	163	57.1	2.8	336	7.1%	89.1	174	277	32.1%	13.8%
1978	3.7	137	52.0	2.6	292	7.1%	70.3	150	238	29.5%	13.5%
1977	4.5	119	31.6	3.7	252	7.3%	69.7	134	219	31.9%	13.9%
1976	5.6	101	31.1	3.3	232	6.7%	66.9	119	200	33.5%	12.9%
1975	20.0	87	18.7	4.7	204	5.4%	65.0	107	184	35.3%	10.1%
1974	2.4	76	32.6	2.3	185	5.3%	41.3	99	151	27.3%	9.7%
1973	2.7	63	20.0	3.1	167	6.3%	43.8	92	146	29.9%	11.4%
1972	2.4	57	13.0	4.3	154	5.9%	46.2	84	140	32.9%	11.2%

Data as orig. reptd. 1. Reflects accounting change. 2. Incl. equity in earns. of nonconsol. subs. 3. Reflects accounting change. 4. Bef. spec. item(s) in 1979.

Standard NYSE Stock Reports
Vol. 49/No. 244/Sec. 15

Standard & Poor's Corp.
25 Broadway, NY, NY 10004

breaking out of its $20 to $30 trading range. When the family rejected the sale of the company, the stock fell back to about $25, at which point we bought more stock because we thought another suitor might come along with a better offer.

In 1981, merger rumors surfaced again. The company announced it was holding talks with a competitor, and the stock jumped to around $43. Once again, the sale was rejected by the family, which apparently considered the offer inadequate. Nevertheless, we did not sell our holdings.

The stated book value had risen to $30 a share, the fundamentals were still sound, and the company had been pursued twice, with a third, perhaps successful, offer a real possibility. The company was obviously thinking seriously enough about a sale to have some earnest merger discussions.

But the real basis for our decision to hold the stock was its good value: a low p/e, a price near book value, no excessive debt, potential for excellent and consistent earnings growth, a going market for the company's products and the possibility for multiple expansion when investors recognized the inherent value of the company.

American Business Products

Our 5 percent rule helped us discover American Business Products, a maker of printed business forms and envelopes. In October 1978, when we started looking at the company, it had a rising trend in all ratios: earnings, return on assets, return on equity and return on sales. Its debt, representing only 20 percent of capitalization, carried a low interest rate, and the firm, which had a strong marketing ability and loyal customers, was in a recession-proof business. Another positive factor was that one family owned 25 percent of the company.

We bought the stock at 7⅜, or about five and a half times earnings, the lowest price/earnings ratio for the stock in ten years. The lowest yearly high for the stock over the previous ten years (excluding 1977) had been $10, so we were aiming for a return of at least $2.50 a share, or 33 percent on our investment. The downside risk on the stock was perhaps $1, and the upside potential was $2.50, or a better than two and a half times risk/reward ratio.

When earnings rose from $1.34 in 1978 to $1.92 in 1979 and $2.15 in 1980, the stock rose to a high of 12½ in 1979 and 15½ in 1980. We exited at 12½ in 1980, content with a nearly 76 percent appreciation in two years, or 35 percent a year.

TABLE 9
AMERICAN BUSINESS PRODUCTS

Per Share Data ($)

Yr. End Dec. 31	1982	1981	1980	1979	1978	1977	¹1976	1975	1974	1973
Book Value	NA	13.32	12.34	10.68	9.18	8.19	7.46	7.22	6.72	5.82
Earnings²	NA	1.87	2.15	1.92	1.34	1.03	0.76	0.73	1.08	0.71
Dividends	0.56	0.48	0.46	0.41	0.34	0.28	0.26	0.23¾	0.16	0.13⅜
Payout Ratio	NA	26%	21%	21%	25%	27%	34%	32%	15%	19%
Prices—High	19⅛	16⅝	15½	12½	11	8⅛	10⅝	14⅛	10	17⅝
Low	11½	10½	7⅞	7⅛	6⅞	5¾	6⅛	6⅜	6⅜	8⅛
P/E Ratio—	NA	9-6	7-4	7-4	8-5	8-6	14-8	19-9	9-6	25-11

Data as orig. reptd. Adj. for stk. divs. of 50% Jun. 1975. 1. Refl. merger or acq. 2. Ful. dil.: 1.32 in 1978, 1.01 in 1977, 0.74 in 1976, 0.72 in 1975, 1.07 in 1974, 0.71 in 1973. NA-Not Available.

Income Data (Million $)

Year Ended Dec. 31	Revs.	Oper. Inc.	% Oper. Inc. of Revs.	Cap. Exp.	Depr.	Int. Exp.	Net Bef. Taxes	Eff. Tax Rate	Net Inc.	% Net Inc. of Revs.
1981	210	17.5	8.4%	²7.40	3.75	1.03	13.1	46.2%	7.06	3.4%
1980	186	19.4	10.4%	5.58	3.30	0.70	15.4	47.6%	8.07	4.3%
1979	166	17.3	10.4%	5.38	2.99	0.85	13.5	46.7%	7.18	4.3%
1978	133	13.2	9.9%	4.07	2.69	0.78	9.7	48.3%	5.01	3.8%
1977	119	10.5	8.9%	4.46	2.50	0.69	7.3	47.8%	3.83	3.2%
¹1976	105	8.3	7.9%	2.93	2.24	0.67	5.4	47.6%	2.83	2.7%
1975	69	5.8	8.3%	1.54	1.61	0.50	3.8	45.7%	2.06	3.0%
1974	70	8.0	11.6%	2.94	1.52	0.63	5.9	48.6%	3.03	4.4%
1973	55	4.9	9.0%	4.79	1.21	0.35	3.5	42.6%	2.01	3.7%
¹1972	46	4.3	9.2%	2.92	1.03	0.25	3.2	47.2%	1.68	3.6%

Balance Sheet Data (Million $)

Dec. 31	Cash	Current Assets	Current Liab.	Ratio	Total Assets	Ret. on Assets	Long Term Debt	Common Equity	Total Cap.	% LT Debt of Cap.	Ret. on Equity
1981	5.41	50.6	17.7	2.9	88.2	9.0%	16.7	51.9	69.9	23.9%	14.3%
1980	3.42	41.0	12.5	3.3	68.8	12.3%	7.9	46.3	55.9	14.1%	18.7%
1979	0.63	36.7	12.6	2.9	62.1	12.1%	7.7	39.8	49.3	15.6%	19.3%
1978	1.19	32.3	11.3	2.9	56.2	9.3%	8.9	34.2	44.7	19.8%	15.4%
1977	2.76	28.1	9.7	2.9	50.9	7.8%	9.1	30.5	41.2	22.0%	13.1%
1976	2.63	25.3	9.1	2.8	46.9	6.3%	8.5	27.7	37.8	22.3%	10.3%
1975	2.69	16.8	6.0	2.8	32.8	6.1%	5.4	20.1	26.8	20.2%	10.5%
1974	2.46	17.9	7.1	2.5	34.1	9.6%	7.1	18.8	27.0	26.2%	17.3%
1973	1.57	14.2	5.6	2.5	29.4	7.4%	6.5	16.2	23.7	27.5%	13.0%
1972	2.27	12.9	4.7	2.7	24.8	7.1%	4.6	14.6	20.0	22.7%	11.8%

Data as orig. reptd. 1. Reflects merger or acquisition. 2. Net of current yr. retirement and disposals.

Standard NYSE Stock Reports
Vol. 49/No. 220/Sec. 3
November 15, 1982
Copyright © 1982 Standard & Poor's Corp. All Rights Reserved
Standard & Poor's Corp.
25 Broadway, NY, NY 10004

Even in the recession of 1981–82, the stock held up, only declining to 10½, despite slightly lower earnings—of $1.87—in 1981. Apparently investors liked American Business Products' recession-resistant business.

P. H. Glatfelter Company

A *Forbes* valuation screen put us onto P. H. Glatfelter, a manufacturer of printing and writing paper, whose customers are book publishing and commercial printing concerns. With minimum long-term debt and a return on equity averaging consistently over 17 percent, the company was selling at 22 in the summer of 1980, or four and a half times earnings. Part of the low stock price was attributable to a projected downturn in earnings caused by a forty-

TABLE 10

P. H. GLATFELTER COMPANY

Per Share Data ($)

Yr. End Dec. 31	1981	1980	³1979	1978	1977	1976	1975	1974	1973	1972
Book Value	32.43	30.35	27.13	22.78	20.04	17.71	16.07	15.02	13.54	12.69
Earnings¹²	3.70	4.83	5.15	3.80	3.25	3.02	2.37	2.63	1.17	0.57
Dividends	1.60	1.60	1.20	0.98	0.90	0.74⅞	0.71½	0.48¼	0.26¼	0.23¾
Payout Ratio	43%	33%	23%	26%	28%	25%	31%	20%	22%	42%
Prices—High	36½	31	34⅞	27½	20¾	18⅜	12⅜	8	7¼	6½
Low	26¼	22⅛	23⅝	17½	15⅝	9⅞	6⅝	5½	4¾	4¼
P/E Ratio—	10–7	6–5	7–5	7–5	6–5	6–3	5–3	3–2	6–4	12–7

Data as orig. reptd. Adj. for stk. divs. of 100% May 1977, 40% Apr. 1976, 50% May 1973. 1. Bef. spec. item of −0.21 in 1972. 2. Ful. dil.: 3.00 in 1976, 2.19 in 1975, 2.16 in 1974, 1.01 in 1973, 0.55 in 1972. 3. Reflects merger or acq.

Income Data (Million $)

Year Ended Dec. 31	Revs.	Oper. Inc.	% Oper. Inc. of Revs.	Cap. Exp.	Depr.	Int. Exp.	Net Bef. Taxes	Eff. Tax Rate	¹Net Inc.	% Net Inc. of Revs.
1981	266	35.0	13.2%	23.7	10.9	0.52	25.4	34.9%	16.5	6.2%
1980	263	42.6	16.2%	38.6	10.0	0.70	36.5	41.2%	21.4	8.2%
²1979	236	48.4	20.5%	14.9	8.4	0.72	43.6	48.1%	22.6	9.6%
1978	121	34.5	28.5%	6.7	6.3	0.85	30.7	51.5%	14.9	12.3%
1977	108	30.8	28.5%	5.7	6.1	0.94	25.9	50.8%	12.8	11.8%
1976	98	29.0	29.6%	5.9	5.8	1.00	23.8	50.7%	11.8	12.0%
1975	80	21.4	26.9%	7.9	5.3	1.04	16.5	48.2%	8.5	10.7%
1974	78	21.0	27.1%	6.8	5.2	0.98	16.5	49.3%	8.3	10.8%
1973	58	12.7	21.8%	3.8	5.1	1.00	7.7	49.5%	3.9	6.7%
1972	48	9.3	19.3%	1.5	4.4	1.03	4.4	50.9%	2.2	4.5%

Balance Sheet Data (Million $)

Dec. 31	Cash	Current Assets	Current Liab.	Ratio	Total Assets	Ret. on Assets	Long Term Debt	Common Equity	Total Cap.	% LT Debt of Cap.	Ret. on Equity
1981	10.6	52.9	26.8	2.0	194	8.5%	5.5	144	168	3.3%	11.8%
1980	21.3	64.7	36.7	1.8	195	11.7%	7.8	134	158	4.9%	16.8%
1979	33.0	71.6	28.5	2.5	173	14.1%	10.0	120	144	6.9%	20.5%
1978	43.6	64.4	16.6	3.9	130	12.0%	12.3	88	113	10.8%	17.9%
1977	36.5	54.1	14.1	3.8	119	11.1%	14.5	78	105	13.8%	17.2%
1976	30.3	45.4	13.3	3.4	111	10.7%	16.8	69	98	17.2%	17.7%
1975	19.5	34.6	10.5	3.3	100	8.4%	18.0	58	89	20.1%	14.9%
1974	16.9	31.5	11.6	2.7	94	8.8%	17.7	49	83	21.4%	17.0%
1973	12.6	24.5	8.8	2.8	86	4.7%	18.3	40	77	23.7%	8.9%
1972	5.8	17.5	5.1	3.4	80	2.7%	18.9	37	75	25.1%	4.5%

Data as orig. reptd. 1. Bef. spec. items. 2. Refl. merg. or acq.

Standard ASE Stock Reports
Vol. 17/No. 71/Sec. 13
September 7, 1982
Copyright © 1982 Standard & Poor's Corp. All Rights Reserved
Standard & Poor's Corp.
25 Broadway, NY, NY 10004

day strike at the company's largest mill. Book value at $27 was highly conservative, in our opinion, since Glatfelter, like many paper companies, had significant timber holdings. In fact, the company owned outright more than 100,000 acres of woodland, which it carried at nominal cost. The family management owned about 33 percent of the stock. In short, here was another neglected company with sound fundamentals.

By 1980, the stock reached 31 and rose to 36½ in 1981. Why? Institutions became aware of so-called asset or natural resource plays and acquired nearly 25 percent of Glatfelter's stock. The takeover of mining companies (e.g., Kennecott) and oil companies (e.g., Conoco) spurred interest in all companies that held valuable resources, and investors began to bid up their stock prices. Once the takeover of resource companies caught the attention of the financial community, the rush to buy complementary or similar companies was on. As so often happens when a fad catches on, Wall Street suddenly "discovers" attractive fundamentals about such companies as Glatfelter that it had previously ignored. The limelight switches quickly, but once it does, bargain prices are a thing of the past.

Ti-Caro, Inc.

The 5 percent rule also helped us find Ti-Caro, a maker of yarn, thread and knit fabrics. In September 1979, when we first looked at the company, we noticed its return on sales was over 6 percent in 1976 and 1977 and had risen to 7.8 percent in 1978. Ti-Caro had a return on equity of over 20 percent in the years 1976–78 and had been enjoying excellent growth since 1973.

As with many textile manufacturers, the current ratio was a top-heavy 6 to 1, and long-term debt was only 15 percent of total capitalization. The stock, trading at 11½, was selling at a substantial discount to the stated book value of $16.50. We were particularly intrigued by a net working capital per share of $13. This meant that if you valued the company's equipment at zero, paid off all the company's long-term debts and other liabilities, the liquid assets (cash, accounts receivable and inventories) would still be worth more than the price of the stock at the time. At 11½, the company was selling at four times earnings. The business was mundane, but nevertheless thriving, and the stock price was clearly

TABLE II
TI-CARO, INC.

Per Share Data ($)

Yr. Ended Sept. 30	1982	1981	1980	1979	1978	1977	1976	1975	1974	[1]1973
Book Value	NA	20.29	18.36	16.59	14.99	12.91	11.15	9.49	9.10	8.48
Earnings	NA	3.16	[2]2.88	[2]2.67	[2]3.03	[2]2.45	[2]2.15	0.82	1.04	0.80
Dividends	1.20	1.14	1.02½	1.00	0.87	0.64	0.47	0.42½	0.42	0.40½
Payout Ratio	NA	36%	36%	38%	29%	26%	22%	52%	40%	50%
Prices[3]—High	17⅛	18⅝	14⅞	13	14½	10	7⅞	5½	5½	9
Low	13¼	12⅝	9⅜	10⅛	9½	7	5	4	3⅛	4½
P/E Ratio—	NA	6-4	5-3	5-4	5-3	4-3	4-2	7-5	5-3	11-6

Data as orig. reptd. Adj. for stk. div(s). of 100% Apr. 1981. 1. Reflects merger or acquisition. 2. Ful. dil.: 2.86 in 1980, 2.65 in 1979, 2.98 in 1978, 2.41 in 1977, 2.14 in 1976. 3. Cal. yr. NA-Not Available.

Income Data (Million $)

Year Ended Sept. 30	Revs.	Oper. Inc.	% Oper. Inc. of Revs.	Cap. Exp.	Depr.	Int. Exp.	Net Bef. Taxes	Eff. Tax Rate	Net Inc.	% Net Inc. of Revs.
1981	272	40.7	15.0%	15.1	6.54	1.74	31.7	45.1%	17.4	6.4%
1980	251	37.2	14.8%	13.0	5.80	2.03	28.8	45.5%	15.7	6.2%
1979	222	34.5	15.6%	9.1	5.28	2.53	26.8	46.1%	14.5	6.5%
1978	209	37.8	18.1%	15.9	4.48	2.26	31.1	47.7%	16.3	7.8%
1977	190	31.1	16.4%	10.4	3.55	1.54	25.4	48.7%	13.0	6.9%
1976	170	27.7	16.3%	3.9	3.20	1.39	22.9	50.2%	11.4	6.7%
1975	119	12.8	10.7%	2.3	3.07	1.55	8.1	46.4%	4.4	3.7%
1974	135	15.9	11.8%	5.0	3.00	2.02	10.7	47.9%	5.6	4.1%
[1]1973	118	12.9	10.9%	4.3	2.93	1.39	8.5	49.5%	4.3	3.6%
[1]1972	106	13.5	12.8%	5.6	2.48	0.98	10.0	49.2%	5.1	4.8%

Balance Sheet Data (Million $)

Sept. 30	Cash	Current Assets	Current Liab.	Ratio	Total Assets	Ret. on Assets	Long Term Debt	Common Equity	Total Cap.	% LT Debt of Cap.	Ret. on Equity
1981	13.7	90.7	19.8	4.6	160	11.4%	17.4	111	140	12.5%	16.3%
1980	10.5	85.1	17.8	4.8-	146	11.4%	18.7	100	128	14.6%	16.4%
1979	5.3	74.2	12.4	6.0	128	11.5%	18.2	90	116	15.8%	16.9%
1978	5.1	72.9	16.9	4.3	123	14.1%	19.3	80	106	18.2%	21.6%
1977	10.0	67.4	11.7	5.8	106	13.1%	20.4	69	94	21.7%	20.3%
1976	7.6	61.4	15.8	3.9	93	13.3%	13.5	59	77	17.6%	20.8%
1975	3.3	46.5	9.3	5.0	78	5.6%	14.4	50	69	21.1%	8.7%
1974	2.6	45.5	10.2	4.5	77	7.4%	15.3	48	67	22.9%	11.8%
1973	4.6	42.4	7.7	5.5	72	6.0%	16.4	45	64	25.5%	9.7%
1972	3.6	35.2	6.8	5.1	61	8.3%	13.9	37	54	25.6%	13.8%

Data as orig. reptd. 1. Reflects merger or acquisition. NA-Not Available.

Standard NYSE Stock Reports
Vol. 49/No. 192/Sec. 23

October 5, 1982
Copyright © 1982 Standard & Poor's Corp. All Rights Reserved

Standard & Poor's Corp.
25 Broadway, NY, NY 10004

the victim of discrimination against anything that even suggested the textile industry.

The weight of numbers and some publicity from a listing on the New York Stock Exchange eventually prevailed, as it always does if one is patient. In early 1981, the stock hit 18½, which, in our view, was still an undervalued price in comparison to many so-called growth companies.

But in 1982, the recession hit in earnest. Nevertheless, as an illustration of the safety-net concept, Ti-Caro's stock price only dipped to 13 despite lower earnings before recovering to 23 by the end of 1982. Reflective of the dramatic discount to book and net working capital, a conservative debt structure and superior track record in normal times, the stock price was cushioned from the worst of the selling deluge.

The Immunity Factor

What we are trying to show by these examples is that excellent investments can be found in other places besides high-growth and glamour areas—namely, in those companies with excellent records that are ignored by institutions and research analysts. The Wall Street professionals usually opt for glamour and high-risk investments because the gains can be dramatic. Yes, Xerox and IBM did provide enormous returns for years. But investors who focus exclusively on growth companies—who go for glory—run large risks. A bad or even a flat earnings quarter can do severe damage to the image of a high-profile company. And if the general market declines sharply, the high-growth, high price/earnings favorites fall much more precipitously than do the plodding secondary stocks.

One of the great dangers of owning a highly visible growth company is that management may not always divulge its plans, policies or problems, and any negative surprise could create havoc with the market price of the stock. Alternatively, a widely followed analyst might turn sour on a high-profile company, lower his earnings estimates, and put out a sell recommendation on the stock. Also surprise announcements that are interpreted negatively, such as an acquisition the financial community dislikes, can often cause a big drop in the price of the stock.

In June 1982, Gulf Oil bid $65 for Cities Service in another gargantuan takeover attempt. Gulf stock plummeted 20 percent, losing close to a billion dollars in market value in two days. Investors were aghast at the high price to be paid for what was commonly seen as an indifferent domestic oil company that always seemed to have good prospects but never could seem to cash in.

Neglected stocks are not subject to many of the vulnerabilities of the high-profile companies, an advantage we call the immunity factor. Institutions and brokers cannot set off a selling panic in the stock because they do not own it and probably haven't heard of it.

Furthermore, if mass psychology produces a major drop in the market as a whole, it is highly unlikely that an overlooked, but profitable, company will suffer a major price collapse. Of course, if the economy and the company's earnings turn down for a quarter or so, the price of the stock might dip, but it probably won't fall drastically.

When an investor buys a company without any sponsorship, he is thumbing his nose at the investment community. In effect, he is making a purchase on the strength of the numbers, the quality of management, and his belief in the ongoing value of the business. The investor who buys neglected stocks is on his own, whether Wall Street agrees or not—or, more to the point, whether Wall Street takes notice or not.

Note that these stocks can fluctuate between 20 and 50 percent a year, especially if they are being accumulated. Thus, we must warn you that it is important to buy these stocks while they are still unknown. Once these neglected companies become known to the public, it is usually too late. The bulk of the price rise usually occurs upon the initial discoverey of the stock's undervaluation.

The Patience Trap

The trap in buying an overlooked stock is mostly a question of the time value of money and its opportunity cost. Frequently, there may not be much of a price advance in such stocks for a long time. And if one buys too early, the stock may decline moderately and stay below the purchase price for many months. As a result, one might become impatient and be tempted to sell the stock if it returns to the original buying price. This is only human nature, and we have lost many opportunities for large profits because we sold out of frustration.

Republic Corporation

Take the case of Republic Corporation, which we bought at 18½ in April 1980. Republic was a miniconglomerate involved in safety devices for mining, mini steel mills, aviation overhaul and repair services, film and videotape processing and printing.

The company had a rather erratic earnings record because of

strikes, and cyclicality in its steel and metal fabricated-products business. However, book value was close to $30 a share, and the company was in good financial shape. Return on equity had averaged over 15 percent in the previous three years, and earnings had increased from $1.37 in 1977 to $3.44 in 1978 and $4.91 in 1979.

What intrigued us about Republic was that management had pared debt radically over the past ten years and had invested wisely in new and modern steel-making facilities to compete with the Japanese. The company was also in the aviation-repair business,

TABLE 12
REPUBLIC CORPORATION

Per Share Data ($)

Yr. End July 31	1981	1980	1979	1978	1977	1976	1975	1974	1973	[3]1972
Book Value	35.23	31.40	26.87	22.11	16.83	11.26	9.96	5.21	1.87	3.22
Earnings[1]	4.05	4.44	4.91	3.44	1.37	0.42	1.90	1.25	0.38	0.46
Dividends	0.60	0.60	0.31¼	0.16¾	Nil	Nil	Nil	Nil	Nil	Nil
Payout Ratio	13%	12%	6%	4%	Nil	Nil	Nil	Nil	Nil	Nil
Prices[2]—High	35¾	30	28	19⅝	11⅛	8⅛	13½	10⅞	17¼	41⅛
Low	20	16¼	14	8½	5⅞	5½	4⅞	4¾	4¾	14
P/E Ratio—	9–5	7–4	6–3	6–2	8–4	20–13	7–3	9–4	46–13	90–31

Data as orig. reptd. Adj. for 20% Oct. 1979 & 1-for-5 reverse split May 1975. 1. Bef. results of disc. opers. of −0.17 in 1977, +0.15 in 1976, −0.13 in 1975, +0.05 in 1974, +0.18 in 1973, +0.28 in 1972, and spec. item(s) of +1.21 in 1977, +0.58 in 1976, +1.86 in 1975, +1.52 in 1974, −2.18 in 1973, −1.18 in 1972. 2. Cal. yr. 3. Reflects merger or acquisition.

Income Data (Million $)

Year Ended July 31[1]	Revs.	Oper. Inc.	% Oper. Inc. of Revs.	Cap. Exp.	Depr.	Int. Exp.	Net Bef. Taxes	Eff. Tax Rate	[3]Net Inc.	% Net Inc. of Revs.
[1]1981	300	25.0	8.3%	37.1	6.57	[4]5.58	15.8	24.9%	11.9	4.0%
[1]1980	296	33.2	11.2%	15.0	6.05	4.32	22.5	44.3%	12.6	4.2%
[1]1979	287	33.6	11.7%	8.2	6.12	4.00	25.6	47.0%	13.6	4.7%
[1]1978	239	24.6	10.3%	9.3	5.47	3.38	15.1	33.3%	10.1	4.2%
[1]1977	241	18.4	7.6%	6.6	5.19	2.73	10.4	55.8%	4.6	1.9%
[1]1976	208	11.6	5.5%	7.3	5.04	3.28	3.2	56.5%	1.4	0.7%
[1]1975	247	22.4	9.1%	9.6	4.71	3.22	14.2	54.9%	6.4	2.6%
[1]1974	226	23.7	10.5%	5.3	4.46	3.98	10.0	58.8%	4.1	1.8%
[1]1973	186	11.6	6.2%	4.7	4.08	4.86	2.4	62.3%	0.9	0.5%
[2]1972	166	10.9	6.6%	5.2	3.84	5.25	2.3	55.2%	1.1	0.6%

Balance Sheet Data (Million $)

July 31[1]	Cash	Current—Assets	Current—Liab.	Ratio	Total Assets	Ret. on Assets	Long Term Debt	Common Equity	Total Cap.	% LT Debt of Cap.	Ret. on Equity
1981	4.7	115	43.0	2.7	201	6.2%	51.4	94.9	156	33.0%	13.2%
1980	34.2	121	34.2	3.6	179	7.5%	52.4	83.5	143	36.7%	16.0%
1979	12.3	102	35.5	2.9	155	9.4%	38.9	72.6	117	33.3%	20.4%
1978	12.1	87	40.0	2.2	134	7.8%	30.5	59.7	92	33.3%	19.0%
1977	5.7	79	37.1	2.1	124	3.7%	30.1	46.2	85	35.3%	11.7%
1976	3.5	78	44.2	1.8	124	1.2%	29.5	32.3	78	37.9%	4.6%
1975	3.3	72	37.1	1.9	117	5.6%	33.2	29.3	78	42.8%	27.3%
1974	3.9	69	40.1	1.7	110	3.6%	34.8	17.9	67	52.0%	29.8%
1973	3.6	60	34.1	1.7	117	0.7%	65.3	9.5	80	81.9%	7.7%
1972	4.8	55	33.7	1.6	118	0.8%	67.1	13.0	80	83.7%	8.1%

Data as orig. reptd. 1. Excludes discontinued operations. 2. Excludes discontinued operations and reflects merger or acquisition. 3. Bef. results of disc. opers. in 1977, 1976, 1975, 1974, 1973, 1972, and spec. item(s) in 1977, 1976, 1975, 1974, 1973, 1972. 4. Reflects accounting change. NM-Not Meaningful. d-Deficit.

April 27, 1982
Copyright © 1982 Standard & Poor's Corp. All Rights Reserved

Standard & Poor's Corp.
25 Broadway, NY, NY 10004

which was rapidly expanding. It also had the potential to reap profits on mine roof supports in its steel fabricated-metal-products business as coal became more of a factor in the nation's energy future. Pension liability was minimal, which was rare for a steel company. Finally, we were able to buy the stock at four times projected earnings (the low end of the p/e range) and at 60 percent of a hard book value.

But in June 1980, we decided to sell the stock at 20¾. The recession was hurting earnings, and we did not have the patience to hold on in the face of a wildly fluctuating stock market. The stock's performance made our caution look exaggerated, as it jumped to 35¾ by mid-1981. This was an expensive mistake, and it happened because we didn't have enough conviction in our initial decision.

Perhaps, in retrospect, we were lucky, because in 1982 Republic's price first eroded and then sank to below 14. The company was considered a steel play, and investors bailed out of anything to do with steel in 1982. Most steel companies were operating at an unprecedented 40–50 percent of capacity (Republic's was 60 percent) and losing big money in the depths of recession. Still, we felt safe enough at 15 and repurchased this usually healthy company in spring 1982.

Cubic Corporation

Another lost opportunity was Cubic Corporation, which was one of the few stocks we have ever bought on a brokerage house recommendation. Cubic was involved in the electronics business (principally for defense systems in reconnaissance and surveillance and for simulation training), automatic fare collectors for mass transit, automatic elevators, data-processing equipment and communications equipment (mainly transmitters and receivers).

In short, this was a sophisticated technology company that historically sold between three and nine times earnings. Earnings had escalated rapidly from a loss in 1974 to a positive $.69 in 1975 and to $1.97 by 1978. We started looking at the company in the middle of 1979 and bought it at 12, or at a p/e of six times earnings.

The company had an after-tax return on sales averaging 5 percent for the previous five years and a return on shareholders' equity of nearly 20 percent in 1977 and 21 percent in 1978. Also, the chief executive officer of the company owned 32 percent of the stock, which he continued to hold through the ups and downs of the fare-collection business.

TABLE 13
CUBIC CORPORATION

Per Share Data ($)

Yr. End Sep. 30[1]	1981	1980	1979	1978	1977	1976	1975	1974	1973	1972
Book Value	15.69	13.42	11.75	10.19	8.68	7.40	6.54	5.89	6.26	5.94
Earnings	2.79	2.06	2.03	1.97	1.63	1.22	0.69	d0.28	0.40	0.36
Dividends	0.47¼	0.45	0.45	0.41⅜	0.31½	0.16⅞	0.11⅜	0.11⅜	0.11⅜	0.11⅜
Payout Ratio	17%	22%	22%	21%	19%	14%	16%	NM	29%	31%
Prices[2]—High	31¾	19½	15⅞	22	12⅞	8	4¾	4	8⅜	12½
Low	14⅛	10⅝	10¼	10⅛	7½	7½	1¾	1¾	2½	5¾
P/E Ratio—	11–5	9–5	8–5	11–5	8–5	7–3	7–3	NM	21–6	34–16

Data as orig. reptd. Adj. for stk. divs. of 33% Nov. 1981 & Mar. 1977. 1. Cal. yrs. pr. to 1976. 2. Cal. yr. NM-Not Meaningful. d-Deficit.

Income Data (Million $)

Year Ended Sep. 30[1]	Revs.	Oper. Inc.	% Oper. Inc. of Revs.	Cap. Exp.	Depr.	Int. Exp.	Net Bef. Taxes	Eff. Tax Rate	Net Inc.	% Net Inc. of Revs.
1981	228	24.3	10.6%	6.7	3.77	2.72	[3]21.1	47.8%	11.0	4.8%
1980	196	21.0	10.7%	3.6	3.33	3.21	[3]15.3	46.7%	8.2	4.2%
1979	172	19.6	11.4%	11.9	2.79	[4]2.63	[3]15.1	46.8%	8.0	4.7%
1978	144	18.8	13.1%	5.4	2.45	1.09	15.7	50.6%	7.8	5.4%
1977	123	14.3	11.6%	4.2	1.95	0.97	13.1	50.8%	6.4	5.2%
1976	110	11.7	10.6%	2.1	1.52	1.06	9.6	50.0%	4.8	4.3%
1975	92	7.4	8.0%	1.7	1.65	1.17	5.2	48.5%	2.7	2.9%
1974	75	d0.1	NM	1.3	1.30	1.14	d2.0	NM	d1.1	NM
[2]1973	67	4.9	7.4%	1.3	1.27	0.96	3.2	50.6%	1.6	2.4%

Balance Sheet Data (Million $)

Sep. 30[1]	Cash	Current Assets	Current Liab.	Ratio	Total Assets	Ret. on Assets	Long Term Debt	Com-mon Equity	Total Cap.	% LT Debt of Cap.	Ret. on Equity
1981	21.8	106	36.1	2.9	133	9.0%	27.5	62.2	96.8	28.5%	19.1%
1980	2.9	86	19.8	4.3	110	7.6%	27.6	53.0	90.7	30.4%	16.3%
1979	2.4	78	20.1	3.9	104	8.5%	28.2	46.8	83.6	33.7%	18.4%
1978	2.8	68	18.4	3.7	84	10.5%	19.5	40.6	65.7	29.6%	20.6%
1977	1.9	50	17.0	2.9	63	10.5%	9.4	34.4	46.4	20.1%	20.2%
1976	2.9	49	20.5	2.4	59	8.9%	8.8	29.4	38.3	23.0%	17.2%
1975	1.2	39	12.4	3.1	48	5.7%	9.6	26.2	35.9	26.6%	10.7%
1974	1.9	37	12.0	3.1	47	NM	10.4	24.4	34.9	29.8%	NM
1973	3.0	38	10.5	3.7	49	3.3%	11.3	26.7	38.2	29.5%	6.1%
1972	6.6	36	18.3	2.0	46	3.4%	2.2	25.5	27.9	8.0%	5.8%

Data as orig. reptd. 1. Prior to 1976 fis. yr. ended Dec. 2. Refl. merger or acq. 3. Incl. equity in earns. of nonconsol. subs. 4. Refl. accounting change. NM-Not Meaningful. d-Deficit.

Standard ASE Stock Reports
Vol. 17/No. 62/Sec. 4

August 5, 1982
Copyright © 1982 Standard & Poor's Corp. All Rights Reserved

Standard & Poor's Corp.
25 Broadway, NY, NY 10004

Although the company's backlog of orders was up in 1979, news started filtering out that Cubic would have a flat year and that there were potential problems with its automatic fare-collection system in London. The bad news depressed the price to 10¼, and we became worried and sold out.

By the end of 1979, when the negative reports proved to be

exaggerated, the stock hit 15⅞. Then the company's defense systems and electronics business improved and earnings jumped, resulting in very favorable quarterly earnings comparisons. Investors took note, and by 1982 the stock rose to 29¾. The moral is this: if you bought the stock cheaply, have the patience to sit out the bad news.

Buying undiscovered or overlooked stocks is not only rewarding, but also generally quite safe. It is the best example of our philosophy of buying price and quantifying downside risk. The problem that most investors have with such an approach is the patience that is required to make it work. We have found that it is easy to look for and find undiscovered companies. The hard part is holding on until the stock has achieved our desired rate of return.

Chapter 6

Buying High-Profile,
Depressed Stocks

IF THERE'S INTELLECTUAL ENJOYMENT in buying undervalued and overlooked stocks, there's emotional satisfaction in making profits on the widely followed stocks that Wall Street has turned against. Such opportunities are provided by short-lived earnings disappointments or financial calamity that creates a selling panic in the stock. These situations usually involve high-profile companies that are carefully followed by analysts and portfolio managers, so that any unexpected event often causes a burst of selling. It's almost as if the analysts and money managers dump the stock in retribution for having had their expectations dashed.

As we said earlier, earnings growth is of paramount importance to portfolio managers and, unfortunately, their obsession with earnings has influenced company managements. Knowing that disappointing earnings will lead to a big drop in their company's stock price, managements are reluctant to report bad news. It is for this reason that the famous stock pickers like John Templeton deprecate the importance of quarterly earnings.

True investors ridicule short-sightedness, contending that no company can be immune to political, economic, legal or social events, and to think otherwise is foolhardy. Often, flat or declining earnings are the result of a specific and rectifiable problem. Is it fair for this kind of problem to lead to a tar-and-feathering of the stock by the financial community when recovery is inevitable and possibly already under way? Unfortunately, the financial community's emotional swing can irreparably damage a company and interfere with its future growth by making it harder to raise needed equity capital.

One might well ask why many so-called investors take such a short-sighted view of a company's problems. There is no logical explanation, but part of the reason is a chain reaction among investors, beginning with the professional traders, who rush to sell at the first hint of bad news. The capital of professional traders is a precious commodity, and they have learned to preserve it by tolerating only a small loss if the stock goes against them. Often these traders are on margin, which further exacerbates the situation.

The next group to sell out are the small funds and the investment advisory services, investors who need to boost quarterly performance and can permit few surprises. Then the big institutions, who fear being caught in a no-growth situation, start to sell. As a result, the stock soon loses its supporters, and the cumulative selling produces a sickening plunge in the stock price. Soon every blemish about the company, whether real or imagined, is exposed, and yesterday's darling is now rejected. The sequence may seem absurd, yet it happens again and again—and not just to individual stocks, but to entire industries. We've taken advantage of selling waves that were caused for many reasons: by management dissension and upheaval, which led to employee turnover; bad or costly mergers or acquisitions; new competition; currency fluctuations; revolution; a nationalization of plant and equipment and/or natural resource holdings; and an unexpected jump in interest rates.

The financial community also seems to have an unfortunate case of tunnel vision. A particular problem, such as interest rates and government deficits in 1981–82 or inflation in 1979–80, often overrides all other considerations. Entire industries, too, are often categorized as unfit for investment. And improving fundamentals or characteristics that were previously highly regarded are often forgotten. It is hard to understand why these attitudes prevail, and, indeed, one could write a whole book about the fickleness of the markets, but that is not our purpose here. Our concern is how to exploit the volatility—when to buy and why.

Many investors balk at trying to buck the trend, arguing that it's dangerous to fight the crowd. There's some merit to their concern, and that's why one should begin buying only when the selling has exhausted itself. Selling will sometimes continue until the stock has declined to such an absurd level that no one is left to sell at that price; the stock is sold out. Of course, it's very difficult, if not impossible, to pick the bottom in a stock. No matter how reasonably valued the stock may be, it could well decline further before it finally turns up.

The best place to discover these outcast stocks is in the daily list of twelve-month lows published in *The Wall Street Journal* or the weekly list published in *Barron's*. If you are keeping a target list of prospective companies, a weekly check of that list might alert you to coming buying opportunities. The list of daily percentage losers is another place to learn about stocks in the throes of a major decline.

Also, be on the lookout for news items that might have a negative impact on earnings or on investors' expectations about a company or its stock, such as a string of resignations by top management, impropriety by the chief executive officer, a major lawsuit or the entry of a major competitor into the company's business, among other things.

Once you have spotted a stock that has declined drastically, don't rush to buy it. The first step is to find out why the stock declined and determine if the reasons for the price retreat stem from long-term considerations or from temporary factors, which could mean a quick turnaround.

In effect, the company, having suffered a crisis of confidence, has shaken the credibility of investors, its most important constituency. For this reason, don't ignore the price decline, even if it appears to be irrational. A bargain hunter should not be arrogant, stubborn or eager to be proven right. Let the selling climax exhaust itself first. Then wait for the invariable rally and the second dip, or "test" of the bottom. After a huge decline, bargain hunters often buy a stock on what Wall Street calls a technical rebound. There is a certain pattern to such situations: First, there is a minor rally after the collapse. Then comes a period of recuperation, or what the market technicians call a market consolidation, which is followed by a large jump in price because investors realize that the company's long-term prospects are better than they seem. The second dip is the time to buy the stock, provided, of course, that from a fundamental viewpoint the price level appears safe on a historical basis.

Most important, study the downside risk. Are underlying assets a cushion to a further decline? Could successive quarters of poor earnings cause a dividend cut and a further decline in the stock? Are negative political or economic events—such as recession, wide currency fluctuations, high interest rates and strikes—expected to persist, or are they temporary or expected to last less than a year? Can the company cope with its dislocations, or are there deeper problems hidden beneath the surface? Carefully scrutinize the major problem. Is it product obsolescence, fiercer competition, a loss of key management personnel, a loss of key suppliers or customers, political nationalization of assets, or a change of government policy that affects the company negatively?

Be sure that the company's basic business and earnings power haven't been dealt a blow so severe that the positives, such as low debt, deep discount to book value or hidden assets, are overridden. Based on our experience, if the business deterioration was unanticipated by management, the recovery could take a long time.

If a fast corporate turnaround appears reasonable, we suggest that investors buy the stock at the low end of its p/e range for the past five years or at a significant discount from book value. Don't buy the stock simply because it has declined a lot or is selling at its 52-week low. Be sure to review the history of the fundamentals and the stock price movement over a five- to ten-year period. Who knows? Perhaps the stock was artificially inflated because of a takeover rumor or overblown expectations for its industry. One must interpret violent swings, whether up or down, objectively. A commonsense review of the company's history will help determine the extent of the underlying value.

One final thought before we move on to some examples of out-of-favor and beaten-down stocks. The opportunities to buy such stocks occur almost invariably in large-capitalization and high-profile companies. The institutions are primarily invested in the big companies and, as we have already discussed, they dominate the market in these stocks, which, as a result, are usually listed on the New York and the American stock exchanges. (Of course, many well-known institutional stocks like Tampax, Coors and Noxell are traded over the counter.)

Probably the best definition of high-profile corporations is that they are the ones traded on the options exchanges, which provide markets for the right to buy and sell stock at specific prices in the future. Traders use options to hedge or speculate because of the fact that the stocks generally show active volume.

Collecting "Fallen Angels"

Although most "fallen angels" will prove to have exhibited good returns on sales, assets and equity in the past, that does not rule out using our checklist once you have focused on one of them and have prepared yourself to take the plunge even though the stock represents a turn-off to others. To repeat, what's most important is to discern what has really tainted the stock and then to resolve in your mind whether the company has the management and financial capability to overcome the problem. Almost invariably, the most mundane cause of a fall from grace is earnings pressure—all of a sudden, the "one-decision perpetual grower" (the buy-never-sell type of stock) stops growing or slows down in its rate of growth and earnings are disappointing. The earnings interruption might be short-term—for example, if the company is laden with heavy start-up costs for a new plant or product—medium-term because of a lousy business climate, or long-term if, for instance, the company's market has changed fundamentally owing to new and strong competition.

Wall Street is slow to forget a snakebite and often remains prejudiced against a particular company or industry for one to two years, despite evidence of a comeback by the stock or industry. This is why contrarian theory stresses patience, because by "going against the tape"—that is, market sentiment—you are usually setting yourself up for a long wait, but you are doing so at very good prices.

As we've pointed out, a 50 percent increase in price at the end of two years is still 25 percent per annum even if the stock price remains mired until sentiment finally becomes rational. Remember that once a stock or industry group is banished from favor, there are very often continual selling waves as institutions use technical rallies to dump their residual holdings that they couldn't unload in the first flush of panic.

Harking back to our checklist and sources, discussed in chapters 3 and 4, let's run through the selection process and point out the important emphasis that we place on buying distressed stocks. First of all, since these are generally large-capitalization companies, there will usually be a lot of publicity when they wilt, so that both the event and cause of decline will be visible, apart from just showing up on the weekly (or daily) "new lows" list in *The Wall Street Journal* or in *Barron's*.

Almost always, there will be a blurb in the financial press or a summary of an analysts' meeting in which the company's immediate problems are explained. Once we take note of this, we write away for the latest quarterly report to see if there is a more complete explanation by the company. Next, we go to the S&P tear sheets or *Value Line* tables to find out what the lowest p/e was in the last five years, if not ten. Now, if analysts have been caught by surprise, they immediately start revising their earnings estimates downward, so that you should look at the *Earnings Forecaster*, if it's available to you, to get an idea of the new forecasts (which may now be all over the map, since analysts, when they scramble to revise, usually overdo it). Again, our habit is to take the last quarter's earnings, multiply it by four, and adjust up or down by 20 percent, based on reading the company's 10Q's. This is not scientific, but we have found from experience that it's not a bad extrapolation.

Since it is risky to buy on a low p/e when earnings are suspect, we look for other evidence of value, such as the lowest discount from end-of-year book value for the past ten years.

So far, we have established what we conceive of as a low target price, but our next emphasis is on two other points on our checklist. What do the company's cash flow and debt burden look like? In short, does the company have the cash to weather the storm and keep up with its debt service, as well as fund necessary capital expenditures and research-and-development costs to stay competitive? When a company is under earnings pressure, conservation of cash and the right priorities for using cash become extremely important. Thus, consulting the annual report is the next step to ascertain the debt structure—its rates and maturities. If the company has excessive debt (by which we mean more than 30 percent of total capitalization and/or a deteriorating current ratio, especially if less than 2 to 1), alarm bells should be triggered in your mind.

Since you have already come up with an earnings forecast for the year, add last year's depreciation figure to it and see if this total is sufficient to meet projected capital expenditures (which is usually in the "management discussion" section of the annual report), dividends and upcoming scheduled debt repayment (a debt repayment schedule is usually found in the debt footnote in the annual report). If cash flow from operations is insufficient to cover these items, be wary of a potential dividend cut, of a capital expenditure cutback that may perhaps harm the company's future competitiveness and profitability, or of the need to go even deeper into debt. Obviously, in this rough equation, you cannot forecast whether the company will resort to asset sales, which is a potential source of cash, but at least you'll get an idea of its cash position, and whether or not the company can rebound quickly.

Finally, after arriving at a fundamental conclusion that the company can earn enough to cover debt service and its other needs, that it is not too debt-heavy, that it is selling at a significant discount to book and at a historically low p/e based on your estimate of earnings, you still should not rashly rush in to buy the stock. Consider how long the stock might be a laggard, given your feelings about overall business conditions and the general health of the company's business, including order backlog, shipments, the prospect of new orders and so forth. Obviously, you would be wary of buying cyclical companies such as International Paper and ASARCO (discussed later in this chapter) in the teeth of the perverse economic recession of 1981 and 1982, with housing starts abysmal, the automobile industry badly hurting, and capital-goods formation at a low ebb. In such circumstances, you may have a longer wait for the stock of such a company to revive. So if you want to be exceedingly safe, knock another 5 percent off your ideal target price for such a company.

Always ask yourself: Are the conditions in place for a one- or two-year turnaround or is there a possibility that the hardship might persist longer? Is the company's output of goods and services going to be stalled by business contraction or high interest rates that will present a barrier to sales if the product line is high-cost, low-volume?

For example, in summer 1982, we were sorely tempted to buy Deere, the premier farm-machinery manufacturer, whose implements we knew were considered top of the line by farmers. But we also knew about the depression on the farm stemming from large debt burdens, high interest rates and low grain prices. New farm equipment appeared beyond the reach of many farmers. Sales and profits would accordingly be severely affected even for blue-chip Deere, which was selling at the lowest price since the last recession and at the largest discount from book value ever. We knew that in the ensuing shakeout, Deere would survive and in fact emerge stronger, since we felt its competitors—such as International Harvester and Massey Ferguson—would either go bankrupt or fold their farm equipment lines. Yet despite the interest we had in buying the stock in the low to mid-20s, we restrained ourselves solely because of our pessimistic view of farm equipment prospects, though not of the fundamental future earnings power of the company. We were wrong; the stock advanced 50 percent within six months, as courageous investors bought for the long term.

Investing in "fallen angels" need not be terribly risky, and the bargains available in stocks of quality companies that have fallen from favor can be enormous even if the stock does not regain its former highflier status and reach its former elevated p/e levels. It is a purely contrarian strategy, and it requires patience and some internal fortitude, but properly applied, the strategy will usually work out, as you will discover from some of the following examples.

International Paper Company

In the March–April 1980 decline in the stock market, we became interested in International Paper, the largest paper and pulp company in the country and a component of the 30 Dow Industrials. The stock first caught our attention when it hit the 52-week "new lows" list. At 32 a share, when we bought the stock, it had a p/e ratio of 5.5 on the average earnings of 1978, 1979 and the first half of fiscal year 1980. The lowest price since 1972 was 31⅝, and that occurred at the bottom of the 1973–74 bear market, when the stock also sold at a p/e ratio of around 5.

In the spring of 1980, paper and forest products companies were viewed as unattractive investments because a poor economic outlook and a disastrous housing market were sure to depress demand for pulp and wood products. Earnings of $7.25 in 1979 would clearly not be matched in 1980, and a reasonable estimate was $5.50 (actual reported earnings turned out to be $5.97). The investment community considered International Paper a laggard—certainly not the premier choice in the group.

On the other side of the coin, we learned that earnings in 1979 were temporarily boosted by the sale of assets. International Paper made $3.55 a share from discontinuing an operation by selling its General Crude Oil subsidiary to Mobil and another $1.99 a share through the sale of a paper mill and 425,000 acres of woodlands in Florida to Southwest Forest Industries. Thus, on an *operating* basis, earnings were only $5.26 in 1979, which were actually below the projected 1980 earnings.

TABLE 14
INTERNATIONAL PAPER COMPANY

Per Share Data ($)

Yr. End Dec. 31	1981	1980	1979	1978	1977	1976	¹1975	1974	1973	1972
Book Value	64.40	56.66	52.96	43.89	40.95	37.88	32.70	29.68	25.47	23.65
Earnings²	10.08	5.97	7.25	4.94	4.98	5.60	4.93	5.95	3.60	2.30
Dividends	2.40	2.40	2.20	2.00	· 2.00	2.00	2.00	1.75	1.75	1.50
Payout Ratio	24%	41%	31%	41%	40%	37%	41%	29%	48%	65%
Prices—High	51½	47⅞	47⅝	49¼	69⅝	79¾	61½	56	57	42¼
Low	37⅛	30½	35⅝	35⅛	39	57⅝	34⅝	31⅝	33	33¼
P/E Ratio—	5–4	8–5	7–5	10–7	14–8	14–10	12–7	9–5	16–9	18–14

Data as orig. reptd. 1. Reflects merger or acquisition. 2. Bef. results of disc. opers. of +3.71 in 1979. 3. Incl. 1.99 capital gain.

Income Data (Million $)

Year Ended Dec. 31	Revs.	Oper. Inc.	% Oper. Inc. of Revs.	Cap. Exp.	Depr.	Int. Exp.	Net Bef. Taxes	Eff. Tax Rate	³Net Inc.	% Net Inc. of Revs.
¹1981	4,983	445	8.9%	716	262	85.3	²778	32.5%	525	10.5%
1980	5,043	605	12.0%	883	264	⁵91.5	²399	21.3%	314	6.2%
⁴1979	4,533	621	13.7%	1,117	250	79.9	²516	32.5%	348	7.7%
1978	4,150	717	17.3%	350	272	85.0	²370	36.6%	234	5.6%
1977	3,669	623	17.0%	355	240	91.5	²339	31.1%	234	6.4%
1976	3,541	644	18.2%	436	213	92.4	²380	33.2%	254	7.2%
¹1975	3,081	618	20.1%	461	193	83.4	²371	41.3%	218	7.1%
1974	3,042	585	19.2%	413	135	45.0	²458	42.7%	263	8.6%
1973	2,314	368	15.9%	142	122	41.4	²246	35.0%	160	6.9%
1972	2,093	289	13.8%	123	112	37.8	²160	35.8%	103	4.9%

Balance Sheet Data (Million $)

Dec. 31	Cash	—Current— Assets	Liab.	Ratio	Total Assets	Ret. on Assets	Long Term Debt	Com- mon Equity	Total Cap.	% LT Debt of Cap.	Ret. on Equity
1981	479	1,813	739	2.5	5,544	9.8%	831	3,194	4,710	17.6%	16.6%
1980	222	1,390	752	1.8	5,197	6.2%	929	2,814	4,334	21.4%	10.7%
1979	620	1,600	851	1.9	4,843	7.7%	1,001	2,586	3,941	25.4%	14.6%
1978	253	1,180	648	1.8	4,099	5.9%	949	2,142	3,407	27.9%	11.3%
1977	288	1,074	500	2.1	3,840	6.2%	1,061	1,979	3,303	32.1%	12.2%
1976	326	1,019	514	2.0	3,640	7.1%	1,054	1,822	3,093	34.1%	14.9%
1975	240	936	498	1.9	3,341	7.2%	1,137	1,496	2,801	40.6%	15.2%
1974	331	1,017	476	2.1	2,730	10.7%	727	1,361	2,207	33.0%	20.7%
1973	222	738	278	2.7	2,197	7.5%	583	1,173	1,858	31.4%	14.1%
1972	160	674	251	2.7	2,076	5.0%	578	1,106	1,762	32.8%	9.3%

Data as orig. reptd. 1. Reflects merger or acquisition. 2. Incl. equity in earns. of nonconsol. subs. 3. Bef. results of disc. opers. in 1979. 4. Excludes discontinued operations. 5. Reflects accounting change.

Standard NYSE Stock Reports
Vol. 49/No. 160/Sec. 8

August 19, 1982
Copyright © 1982 Standard & Poor's Corp. All Rights Reserved

Standard & Poor's Corp.
25 Broadway, NY, NY 10004

Based on the purchase price of the timberland sold to Southwest Forest, our conclusion was that the company's remaining 8.3 million acres of timberland were carried at a large discount from their present value. In fact, we estimated that the real book value of the company was at least 50 percent higher than the $53 the company showed in its annual report.

Another plus was the fact that the stock had traded as high as 47⅝ in every year since 1972. What's more, in three of the years since 1975, the stock rose above $60, and earnings during those years were lower than the trailing twelve months' earnings at the time of our analysis. Finally, in February 1980, only a month or so before the market break, the stock sold at $44. Despite the company's lackluster image, was there any solid reason for the stock to drop some 30 percent within a month?

We concluded that the price risk was minimal, since we were buying the stock near a ten-year low and we believed the price would soon rise to a more reasonable valuation. Sure enough, within a year, the price recovered to a more normal level, hitting $51 by the spring of 1981. The result was an appreciation of close to 60 percent, with practically no risk. As it turned out, the investment community had overstated the negatives and pushed down the company's stock to an artificially low level. Ironically, recession fears again caused International Paper's stock to decline to the low 30s in early 1982. The company had posted operating profits of $5.74 in 1981, a respectable performance, which was augmented to $10.08 by a $4.34 a share gain on the sale of its Canadian subsidiary. The sale, in our opinion, was a plus since the company rid itself of a subsidiary that had lagged behind the corporate goals for return on assets and equity and also received cash to help pay down debt. Though we expected weak earnings comparisons throughout 1982, we remained favorably inclined toward the stock in the low 30s and reestablished an investment at those levels, willing to look over the valley.

General Foods Corporation

Another classic example of an "oversold" large capitalization company was General Foods, a well-known company with such established brands as Maxwell House coffee, Sanka, Jell-O and Post cereals. We first became interested in General Foods in February 1980, when the institutions, which normally hold about 40 to 50 percent of the capitalization of the company, decided to reduce their positions because earnings were expected to decline by 10 percent. (In reality, earnings actually rose by 2 percent.) This selling drove the stock price down to 27, at which point we thought it was a good buy.

General Foods' return on equity had exceeded 15 percent since 1974, and long-term debt was only 18 percent of capitalization. Book value was 29, and the company had shown moderate growth, earning $5.12 in 1979, up from $3.40 in 1977. At five and a half times earnings, the lowest p/e ratio in some ten years, we felt General Foods was a good percentage play, since the stock had reached 34 in every year since 1976.

The general stock market environment worsened soon after our purchase of General Foods, and the stock fell to below $25. But,

TABLE 15

GENERAL FOODS CORPORATION

Per Share Data ($)

Yr. End Mar. 31[1]	[6]1981	1980	1979	1978	1977	1976	1975	[2]1974	1973	1972
Book Value	30.86	32.11	29.15	25.98	23.00	21.18	18.95	17.09	15.81	14.78
Earnings[3]	4.47	5.14	[4]5.12	[4]4.65	[4]3.40	[4]3.56	[4]3.02	2.43	2.40	[4]2.21
Dividends	2.20	2.20	1.95	1.72	1.64	1.53½	1.42½	1.40	1.40	1.40
Payout Ratio	49%	43%	38%	37%	48%	43%	47%	58%	58%	63%
Prices[5]—High	35	34¼	37	35¼	36⅛	34¾	29⅜	28⅝	30½	36¼
Low	27¾	23½	28¼	26½	29	26⅛	18⅜	16	21¾	23½
P/E Ratio—	8-6	7-5	7-6	8-6	11-9	10-7	10-6	12-7	13-9	16-11

Data as orig. reptd. 1. Of fol. cal. yr. 2. Reflects acctg. change. 3. Bef. results of disc. opers. of −0.42 in 1981, −0.43 in 1974. 4. Ful. dil.: 5.02 in 1979, 4.56 in 1978, 3.33 in 1977, 3.49 in 1976, 2.97 in 1975, 2.18 in 1972. 5. Cal. yr. 6. Reflects merger or acquisition.

Income Data (Million $)

Year Ended Mar. 31[1]	Revs.	Oper. Inc.	% Oper. Inc. of Revs.	Cap. Exp.	Depr.	Int. Exp.	Net Bef. Taxes	Eff. Tax Rate	[4]Net Inc.	% Net Inc. of Revs.
[5]1981	8,351	694	8.3%	283	131	152	[3]418	47.1%	221	2.6%
1980	6,601	565	8.6%	187	89	50	[3]473	46.0%	255	3.9%
1979	5,960	534	9.0%	262	78	39	[3]470	45.6%	256	4.3%
1978	5,472	524	9.6%	121	77	31	[3]452	48.6%	232	4.2%
1977	5,376	425	7.9%	126	70	38	[3]331	48.7%	170	3.2%
1976	4,910	448	9.1%	112	70	27	[3]368	51.8%	177	3.6%
1975	3,978	384	9.6%	96	57	24	[3]319	52.8%	150	3.8%
[2]1974	3,675	326	8.9%	104	56	44	[3]241	49.8%	121	3.3%
1973	2,987	298	10.0%	88	55	25	[3]232	48.6%	119	4.0%
1972	2,632	284	10.8%	89	53	24	220	49.7%	110	4.2%

Balance Sheet Data (Million $)

Mar. 31[1]	Cash	Current— Assets	Current— Liab.	Ratio	Total Assets	Ret. on Assets	Long Term Debt	Common Equity	Total Cap.	% LT Debt of Cap.	Ret. on Equity
1981	163	2,254	1,215	1.9	3,861	6.3%	731	1,626	2,499	29.2%	13.6%
1980	309	2,019	929	2.2	3,130	8.4%	391	1,610	2,121	18.4%	16.6%
1979	178	1,951	1,047	1.9	2,978	9.2%	255	1,480	1,845	13.8%	18.3%
1978	291	1,736	845	2.1	2,565	9.3%	251	1,321	1,681	14.9%	18.6%
1977	132	1,618	860	1.9	2,433	7.1%	260	1,174	1,535	16.9%	15.0%
1976	129	1,569	850	1.8	2,345	8.1%	253	1,085	1,448	17.4%	17.1%
1975	216	1,252	654	1.9	2,013	7.7%	235	983	1,312	17.9%	15.9%
1974	53	1,150	602	1.9	1,897	6.4%	259	903	1,238	20.9%	13.6%
1973	132	1,102	585	1.9	1,855	6.7%	271	873	1,207	22.4%	14.1%
1972	142	987	554	1.8	1,729	6.6%	216	829	1,096	19.7%	13.7%

Data as orig. reptd. 1. Of fol. cal. yr. 2. Excludes discontinued operations and reflects accounting change. 3. Incl. equity in earns. of nonconsol. subs. 4. Bef. results of disc. opers. in 1981, 1974. 5. Excl. disc. opers. and reflects merger or acquisition.

Standard NYSE Stock Reports
Vol. 49/No. 224/Sec. 13

November 19, 1982
Copyright © 1982 Standard & Poor's Corp. All Rights Reserved

Standard & Poor's Corp.
25 Broadway, NY, NY 10004

we weren't alarmed because we believed both General Foods and the stock market itself were oversold. General Foods was not a glamour stock, but it certainly offered the prospect of a move to 34, or a 25 percent gain, over the next twelve months. And that didn't include an annual dividend that provided an 8 percent yield and a cushion against further erosion in the stock price.

In 1980, General Foods was not a stock that appealed to the investment managers and traders. It represented an ignored stock that gets knocked down in a market sell-off, only to rebound again. Our strategy here was to wait for General Foods to move up with the rest of the market. Since the market had declined sharply in anticipation of the 1980 recession, it appeared likely that both General Foods and the stock market would rebound nicely in the next few months. As it turned out, the market did rebound, and we were able to sell the stock one year later at our objective of 34. Of interest is that even in the worst moments of 1982, the stock never fell below 32 and, in fact, was a star performer as analysts and institutions favored food processors as being conceptually "recession-proof."

ASARCO Incorporated

ASARCO, a leading producer of copper and silver, as well as other by-product metals, was a classic case of a commodity company that experienced a cyclical rebound. We first became interested in the company in 1978, when we read in *The Wall Street Journal* that Bendix Corporation, a diversified manufacturer, was taking a position in the stock. Ultimately, Bendix acquired close to 20 percent of ASARCO at an average price of about 19. At the time, Wall Street had little interest in the metal stocks, or so-called asset plays.

By late 1978, when we bought the stock, strikes and very depressed prices for nonferrous metals had driven the stock price down to $15 a share. Despite the low stock price, the outlook at ASARCO was picking up. The supply and demand for copper was in better balance, and a loss of $1.10 in 1977 had been reversed to a profit of $1.69 in 1978.

On the positive side, long-term debt was only some 25 percent of total capitalization, which was low for a metal company. Furthermore, official book value was $30—understated, in our opinion. ASARCO had properties in Peru, in Mexico and throughout the

West, as well as a 49 percent interest in MIM Holdings in Australia, reputed to own the richest silver mine in the world.

TABLE 16

ASARCO Incorporated

Per Share Data ($)

Yr. End Dec. 31	1982	1981	1980	1979	1978	1977	1976	1975	1974	1973
Book Value	NA	39.15	44.37	38.26	30.61	30.28	32.07	32.20	32.30	29.00
Earnings[1]	NA	1.54	7.31	8.56	1.69	d1.10	1.58	0.95	4.71	4.25
Dividends	0.50	1.40	1.85	1.30	0.40	0.70	0.70	1.05	1.42½	1.20
Payout Ratio	NA	91%	25%	15%	25%	NM	44%	110%	30%	28%
Prices—High	28¾	48½	58½	37⅞	20⅜	23⅝	20	19¾	27⅜	26⅛
Low	17¼	24¾	25½	13⅝	13¼	13	13⅛	12	13	17¼
P/E Ratio—	NA	31–16	8–3	4–2	12–8	NM	13–8	21–13	6–3	6–4

Data as orig. reptd. 1. Bef. spec. item(s) of +0.71 in 1980. NA-Not Available. NM-Not Meaningful. d-Deficit.

Income Data (Million $)

Year Ended Dec. 31	Revs.	Oper. Inc.	% Oper. Inc. of Revs.	Cap. Exp.	Depr.	Int. Exp.	Net Bef. Taxes	Eff. Tax Rate	[3]Net Inc.	% Net Inc. of Revs.
1981	1,532	51	3.3%	163	58.4	47.0	[1] 56	10.9%	[2] 50	3.3%
1980	1,817	132	7.3%	130	[2]49.4	[2]26.4	[1]276	21.7%	216	11.9%
1979	1,724	214	12.4%	70	56.1	29.9	[1]317	18.2%	259	15.0%
1978	1,175	104	8.9%	79	54.5	38.4	[1] 72	31.1%	49	4.2%
1977	1,046	60	5.7%	96	52.6	37.0	[1] d24	NM	d30	NM
1976	1,104	99	9.0%	76	50.7	33.9	[1] 54	21.9%	42	3.8%
1975	1,005	61	6.1%	167	36.5	22.7	[1] 15	NM	25	2.5%
1974	1,344	120	9.0%	138	34.9	11.8	[1]159	21.0%	126	9.4%
1973	1,068	78	7.3%	97	26.8	8.9	[1]137	17.1%	113	10.6%
1972	814	49	6.1%	67	23.9	5.2	[1] 59	16.8%	49	6.0%

Balance Sheet Data (Million $)

Dec. 31	Cash	Assets (Current)	Liab. (Current)	Ratio	Total Assets	Ret. on Assets	Long Term Debt	Common Equity	Total Cap.	% LT Debt of Cap.	Ret. on Equity
1981	25	538	383	1.4	2,093	2.6%	388	1,019	1,623	23.9%	3.5%
1980	128	546	278	2.0	2,045	10.8%	278	1,314	1,679	16.5%	17.7%
1979	83	644	404	1.6	1,970	14.6%	285	1,131	1,484	19.2%	25.5%
1978	28	421	216	2.0	1,623	2.9%	337	934	1,326	25.5%	5.3%
1977	9	370	198	1.9	1,530	NM	393	809	1,249	31.5%	NM
1976	30	380	154	2.5	1,544	2.8%	400	857	1,304	30.7%	4.9%
1975	35	442	174	2.5	1,502	1.8%	342	861	1,247	27.4%	2.9%
1974	20	408	234	1.7	1,329	10.1%	116	863	1,025	11.4%	15.4%
1973	20	364	196	1.9	1,149	10.6%	92	774	907	10.1%	15.6%
1972	15	333	202	1.6	990	5.2%	51	683	770	6.6%	7.3%

Data as orig. reptd. 1. Incl. equity in earns. of nonconsol. subs. 2. Reflects accounting change. 3. Bef. spec. item(s) in 1980. NM-Not Meaningful. d-Deficit.

Standard NYSE Stock Reports
Vol. 49/No. 224/Sec. 4

November 19, 1982
Copyright © 1982 Standard & Poor's Corp. All Rights Reserved

Standard & Poor's Corp.
25 Broadway, NY, NY 10004

In 1979, as the commodity markets rose because of inflation fears, precious-metal prices jumped and their spectacular advances spilled over to copper, lead and zinc. From almost one day to the next, investor sentiment changed, and suddenly investors weren't able to buy enough metal and mining stocks. Because of double-digit inflation, investors wanted an inflation hedge, and resources in the ground were seen as a good refuge. By 1979, ASARCO's price leaped to the high 30s, eventually hitting $58½ in early 1980, when gold reached $850 an ounce and silver $50 an ounce.

We sold the stock at $31, which once again was too early, but still a return of more than 100 percent. At $31, the stock was selling close to stated book value, and we didn't want to be greedy. Our caution proved to be well founded. While ASARCO's profits hit $8.56 in 1979, because of the surge in silver, gold and copper prices, earnings slipped to $7.31 in 1980. Commodity price increases were overdone because of a mania for inflation hedges—which boosted ASARCO's earnings artificially and temporarily. By 1981, with housing, autos and utility capital spending in the doldrums, copper and metal prices retreated to much lower levels, far below even production costs, and ASARCO's earnings were cut to less than half of the 1980s level.

Nevertheless, ASARCO's stock held in the 30s and 40s throughout most of 1981. For one thing, investors thought it was a potential takeover situation. They were further intrigued when ASARCO bought back Bendix's holdings for $55 a share, thereby reducing its own outstanding shares by 20 percent. Perhaps Wall Street believed that ASARCO knew more about its own value than the metals analysts.

Finally, in order to forestall takeover attempts, ASARCO allowed MIM to buy up to 18 percent of its shares. The dimming prospects of a takeover and the literal shutdown of orders for copper in 1982 ended up with ASARCO stock falling below $20, a testimonial to the cyclical fortunes of a commodity producer.

Simmonds Precision Products, Inc.

A good example of a roller-coaster ride in popularity was Simmonds Precision, a classic high-technology growth company, principally engaged in electronic instrument and motion and engine control systems for the aerospace industry. In 1980, we read an announcement by the company's management in *The Wall Street Journal* that earnings would decline in that year because of a write-off of the company's medical instrumentation division. This statement intrigued us, and we took a closer look at the company especially since it had hit a yearly low after the announcement.

Earnings had risen every year since 1971, jumping from $.26 to $1.35 in 1979. Book value also rose from about $2 to $7.80 during the same period, and return on equity jumped from 6.5 percent in 1971 to more than 15 percent by 1979. Debt was only about one

TABLE 17

SIMMONDS PRECISION PRODUCTS, INC.

Per Share Data ($)

Yr. End Dec. 31	1982	1981	1980	1979	1978	¹1977	1976	1975	1974	1973
Book Value	NA	9.21	7.67	7.80	5.56	5.27	4.59	3.85	3.31	2.81
Earnings²	NA	1.97	1.74	1.35	1.22	³1.03	³0.84	³0.77	0.60	0.48
Dividends	0.38	0.34	0.30	0.26	0.22	0.19	0.15	0.12	0.10	Nil
Payout Ratio	NA	17%	17%	20%	18%	18%	18%	15%	17%	Nil
Prices—High	26⅞	19½	19¼	20⅜	21⅛	9¼	9⅛	9⅜	4	5¼
Low	10⅝	10¼	7¾	11	7½	5½	5	2½	2¼	2⅞
P/E Ratio—	NA	10-5	11-4	15-8	17-6	9-5	11-6	12-3	7-4	11-6

Data as orig. reptd. 1. Reflects merger or acquisition. 2. Bef. results of disc. opers. of − 1.64 in 1980, and spec. item(s) of +0.05 in 1976. 3. Ful. dil.: 1.02 in 1977, 0.83 in 1976, 0.76 in 1975. NA-Not Available.

Income Data (Million $)

Year Ended Dec. 31	Revs.	Oper. Inc.	% Oper. Inc. of Revs.	Cap. Exp.	Depr.	Int. Exp.	Net Bef. Taxes	Eff. Tax Rate	³Net Inc.	% Net Inc. of Revs.
1981	139	23.5	16.9%	4.80	2.59	3.43	17.1	43.1%	9.72	7.0%
²1980	132	20.7	15.7%	6.40	2.10	2.55	11.9	28.9%	8.47	6.4%
1979	119	14.1	11.9%	3.85	1.79	1.51	11.0	43.1%	6.25	5.3%
¹1978	98	12.4	12.6%	3.54	1.44	1.46	9.3	44.9%	5.13	5.2%
¹1977	66	7.8	11.9%	3.79	0.94	1.20	5.7	45.6%	3.10	4.7%
1976	50	6.3	12.6%	2.83	0.81	0.61	4.8	47.4%	2.50	5.0%
1975	52	5.9	11.3%	1.36	0.75	0.69	4.2	45.3%	⁴2.31	4.4%
1974	43	4.5	10.6%	0.78	0.70	0.63	3.4	45.9%	1.82	4.3%
1973	39	4.1	10.5%	0.89	0.65	0.45	3.1	50.2%	1.54	3.9%
1972	35	3.3	9.2%	0.84	0.63	0.56	2.0	42.5%	1.17	3.3%

Balance Sheet Data (Million $)

Dec. 31	Cash	——Current—— Assets	Liab.	Ratio	Total Assets	Ret. on Assets	Long Term Debt	Com- mon Equity	Total Cap.	% LT Debt of Cap.	Ret. on Equity
1981	3.52	63.2	17.0	3.7	90.8	10.6%	19.0	52.4	72.8	26.2%	20.0%
1980	1.37	65.3	22.3	2.9	90.7	9.9%	22.6	44.2	67.3	33.5%	19.0%
1979	3.37	56.0	16.5	3.4	78.4	8.2%	14.8	44.1	60.9	24.3%	15.9%
1978	2.84	42.7	18.7	2.3	62.6	8.1%	11.0	29.6	42.6	25.9%	17.0%
1977	2.65	30.0	10.0	3.0	47.5	7.2%	11.6	22.8	36.4	31.8%	14.4%
1976	3.01	25.0	6.9	3.6	38.7	6.9%	8.7	20.1	30.7	28.2%	13.2%
1975	1.18	21.7	7.2	3.0	33.5	7.1%	5.6	17.8	25.2	22.2%	13.6%
1974	1.67	20.9	7.6	2.7	32.2	6.0%	5.3	16.4	23.6	22.5%	11.6%
1973	1.01	17.5	7.6	2.3	28.8	5.6%	3.4	14.8	19.9	16.9%	10.8%
1972	1.18	17.4	6.0	2.9	28.6	4.1%	5.6	14.5	21.7	25.6%	8.3%

Data as orig. reptd. 1. Reflects merger or acquisition. 2. Excludes discontinued operations. 3. Bef. results of disc. opers. in 1980, and spec. item(s) in 1976. 4. Reflects accounting change.

Standard NYSE Stock Reports
Vol. 49/No. 246/Sec. 21

December 23, 1982
Copyright © 1982 Standard & Poor's Corp. All Rights Reserved

Standard & Poor's Corp.
25 Broadway, NY, NY 10004

third of total capitalization and carried reasonable interest rates. Although there were only about 4½ million Simmonds shares actively traded, institutions had become interested in the company and by 1980 held about 15 percent of the stock. Up to the time of the announcement of the write-off, the stock price history reflected this good performance, having jumped from 9 in 1978 to 20 in 1980.

As it turned out, the write-off led to a $1.64 nonrecurring loss in 1980. But without the write-off, earnings would have risen above 1979's results. Management, in a realistic and wise move, decided to rid the company of a money-losing albatross, which we viewed as a positive development for the company. The institutions did not agree with us, however, and they unloaded the stock. By the spring of 1980, Simmonds sold at 8 a share, or four times continuing earnings from operations, at which price we acquired stock.

Later in the year, the stock recovered because bargain hunters realized the selling was overdone and the company was actually in a much healthier state now that the losing operation had been removed. By November 1980, the stock had rebounded to 18, or to a more normal p/e of 9. Here was another instance of an emotional reaction by investors, who focused on superficial news and failed to see the write-off as a plus for the future and a sign of strong and decisive management.

Stewart-Warner Corporation

One of the best illustrations of how a recession or a downturn in an industry created unwarranted selling in a stock is Stewart-Warner, a company that derived about 30 percent of its revenues from truck parts, mostly original equipment, about 18 percent from industrial lubricating equipment and 20 percent from casters, with the balance derived from electrical equipment. In essence, it was a diversified manufacturing company.

In the first quarter of 1980, as the odds of a severe recession increased, it became apparent that Stewart-Warner's earnings might be affected by the cyclical fluctuations in capital goods and the automotive industries. (And, in retrospect, earnings did fall to $2.86 in 1980 from $3.35 the year before.) But did lower earnings expectations justify a price drop from 22½ in February 1980 to 14 a month later?

At 15¼ a share, which is where we bought the stock, the last twelve months' earnings of $3.35 indicated a p/e of 4½. Even discounting a 20 percent drop in earnings for 1980 to $2.56, as reported by the Standard & Poor's *Earnings Forecaster*, the p/e was still below 6, which was at the low end of the historical range. Other pluses: the stock was selling at a 60 percent discount from book value and yielded 9.6 percent, with little likelihood of a dividend

TABLE 18
STEWART-WARNER CORPORATION

Per Share Data ($)

Yr. End Dec. 31	1981	1980	1979	1978	1977	1976	1975	1974	[1]1973	1972
Book Value	27.68	26.98	25.62	23.73	21.79	20.08	18.55	17.75	16.81	15.74
Earnings[2]	2.38	2.86	3.35	3.28	2.99	2.78	2.03	2.18	2.24	1.82
Dividends	1.54⅞	1.50½	1.46½	1.34½	1.27¾	1.25½	1.23½	1.22⅞	1.19⅝	1.18½
Payout Ratio	65%	52%	44%	41%	43%	45%	61%	56%	54%	65%
Prices—High	24⅜	28½	33	24⅝	24⅛	22⅝	17⅛	19¼	22⅞	25⅞
Low	20⅛	13⅞	18½	17⅝	18⅜	15¼	10⅞	10⅜	14½	22⅛
P/E Ratio—	10–8	10–5	10–6	8–5	8–6	8–5	8–5	9–5	10–6	14–12

Data as orig. reptd. Adj. for stk. div(s). of 25% Dec. 1981, 25% Jun. 1979. 1. Reflects accounting change. 2. Bef. spec. item(s) of +0.04 in 1972.

Income Data (Million $)

Year Ended Dec. 31	Revs.	Oper. Inc.	% Oper. Inc. of Revs.	Cap. Exp.	Depr.	Int. Exp.	Net Bef. Taxes	Eff. Tax Rate	[3]Net Inc.	% Net Inc. of Revs.
1981	329	31.5	9.6%	6.2	6.10	0.26	[2]26.6	42.1%	15.4	4.7%
1980	336	38.3	11.4%	8.8	5.66	0.31	[2]33.8	45.0%	18.6	5.5%
1979	366	43.6	11.9%	12.0	5.12	0.24	[2]40.8	46.7%	21.7	5.9%
1978	334	44.8	13.4%	8.8	4.87	0.21	[2]41.6	48.8%	21.3	6.4%
1977	292	40.7	13.9%	7.9	5.08	0.16	[2]37.8	48.6%	19.4	6.6%
1976	274	39.3	14.3%	6.8	5.15	0.20	[2]35.2	48.8%	18.0	6.6%
1975	241	30.3	12.6%	4.5	5.27	0.24	[2]25.6	48.7%	13.1	5.4%
1974	261	31.9	12.2%	5.3	5.20	0.24	[2]27.7	49.3%	14.0	5.4%
[1]1973	244	31.0	12.7%	5.7	5.14	0.16	[2]27.9	48.5%	14.4	5.9%
1972	198	26.8	13.5%	7.4	4.69	Nil	[2]23.0	49.3%	11.6	5.9%

Balance Sheet Data (Million $)

Dec. 31	Cash	Assets	Current Liab.	Ratio	Total Assets	Ret. on Assets	Long Term Debt	Common Equity	Total Cap.	% LT Debt of Cap.	Ret. on Equity
1981	10.9	181	47.8	3.8	235	6.5%	0.66	178	183	0.4%	8.7%
1980	6.7	182	53.2	3.4	236	7.9%	0.77	175	181	0.4%	10.9%
1979	6.1	178	61.1	2.9	234	9.7%	1.93	166	170	1.1%	13.6%
1978	13.4	164	55.4	3.0	216	10.2%	2.05	154	158	1.3%	14.4%
1977	16.5	151	52.3	2.9	200	10.1%	2.05	142	145	1.4%	14.3%
1976	21.6	136	47.1	2.9	184	10.1%	2.07	130	134	1.5%	14.4%
1975	11.7	125	45.5	2.8	172	7.6%	2.11	120	123	1.7%	11.2%
1974	6.1	129	53.7	2.4	174	8.4%	1.12	114	117	1.0%	12.6%
1973	4.7	116	46.3	2.5	160	9.7%	1.42	108	110	1.3%	13.7%
1972	7.6	96	35.8	2.7	136	8.8%	Nil	101	101	Nil	11.8%

Data as orig. reptd. 1. Reflects accounting change. 2. Incl. equity in earns. of nonconsol. subs. 3. Bef. spec. item(s) in 1972.

Standard NYSE Stock Reports
Vol. 49/No. 173/Sec. 26

September 8, 1982
Copyright © 1982 Standard & Poor's Corp. All Rights Reserved

Standard & Poor's Corp.
25 Broadway, NY, NY 10004

cut. In addition, earnings had grown steadily since 1971. The company was virtually debt-free, its current ratio was 3 to 1, the after-tax return on sales had been consistently above 5.5 percent for the previous ten years and return on equity had averaged 13½ percent for the previous 5 years.

The downside risk was not significant and we felt the fundamentals were being ignored. We figured the stock had a good chance of hitting 20 within a year, which would give us an annual return of 40 percent, including dividends. As it turned out, the stock actually rose to a high of 28½ by the end of 1980, and even in 1981–82 never dipped below 20.

Armstrong World Industries, Inc.

Another example of how recessionary concerns can bring about an overreaction in a stock was Armstrong World Industries (ACK),

TABLE 19
ARMSTRONG WORLD INDUSTRIES, INC.

Per Share Data ($)

Yr. End Dec. 31	¹1981	1980	1979	1978	1977	1976	1975	1974	1973	¹1972
Book Value	24.12	23.29	22.45	20.77	19.41	18.86	17.27	17.32	16.76	15.45
Earnings²	1.88	1.94	2.58	2.36	1.55	2.01	1.34	1.45	2.15	1.60
Dividends	1.10	1.10	1.07½	1.00	1.00	0.91	0.83	0.90	0.82	0.80
Payout Ratio	58%	57%	41%	42%	64%	45%	62%	62%	38%	50%
Prices—High	18¾	18⅝	19	21⅜	27¾	32⅞	28	32¾	34¼	44⅞
Low	14	12⅜	14⅝	14¾	16⅝	23⅞	17¼	14¾	21	31
P/E Ratio—	10-7	10-6	7-6	9-6	18-11	16-12	21-13	23-10	16-10	28-19

Data as orig. reptd. **1.** Reflects merger or acquisition. **2.** Bef. spec. item(s) of +0.48 in 1976. d-Deficit.

Income Data (Million $)

Year Ended Dec. 31	Revs.	Oper. Inc.	% Oper. Inc. of Revs.	Cap. Exp.	Depr.	Int. Exp.	Net Bef. Taxes	Eff. Tax Rate	²Net Inc.	% Net Inc. of Revs.
¹1981	1,376	136	9.9%	60.5	49.2	13.8	79	39.1%	47.1	3.4%
1980	1,323	158	11.9%	64.6	45.6	14.2	100	50.4%	48.6	3.7%
1979	1,341	180	13.4%	56.1	41.6	13.8	126	47.5%	66.0	4.9%
1978	1,244	184	14.8%	43.7	42.7	14.6	128	52.4%	61.1	4.9%
1977	1,089	150	13.8%	50.7	37.7	15.0	95	57.6%	40.4	3.7%
1976	981	144	14.6%	62.4	35.3	13.1	103	48.9%	52.3	5.3%
1975	859	102	11.8%	38.3	32.2	16.6	61	42.4%	34.9	4.1%
1974	889	111	12.5%	68.8	30.4	12.3	68	42.2%	37.8	4.2%
1973	795	139	17.5%	53.4	27.6	7.9	105	45.9%	55.7	7.0%
¹1972	684	106	15.4%	37.7	27.0	6.5	79	46.3%	41.8	6.1%

Balance Sheet Data (Million $)

Dec. 31	Cash	—Current— Assets	Liab.	Ratio	Total Assets	Ret. on Assets	Long Term Debt	Common Equity	Total Cap.	% LT Debt of Cap.	Ret. on Equity
1981	31.7	455	182	2.5	939	5.2%	98	589	756	13.0%	8.1%
1980	37.8	446	148	3.0	892	5.5%	104	576	743	14.0%	8.5%
1979	35.3	447	139	3.2	876	7.8%	126	556	737	17.1%	12.3%
1978	50.4	420	137	3.1	849	7.3%	130	535	712	18.2%	11.7%
1977	54.7	387	121	3.2	822	5.0%	156	500	702	22.2%	8.1%
1976	48.7	352	110	3.2	788	6.8%	148	486	678	21.9%	11.1%
1975	37.6	329	111	3.0	741	4.7%	138	445	630	21.9%	7.7%
1974	8.0	320	101	3.2	734	5.5%	143	446	633	22.7%	8.5%
1973	16.5	271	93	2.9	647	9.0%	82	431	554	14.7%	13.3%
1972	20.6	239	74	3.3	588	7.3%	75	397	515	14.6%	10.7%

Data as orig. reptd. **1.** Reflects merger or acquisition. **2.** Bef. spec. item(s) in 1976.

Standard NYSE Stock Reports
Vol. 49/No. 171/Sec. 4

September 3, 1982
Copyright © 1982 Standard & Poor's Corp. All Rights Reserved

Standard & Poor's Corp.
25 Broadway, NY, NY 10004

one of the world's largest manufacturers of floor coverings, ceiling systems and interior furnishings and furniture. Like many housing-related stocks, the company had a cyclical earnings record, and when higher interest rates and inflationary pressures seemed sure to bring about a credit crunch and recession, most housing-related stocks dropped sharply. As a result, the institutions, which held 50–60 percent of ACK, wanted to reduce their holdings, and the stock plummeted to 12½ in 1980 from a high of 19 in 1979 and 21 in 1978.

At 12½ a share, the stock was selling at five times 1979 earnings and six and a half times the expected lower earnings for 1980—which was at the low end of its historical p/e range. By our calculation, ACK had a hard book value of $20, and net current working capital on the order of $9 a share. Also, long-term debt was only about 15 percent of total capitalization. Moreover, a good deal of ACK's business was in refurbishing and repair, areas that actually pick up in a recession. Thus, we believed that earnings might hold up fairly well, even during bad economic times.

Our analysis indicated the risk was small, especially because the stock carried a yield of over 8 percent. We believed a recovery to 20 over the next twelve months was a good bet, since the lowest yearly high over the previous ten years was 19. And, we reasoned, if there was any recovery in the housing market, the stock might go even higher, which it did, eventually hitting 25 in 1982.

RCA Corporation

By 1980, RCA had become a perfect illustration of Murphy's Law—of how nearly everything that could go wrong went wrong. The company had become highly visible to Wall Street, partly because of a takeover of CIT Financial in January 1980, one of the largest consumer finance companies, and partly because of many well-publicized management changes, which had created a negative image for the company. RCA had also had several chief executive officers, some of whom had resigned under fire. NBC, the company's broadcasting subsidiary, was under great pressure because it had lost ground to ABC and CBS during the previous three years. Fred Silverman, the media genius who was hired away from ABC to run NBC, did not have the instant success that everyone had expected, and NBC's slump in the ratings caused many of its television station affiliates to switch to other networks.

TABLE 20

RCA CORPORATION

Per Share Data ($)

Yr. End Dec. 31	1981	1980	1979	1978	1977	1976	1975	[1]1974	1973	1972
Book Value	19.06	21.23	21.71	19.59	17.34	15.30	14.01	13.63	13.19	11.22
Earnings	d0.19	[2]3.35	[2]3.72	[2]3.65	[2]3.23	[2]2.30	1.40	1.45	[2]2.39	[2]2.05
Dividends	1.80	1.80	1.60	1.40	1.20	1.00	1.00	1.00	1.00	1.00
Payout Ratio	NM	54%	43%	38%	37%	43%	71%	69%	42%	49%
Prices—High	32¼	33	28¼	33⅞	32½	30⅛	21⅜	21½	39⅛	45
Low	16¾	18½	21⅛	22⅝	24⅜	18⅞	10⅜	9¼	16½	32⅛
P/E Ratio—	NM	10-6	8-6	9-6	10-8	13-8	15-7	15-6	16-7	22-16

Data as orig. reptd. **1.** Reflects merger or acquisition. **2.** Ful. dil.: 3.19 in 1980, 3.57 in 1979, 3.50 in 1978, 3.11 in 1977, 2.24 in 1976, 2.33 in 1973, 2.01 in 1972. NM-Not Meaningful.

Income Data (Million $)

Year Ended Dec. 31	Revs.	Oper. Inc.	% Oper. Inc. of Revs.	Cap. Exp.	Depr.	Int. Exp.	Net Bef. Taxes	Eff. Tax Rate	Net Inc.	% Net Inc. of Revs.
1981	8,005	983	12.3%	1,739	497	401	[3] 98	45.1%	[2] 54	0.7%
1980	8,011	972	12.1%	986	494	279	[3]507	37.8%	315	3.9%
1979	7,455	976	13.1%	865	438	[2]163	[3]472	39.8%	284	3.8%
1978	6,601	942	14.3%	700	364	113	[3]515	45.9%	278	4.2%
1977	5,881	848	14.4%	869	332	97	[3]470	47.5%	247	4.2%
1976	5,329	689	12.9%	780	300	94	[3]343	48.3%	177	3.3%
1975	4,790	518	10.8%	681	272	98	[3]189	41.7%	110	2.3%
[1]1974	4,594	525	11.4%	749	260	96	202	43.8%	113	2.5%
1973	4,247	602	14.2%	621	232	69	335	45.2%	184	4.3%
1972	3,838	532	13.9%	464	230	58	269	41.3%	158	4.1%

Balance Sheet Data (Million $)

Dec. 31	Cash	Current Assets	Current Liab.	Ratio	Total Assets	Ret. on Assets	Long Term Debt	Common Equity	Total Cap.	% LT Debt of Cap.	Ret. on Equity
1981	175	3,619	3,063	1.2	7,857	0.7%	1,856	1,438	4,096	45.3%	NM
1980	175	3,403	2,277	1.5	7,148	4.8%	1,771	1,597	4,183	42.3%	15.6%
1979	206	3,230	2,136	1.5	5,990	5.2%	1,474	1,625	3,234	45.6%	18.0%
1978	241	2,758	1,612	1.7	4,873	6.0%	1,118	1,464	2,717	41.1%	19.8%
1977	264	2,376	1,400	1.7	4,352	6.0%	1,076	1,295	2,507	42.9%	19.8%
1976	178	2,038	1,261	1.6	3,838	4.7%	944	1,142	2,222	42.5%	15.7%
1975	280	2,047	1,287	1.6	3,728	3.0%	958	1,044	2,137	44.8%	10.2%
1974	318	1,898	1,162	1.6	3,647	3.3%	1,054	1,015	2,204	47.8%	10.8%
1973	287	1,835	1,043	1.8	3,301	5.7%	908	982	2,024	44.8%	19.6%
1972	394	1,807	1,026	1.8	3,137	5.1%	909	836	1,885	48.2%	19.2%

Data as orig. reptd. **1.** Reflects merger or acquisition. **2.** Reflects acctg. change. **3.** Incl. equity in earns. of nonconsol. subs.

As if this weren't enough, Hertz, another large division of the company, was being squeezed by the recession and fierce competition for car rentals at the airports. The final catastrophe was NBC's losing the coverage of the Moscow Olympics (due to President Carter's boycott), the company's only hope for better earnings. All these factors pushed the stock to 19 in the spring of 1980, or to a p/e of 6 on 1980 estimated earnings. The big holders rushed to get out of the stock on the bad news, and RCA sold at its lowest p/e since 1974.

But there were positives too. The stated book value was 21, but was probably far greater, since the company's NBC Broadcasting Company and its affiliates were worth substantially more than they were carried for on the books. Return on equity had averaged 15½ percent since 1976. Not only was the company a leader in consumer electronics, but it also had strong research and development in state-of-the-art electronics technology. Other pluses: marginal operations bought in a conglomeration binge in the early 1970s were being sold off, and NBC had probably stopped losing market share.

Indeed, propelled by a better overall stock market and hopes for its new videodisc system, RCA's stock rallied to 33 by the end of 1980, for a 75 percent gain. At that point we decided to take profits because the stock had reached our objective.

However, less than a year later, the fickleness of the markets gave us another buying opportunity in the stock. By the fall of 1981 RCA stock had dropped to 16 as problems continued to plague the company. The litany of investor woes was similar to those in 1980: large start-up losses for the vaunted videodisc, the recession's effect on Hertz, the squeeze of high interest rates on CIT and the departure of Fred Silverman and Edgar Griffiths, the chief executive for the previous five years. If anything, the outlook was even worse in 1981 and 1982 than it had been in 1980. RCA wrote off $150 million in the third quarter of 1981 and cut its dividend in the first quarter of 1982. NBC dumped several pilot TV programs, and sales of the videodisc were not coming anywhere near expectations. And, in fact, the venture looked like a white elephant.

While not underestimating the problems, we did note some encouraging signs. The new chief executive officer, Thornton Bradshaw, had apparently put an end to board-room intrigue and had hired a top broadcasting executive to replace Silverman. Most important, there was increasing speculation that RCA might sell either CIT or Hertz. That would enable the company to reduce its debt burden and high interest expenses, which had penalized earnings in the past few years. The always opportunistic Bendix and its aggressive CEO, Bill Agee, having made a bundle on ASARCO stock, also saw the attraction of a revamped RCA and announced intentions to buy up to 10 percent of RCA. This renewed speculative interest in the stock, which quickly rose to 22—only to decline to 16 when no immediate deal was forthcoming. The jury is still out on RCA at this writing.

Possible Traps

Based on the examples discussed above, it may appear easy to invest in beaten-down, high-profile stocks, which is certainly not the case. To make money in such stocks, investors must correctly evaluate one very difficult question: Have the company's recovery powers been seriously or irreparably damaged? An obvious example of a company that could not recover was W. T. Grant. And without federal aid, Chrysler would have failed in 1980 or 1981.

Even if a company doesn't go out of business, its problems could linger far longer than anyone expects, and the outcome may remain in doubt for years. If that happens, investors might be locked into an unattractive investment for years. Therefore, investors must analyze the company's problems very carefully. One major mistake in a portfolio could offset many profits and undermine total performance.

Even if a stock is at the low end of its p/e range or sells substantially below its asset value, it may not be a good investment. Consider International Harvester. A debilitating strike in 1979 that lasted for six months and the high fixed costs of the company produced huge losses. Meanwhile, short-term debt ballooned, and more important, the company lost credibility with its dealers and many of its customers. Labor problems reduced the quality of the company's products, and its image suffered substantially. For 1980 as a whole, the company lost $12 a share, and productive assets had to be sold and modernization programs deferred. Meanwhile, the stock declined to $22 a share, or 40 percent of book value, the lowest price since 1976. At first glance, some investors probably thought the stock was a buy. As it turned out, the stock eventually fell to less than $5 in 1982 as cash-flow problems and mounting losses caused a mass exodus out of the stock. At this writing, the fate of the former blue chip hangs in the balance.

Similarly, Burroughs Corporation, the once proud member of

the glamour/growth stocks of the 1960s and early 1970s, and a leading computer main frame manufacturer, also encountered major selling pressure in 1980. Manufacturing snafus and publicity about customer service complaints weakened demand for the company's product lines and caused the stock price to drop from a high of 87½ in early 1980 to 46¼ by the end of 1980. We made the mistake of buying the stock at 54, the lowest price since 1977. We thought the damage was done and believed the selling by the institutions had run its course. As it turned out, we misjudged the magnitude of investor dissatisfaction, and when quarterly earnings comparisons continued to be poor, the stock declined to the high 20s.

The point here is: Don't underestimate the severity of investor disillusion. Once the apparent price storm appears to have stabilized, ask whether all the bad news is out, what else could go wrong, how secure the safety nets are (asset value, dividend yield, book value). Also, be sure to read as much as possible about the company, its problems and the industry outlook.

A diligent investor should even consider contacting the company and talking to the shareholders-relations department. At the very least, learn how management views the company's problems. The most important thing to focus on is whether management's assumptions about the future are heavily dependent on imponderables or events out of their control. If so, it may be better to stay away from the company.

The most accessible, although probably not the most illuminating source in judging management's perception of its problems and its proposed solutions, is the president's letter to shareholders in the annual report and his statements in the quarterly earnings reports (10Q's). In addition, most larger corporations have a public relations department that periodically issues releases on corporate news and events. To be sure, a little bit of reading between the lines is necessary in digesting this kind of information. Nevertheless, if management is predicting unsatisfactory results and blaming it on the economy or interest rates, for example, without specifying remedial steps that are to be made to correct or mitigate the falling orders or margin squeezes, then management may be reacting too slowly. Management could cut overhead, reduce prices to pare inventory, write off and close down unprofitable segments of its business rather than just endure possible losses or earnings declines.

If you don't hear aggressive noises in times of business contraction, earnings may be penalized and with them the stock price.

If published material is sketchy, then call the company, indicate that you are a potential shareholder and ask questions. Answers may be evasive, but generally the corporate public relations officer or treasurer will give you some comments on what is going on and what actions the company is taking to correct problems.

To sum up: Out-of-favor stocks involve a certain amount of speculation, even if the stock is selling at a historically low price/earnings ratio. The recovery of the company and the stock can take much longer than first expected. Moreover, the stock can continue to fall after it is bought, which can be quite upsetting. And when the stock does return to one's purchase price, the temptation to sell can often be overwhelming. A premature sale can be a big mistake. We have often found that a stock that returns to our original purchase price may be at the beginning of a major advance. The way to avoid selling too early is to monitor closely the company's prospects. Read the shareholder reports, articles on the company in the financial journals, publicity releases by the company, and any brokerage house reports. If the company is successfully dealing with its problems, make a point of knowing about it.

The Investment Paddy Wagon

Among old Wall Street hands, there's an old cliché that "when the paddy wagon comes, it even takes the good girls to jail." Freely translated, it means that when the investment climate turns really negative, even the blue bloods of the market, the so-called glamours, fade and fall sharply in price. To us, this is an ideal time to buy cheap and hold for the long term. Quality companies such as Deere, Boeing, Lilly, Minnesota Mining & Manufacturing, NCR, General Electric, Avon and many others had large declines in the 1981–82 recession. Investors, especially the institutions, place too much emphasis on news—both good and bad—which helps to distort prices.

A loss of investment perspective in a stock due to fear in the market almost invariably is fertile ground for profit. Even if the "fallen angels" never recover to their historical or traditional price/earnings ratios or to their former return on equity, usually 15 percent or greater, their recovery potential is enormous, given their financial stability and earning power in a normal year. So when the "good girls" get caught in a bear market, when everyone is selling, that is the time for value-oriented investors to swoop in and buy the aristocrats of the market and wait it out until the market sentiment again turns positive and the underlying values reassert themselves.

Chapter 7

Special Situations:
Turnarounds and
Takeovers

THE TERM "SPECIAL SITUATIONS" has many different connotations on Wall Street. Our definition of the term is those stocks that rise dramatically in price because of a fundamental change in the company's outlook. Such a change is usually brought about by one of the following events:

1. The prospect of a radical turnaround of a company that has had a negative image for a long time.

2. A takeover by another company. Or a purchase of a large interest by another company or group that seeks control of the target company, or at the very least, an important influence on management policies.

The stocks of these two types of special situations are usually selling at depressed and undervalued levels. Thus, once the investment community becomes interested in the stock, the price advances can often be considerable.

Nevertheless, one must analyze why the stock is selling at such a low price. We have repeatedly argued that it is risky to contradict the general consensus, and nowhere is that more important than with special situations. Any investment in a stock that is considered a potential turnaround or takeover must be considered a speculation. Accordingly, we try to avoid having more than 20 percent of a portfolio in these kinds of stocks. For one thing, they are highly vulnerable to a sudden drop in the stock market because they have little, if any, sponsorship or support in the market. Second, one may have to hold these stocks longer than most other bargain-hunting investments. In the case of a turnaround, the company's image may be so negative that the investors require substantial proof that the turnaround is for real. And in the case of a prospective takeover, a purchase of a block of stock by another company or investor group may not be enough to capture the interest of the financial community. Such a purchase may be for investment purposes only and may not lead to an immediate buy-out. Wall Street speculators have learned not to run up the stock prices of a target company unless they have solid reasons for believing that a serious attempt will be made to get control.

The speculative nature of special situations underscores the need to examine the stock's downside risk thoroughly, to scrutinize the company's annual report and proxy statement, and to have a very good reason to believe you've bought at the bottom if the turnaround falters or the takeover prospects dim.

Turnarounds: The Phoenix Syndrome

Precisely because turnaround stocks are characterized by a terrible image and chronic disappointment for shareholders, the important item to focus on is the reason for the expected turnaround. The poor image of the company may stem from one or more of the following reasons, among others: bad management policies, poor products and services, mature markets for the company's products, chronic legal problems, suggestions of impropriety by the company or its management, consistently poor earnings and inadequate return on assets and shareholders' equity, poor use of assets, abysmal labor problems, or asset or revenue exposure in countries with big political risks. A turnaround in a company's fortunes usually requires a radical change in management policy, which can be painful in the short turn but will eventually produce the desired results.

The major cause of the problem areas listed above is the inability or unwillingness of management to come to grips with them and to launch remedial action. Sometimes this is a result of incompetence or complacency, but more often the stumbling block is management's ego. Management often finds it easier to avoid matters than to acknowledge past mistakes. Thus, even if it is obvious to most objective observers that a division or product line should be sold, management may not do so. Either the managers are reluctant to admit an error or they are unwilling to see their company shrink in size, even if a division is undermining earnings. Many managers feel they have to justify their jobs and without a certain volume of sales, stockholders might question management's high salaries and fancy perquisites.

Although lip service is paid to the concept of corporate democracy in this country, most shareholders take very little interest in management policy unless there is evidence of blatant negligence or mismanagement. Typically, shareholders vote for management's proposals year after year, and with the many regulations imposed by the SEC, it is hard to challenge managers even if they are doing a bad job. The managers have a powerful advantage because they can use the company's resources to fight any usurpers seeking control of the company through a proxy battle.

What circumstances, then, will force management to take the appropriate action? Sometimes negative publicity in the financial press about a company's policies will do the trick. Occasionally dissident shareholders who are disgusted with bad earnings and a low stock price can force a change in management policies. Or sometimes dissident members of the board of directors can push through a change of policy. Indeed, one of the first tip-offs of a potential turnaround is the formation of shareholder committees or the existence of dissatisfied directors who seek to influence the direction of the company.

A successful turnaround is usually prompted by action on one or more of four fronts:

1. Infusion of new equity or a conversion of debt into equity. Such an event is drastic and amounts to a massive reorganization of the company. Both Penn Central and Lockheed were technically insolvent but received large amounts of federal aid, which enabled them to achieve a remarkable turnaround.

2. Change of management. New managers are brought in who are capable of identifying the problem and dealing with it.

3. Asset redeployment. This occurs when management takes a hard look at the entire business, laying off personnel and selling off assets or unprofitable product lines. The cash generated by the sale of assets is then redeployed into what is hoped will be a more profitable business.

4. A new product or service that provides a proprietary edge

to the company and that could revitalize it. The new product could be a result of corporate research and development, a new license or the purchase of a business that offers excellent growth potential.

There is no set formula to follow when buying a turnaround situation and you should recognize that there is significant risk in these kinds of investments. In our experience, the most dramatic turnarounds occurred in companies that we would totally shun based on our checklist criteria. This is why the actions listed above are necessary catalysts of revival. By definition, companies that are candidates for recovery have undergone a period of decline in sales and earnings and are often saddled with excessive debt. This is what necessitates a fresh start if the company is to survive, whether it comes in the form of (1) debt restructuring, (2) new equity, (3) management with enough guts to shake up the business, even amputating divisions or businesses, or (4) the luck of either internally generating a new product or service or acquiring a license for one that gives the company an earnings lever to prop itself up so that it may shed its bad image, unprofitable businesses and overloading debt.

In using our checklist, if you are going to take the plunge in this kind of risk venture, make sure of two factors: that you are buying, first, at a five-to-ten-year rock-bottom *price* (forget about the price/earnings ratio, since earnings are hard to predict—if they exist at all), and second, at the lowest discount from book value, or even better, net current working capital in ten years. This won't save you from losses if the company continues to falter and no turnaround materializes, but at least you are somewhat protected by a low purchase price. What you are really looking for is a better-dead-than-alive situation, where even if the company goes out of business, there would be sufficient realization of cash to pay off all debt and disburse the rest to shareholders even if cost on the books for inventory, plant and equipment is only realized at $.50 on the dollar or less.

With this in mind, one way to look for turnarounds, and indeed potential takeovers, is to scan screens of these very undervalued situations that appear in *Value Line* and *Forbes* or are produced by stockbrokers, such as Oppenheimer & Company. This is as good a starting point as any for crippled stocks.

One last item to seek in potential turnarounds: does the company have forgotten or hidden assets that it could potentially turn to its advantage by selling and thereby realizing an infusion? CI Realty (see below) exemplifies such a situation.

The real source of finding turnarounds, though, is your own ability to interpret the four types of catalysts in a favorable light, either by reading about them yourself or having the potential pointed out by a broker or someone else. Then climb on, hold tight and hope for a big score. Most of all, as we have just said, try to buy at historically low levels with respect to price, book value and maybe net current working capital, but be aware that you aren't in conformity with any checklist and thus keep your exposure to turnarounds low as a percentage of your overall portfolio. Remember that the phoenix was a rare mythical bird.

Debt Restructuring

The Real Estate Investment Trusts (REITs) present a good example of successful debts restructuring. In the early 1970s, REITs borrowed billions of dollars from the banks and invested the money directly in real estate or lent it to real estate developers. But the 1973–74 credit crunch and the ensuing recession caused a debacle in the real estate industry, and many REITs began to lose money. They attempted to foreclose on their loans to developers but were not successful in getting paid because of the depressed real estate markets. Seeing that their customers' loans were in default, the banks began to foreclose on the REITs. But since the REITs couldn't get paid, neither could the banks, and what resulted was insolvency for the REIT industry.

Instead of writing off the loans to the REITs, many banks forgave the debt in return for real estate assets. This usually proved to be a wise decision because real estate properties rose sharply in value in the late 1970s and most banks were able to liquidate the assets they took back, without significant loan losses. But many of the REITs still held valuable properties, whose worth was eventually recognized by the financial community. In fact, by 1979 REITs became one of the leading stock groups and their shares jumped sharply. Thus, what might have been a series of large bankruptcies eventually became successful turnarounds.

CI Realty: A Case of an Asset Turnaround

In 1975 we noticed an announcement in the newspaper that CI Realty, an "equity REIT" that owned real estate properties, planned to merge with CI Mortgage, a virtually bankrupt "mortgage REIT" that had made many bad mortgage loans. Both REITs had been started by City Investing as a way of expanding its home-building efforts and were still managed by a subsidiary of City Investing.

The proposed merger of the two REITs was an indication to us that City Investing was trying to prop up CI Mortgage with the real estate properties of CI Realty. For obvious reasons, shareholders of CI Realty opposed the merger, sought refuge in the courts and won. All this prompted our interest because we suspected that CI Realty might have some hidden assets.

Upon closer examination, we discovered that CI Realty owned 1.5 million square feet of prime office space in New York City and some three thousand garden apartments located mainly in the South and Midwest. Despite the underlying value, the stock of CI Realty languished between 3 and 5 a share for most of 1975. Of course, real estate fundamentals at the time were terrible. Apartment vacancy rates around the country had jumped sharply because of the 1974–75 recession, and New York City office space was almost being given away because of a temporary surplus of office space and the near bankruptcy of New York City.

We believed the office space and the garden apartments were worth substantially more than CI Realty's official book value and we accumulated almost 5 percent of the stock between 3 and 7. Two years later, when real estate started a major renaissance and investors recognized the undervalued real estate assets, CI Realty rose to 14. We sold our shares to City Investing, the parent of the sponsor, in 1978 at 13½ a share. Once again, we sold much too early. Subsequently a group of investors purchased CI Realty with the acquiescence of City Investing for a price of nearly $20 a share from several other groups and ultimately liquidated the real estate assets for more than $40 a share.

Penn Central: An Example of a Public Bailout

Penn Central is another turnaround situation that survived and eventually prospered because of federal aid and the patience of its creditors. Penn Central became insolvent in 1970 and remained in bankruptcy for over eight years. All of the company's railroad assets were liquidated or sold to Conrail, and a five-year court battle ensued over the amount of money due Penn Central from Conrail for the railroad right of way.

However, Penn Central's remaining assets were quite substantial. It owned a pipeline and a refining operation, large land holdings (particularly in Florida), certain railroad rights of way and eight Six Flags amusement parks across the country. These operations were so profitable that when Penn Central emerged from bankruptcy in 1978, the company actually earned $1.03.

We became interested in the stock in 1979, at between 9 and 11½ a share. The company had a number of good things going for it. For one thing, its remaining assets were undervalued and no doubt some of them would be sold at a profit. Second, the company was redeploying assets, having purchased Marathon Manufacturing, a producer of drilling rigs and mining equipment. The company also had huge tax-loss carryforwards, which shelter its profitable operations. Finally, a large cash settlement from the government for the railroad right of way seemed likely at some future date.

By 1980, progress was dramatic. The company made $2.80 a share and indicated that a large cash settlement might soon be forthcoming. (As it turned out, in 1981 the company did receive a $2.1 billion settlement from the government.) It was estimated that such a settlement might give Penn Central a book value of $50 a share, even after paying off its reorganization debts. The news quickly pushed the stock over $30. Investors realized that a large cash payment would allow Penn Central to make a substantial acquisition and shelter the profits of that acquisition with its huge tax-loss carryforward.

One of the bargain hunters mentioned previously, Carl Lindner, as well as the Hunt family, also started acquiring the stock and led the fight to prevent Penn Central's management from acquiring Colt Industries, a steel producer. Penn Central's president had wanted to utilize the tax losses and was desperate to buy something that earned enough to offset them. Fortunately, the presence and power of large investors in his company stymied the idea in one of those rare instances where corporate democracy prevailed. Colt ended up having real difficulties in 1982 in the recession, and the price that Penn Central would have paid for it appeared far too high in retrospect. Incidentally, the publicity about Lindner and the Hunts gave speculative appeal to Penn Central, so that the price held up well in 1982.

G. D. Searle: The Catalyst of New Management

Penn Centrals and REITs don't come along too often, but a turn-around produced by new management often does. Take the case of G. D. Searle, a leading ethical drug company that tried to diversify its operations away from drugs, which require a constant stream of large research and development expenditures. In the mid-1970s Searle made a series of unwise acquisitions in optical products, sun glasses, hospital linen and other businesses unrelated to drugs. The inevitable result was a burgeoning debt load, poor financial controls and a drop in earnings from $1.56 in 1975 to $1.18 in 1976 and to $0.68 in 1977.

New management was installed to solve the problems in the person of Donald H. Rumsfeld, who had been Secretary of Defense in the Ford Administration. A brilliant administrator, Rumsfeld took over as chief executive officer and weeded out unprofitable businesses, fired many middle managers, reduced debt and switched the corporate emphasis from sales volume to profits. Furthermore, those divisions that could not conform to strict standards of profit-ability were sold or liquidated. Earnings responded well, jumping to $1.88 in 1980, while return on shareholders' equity increased to 18 percent, up from 8.6 percent in 1977.

Searle's stock, which had plummeted from the mid-20s to 10–20, gradually moved up and, by 1981, had reached the mid-30s. The turnaround was directly attributable to Rumsfeld and the manage-ment team he put together. Once Wall Street became convinced that Rumsfeld meant business, the stock price began to rise and Searle's price/earnings ratio came into line with the other better drug companies.

Sherwin-Williams: Management by Brinksmanship

In 1976 Sherwin-Williams was close to insolvency. Its product line was outmoded, its stores were shabby and in poor locations, its financial controls were in disarray and unable to deal with rising costs, and its customers were being wooed away by competitors. Demand for its products slumped, the company lost $0.86 a share in 1977, and there was serious talk among analysts that the company might seek a bankruptcy reorganization.

The chief executive officer resigned because of "fatigue" and a sense of helplessness, the newspapers reported, and he was replaced by J. G. Breen, who proposed radical surgery. Breen ordered the closing of unprofitable stores, fired personnel and put into effect a drastic program of cost reductions. He reoriented corporate strategy toward the do-it-yourself market and new decorating products, such as wallpaper and drapes. He also tried to lessen the company's dependence on contractors and institutional buyers by launching an advertising campaign aimed directly at the consumer.

A calculated gamble that such a strategy would work out was not too risky, in our opinion. The stock was selling at half of a hard book value and had enough assets to survive even such a drastic fate as a Chapter XI reorganization. We believed the company had the assets to back up its business and only needed the proper management to utilize them.

Indeed, Breen's policies were very successful. Earnings recovered and the stock price doubled in less than two years.

N. L. Industries: Rejuvenation through Asset Redeployment

Sometimes existing management takes a gamble on the future and shifts the company's resources into an entirely new area. Take the case of N. L. Industries, the old National Lead Company, which had such a lackluster stock performance that it was once known as National Dead. The company was saddled with low-margin, lead-products business and sold additives for paints and gasoline, a mature market with declining demand.

The company's one attractive business was its Baroid Division, which supplied drilling mud to the oil-service industry to cool and lubricate the oil well during the drilling operation. N. L. saw the opportunity in that business and started to shift its resources into the oil-service industry. By 1977 it had divested a good portion of the lead business and used the cash to acquire Rucker Company, a major supplier of drilling fluids and equipment to the oil and gas exploration industry.

The redeployment was highly successful. By 1980 petroleum services accounted for some 60 percent of N. L.'s revenues and 40 percent of profits, up from 30 percent previously. Meanwhile, during the same period, return on equity climbed from 10 percent to 19½ percent, and return on assets doubled. And as so often happens, the institutions, which had previously ignored National Lead, loved N. L. Industries because it was now seen as a growth company in a growth industry.

By 1980 the stock had quadrupled from our $10 purchase price in 1978. With a much higher p/e multiple and increased recognition on Wall Street of the changed nature of the company, we decided to take our profits at around $36 a share. It was lucky we did because when the oil glut of 1982 hit, the institutions bailed out; by March 1982 N. L. was selling under 20, as anything that was tainted with the energy label got slaughtered in the market. Still, because of the change in business and even with expectations of lower earnings in 1982, the stock held in the mid-teens, far above its low of 8 in the 1974 recession.

Esmark: Raising Cash through Asset Redeployment

Another example of a company that changed its image through asset redeployment was Esmark, the old Swift Meat Company. We first became interested in the company at around $30 a share, noting that book value was probably between $60 and $70. But the real attraction was the company's valuable oil properties and lease holdings, which Wall Street ignored, still viewing the company as a stodgy meat-packing operation beset by labor problems.

All this changed in 1980, when Mobil acquired about 12 million shares of Esmark's stock through a tender offer at $60 a share. In order to avoid being taken over by Mobil, Esmark negotiated a settlement whereby Mobil would exchange its Esmark holdings in return for Esmark's Trans Ocean Oil Division. Not satisfied with that, management instituted a total financial restructuring. First, management sold the company's remaining oil operations for $375 million, and then spun off 60 percent of the meat-packing business to the public. As a result, the company recorded a capital gain of $18 a share in 1980, received enough cash to reduce all of its debt and had its capitalization trimmed to only 10.2 million shares.

Also, the company's remaining businesses were attractive. It had operations in processed food, fertilizer production, personal-care products (Playtex) and auto products (STP). The company's financial engineering had changed its basic nature and put it on a stronger financial footing, which largely shielded it from the 1981–82 recession.

Union Carbide: The Emphasis of Profits Instead of Volume

Union Carbide Corporation, the second-ranking chemical company in the country and one of the 30 Dow Industrials, was a classic case of a company that concentrated too much on volume, at the expense of profits. The company had invested in a number of product lines, such as fish farming, seed production and medical supplies, which were far afield from its basic chemical, industrial gas and battery-product business. Carbide also had acquired refineries in Europe in order to lower its cost of raw materials. The new operations and the company's traditional dependence on cyclical, basic chemicals had slowed earnings growth by the late 1970s.

Meanwhile, the stock sank to the mid-30s from a high of over 75 in early 1976. Faced with a sharply declining return on assets, poor earnings projections and a weakening stock price, management initiated a divestiture program. Based on early indications of success in its divestitures and a book value of close to $60 a share, Union Carbide represented a good value in our opinion.

By 1980 the results of the divestiture program became evident to the financial community, and the stock recovered to the 50s. At this writing, we still hold the stock. Losing or marginal businesses have been eliminated and Carbide is focusing its resources on growth areas such as batteries, specialty chemicals, strategic metals, carbon and high-margin industrial gases. At five times projected earnings and a book value that has risen to $70, the stock continues to be undervalued.

Turnaround through New Products

The introduction of a new product or service can often be the catalyst to shift investor sentiment about a stock. However, no matter how attractive the new product or service may be, it should not carry too heavy a weight in one's investment analysis. The company should be analyzed in the same way that we've emphasized all the way through. To be on the safe side, the company should be sufficiently undervalued to merit investor interest even if there were no new products. We like to look upon the product as a bonus that could hasten and heighten the expected rate of return.

Tandy Corporation: Personal Computers

In the late 1970s we became interested in Tandy, the largest retailer of consumer electronics. It was recommended strongly by one of our brokers in a report. On the negative side, the interest rate on Tandy's long-term debt was very costly, and debt accounted for a high proportion of total capitalization. Another drawback was that retailers, even high-margin ones like Tandy, were not popular with the investment community at the time.

On the positive side, earnings had grown steadily since the mid-1960s, and return on equity had exceeded 40 percent for each of the past few years. The stock was selling in a range between 4 and 8 and appeared to be quite undervalued.

Unfortunately, the high debt ratios of the company scared us off, and we missed out on an excellent buying opportunity. What we overlooked at the time was that the company would soon market personal computers, a business with dramatic growth potential. As it turned out, the growth in personal computer sales allowed the company to cover the debt service easily. Within two years, earnings had doubled and the stock hit the high 30s.

Carlisle Corporation: A New Roofing Process

A write-up in *Value Line* alerted us to a new product recently developed by Carlisle Corporation, a relatively unknown purveyor of rubber products and wire cable. We first took a look at the company in 1980, when it was selling at around 13, and we liked what we saw. Return on shareholders' equity had jumped from 12 percent in 1976 to 25 percent in 1979, and earnings had risen steadily since 1975. However, there was little interest in the stock because investors classified it as part of the tire-and-rubber industry, a business that was in a severe slump at the time.

The catalyst for renewed investor interest was the development by the company of a new single-ply roofing system that utilized rubber sheeting. The material was much more durable and cheaper to install than the regular asphalt and asbestos roofing, especially in the case of commercial and industrial buildings.

The new product helped boost the stock to $54 a share by 1981, or a p/e ration of 15, nearly twice the highest p/e since 1975. We decided to sell the stock then because the p/e ratio had obviously gotten ahead of itself and we felt the roofing process was not proprietary, a view that was confirmed when competing companies subsequently announced plans to market a similar roofing system.

Iowa Beef: Innovation in Meat Packing

In the mid-1970s, Iowa Beef was about as unpopular a stock as one could find on Wall Street. The stock sold at a third of book value and as low as two times earnings because of labor problems, rumors of Mafia influence and classification by investors as a meat packer, a notoriously low-margin business. However, earnings were increasing because the company had developed an innovative process of fabricating and boxing meat for food retailers that had squeezed the competition and made Iowa Beef the largest meat processor in the country. Even labor problems improved when the company closed outmoded plants and opened new and modern facilities that employed nonunion workers. The progress of the company was eventually recognized and the stock advanced sharply.

As we mentioned earlier, David Murdock, one of the bargain hunters we talked about in chapter 1, had acquired a substantial position in Iowa Beef in the late 1970s. A few years later, when the company was showing good earnings progress and had come to dominate the meat-packing business, Murdock tried to interest Armand Hammer, head of Occidental Petroleum, in a takeover of Iowa Beef. The net result was that in 1981 Occidental tendered for Iowa Beef at 76 a share. In 1974 the stock sold as low as 4, quite a contrast to its eventual takeover price but clear evidence of what revitalization through a new process can accomplish.

Takeovers—Wall Street's Holy Grail

In 1980–82 there were times when it appeared as if the only way to make any money in the financial markets was in the takeover game. In fact, many investors concentrated their entire investment strategy in trying to pick the next takeover candidate. Almost every day, announcements were made of one company's investment in another's shares.

The idea of buying cheap assets is the real motivation behind the takeovers. Management may put forth many justifications to its board of directors or shareholders, but the real reason is usually a question of undervalued assets. As a general statement, the U.S. stock market was cheaper than any other market in the world in the late 1970s and early 1980s, a point not lost on astute corporate managements. Thus, an investment in the stock of certain companies was and is seen as a cheap way of buying the assets that have risen so much in price because of inflation.

Secondary motivations behind the merger mania were as follows:

1. It's cheaper to buy existing assets, such as real estate, natural resources or plant and equipment, than to build or develop them, especially in a time of historically high interest rates.

2. Rising costs of raw materials encouraged backward integration to the production of raw materials.

3. Management of companies with cheap stock prices or large holdings of cash worry about being taken over and see the best defense as a buy-out of another company.

The takeover game has attracted a lot of attention, and now many investors buy on rumors or speculations. We believe such an approach is highly risky. Obviously, the best time to get involved with a potential takeover candidate is before the rumors push up the stock price. In other words, buy on fundamentals and not on a story. That's because the takeover game has become very competitive and you are up against a cadre of sophisticated operators. Corporations are constantly on the lookout for new businesses to buy or invest in, and their mercenaries, the investment bankers, are also active because the investment stakes and the commensurate fees of the investment bankers are enormous.

For these reasons, we would advise you against buying a stock because it appears to be a potential takeover candidate. You should always focus on fundamental value: low stock price, discount to book value, low p/e, earnings progress, low debt to capitalization, and hidden assets. The potential takeover aspect should be viewed as a bonus, not the reason for making an investment.

Once takeover discussions or a large investment position in a company's shares come out into the open, the stock price will inevitably rise to a higher level. But even then, there can be some attractive investment opportunities, as long as one can safely ascertain that the stock still remains cheap at the higher price.

A number of market professionals, called arbitrageurs, speculate almost exclusively on takeover possibilities that have already been announced. The challenge they face once the rumor surfaces is to determine whether a potential takeover is for real, whether the government will prevent the merger or takeover from taking place, and whether the target company will be successful in fending off the buyer if it chooses to oppose the buyer.

Sometimes a mere rumor of a potential takeover becomes a self-fulfilling process. Upon hearing that a particular cheap stock may be for sale, bargain hunters, acquisition-minded companies and professional investors start planning a raid of their own. This happened in the summer of 1978, when rumors surfaced that Mead Corporation, a paper and forest products concern, was for sale. The rumors intrigued Occidental Petroleum and it launched a tender offer for Mead. As it turned out, Mead was not interested in selling out, and Occidental and Mead became involved in a lengthy court battle, which Mead eventually won after incurring enormous legal expenses.

Another self-fulfilling prophecy was the famous battle for Conoco that took place during the summer of 1981. The fears of an oil glut drove down Conoco's stock from a high of 73 in 1980 to the high 40s in the first half of 1981. The selling was apparently overdone because Conoco was still expected to earn $9 a share in 1981 and owned reserves of oil, gas, coal and other natural resources that gave it a conservative economic value of $125–$150 a share.

In May 1981 Dome Petroleum of Canada offered $65 a share for 22 million of Conoco's shares. To everyone's surprise Conoco shareholders rushed to sell, eventually tendering 55 million shares. However, Dome was interested in buying only enough shares to force Conoco to sell its interest in Hudson's Bay Oil & Gas Company and stuck to the original offer. The surprising response by Conoco shareholders alerted other large companies to Conoco's vulnerability, and what followed was a bidding war between Seagram, Mobil and Du Pont, which Du Pont finally won after paying $98 in cash and its own shares.

The takeover game has become so successful since the late 1970s that takeover experts now abound. A number of Wall Street partnerships and investment firms currently specialize in leveraged buy-outs. In addition, countless others have discovered the knack of buying a company's stock at wholesale prices and selling at retail. These bargain hunters seek either a controlling interest or a large enough ownership position to exploit to their advantage. Most typically, in such situations, one of three basic scenarios develops, although there are variations on each of them:

1. The target company buys out the bargain hunter at a premium over the current market price. Members of management, often fearful for their jobs, are relieved to buy out the holdings of any interloper.

2. The target company looks for a "white knight" because it does not have the resources to buy out the bargain hunter's interest. Often the target company lets itself be acquired by the white knight rather than be taken over by an unattractive suitor.

3. The bargain hunters keep on buying the target company's stock until they have acquired control, at which time they sometimes replace management, redeploy assets, merge the company into another corporation they control or liquidate the assets.

Any one of these alternatives will enhance the value of the target company's stock. If an investor is a shareholder before one of these actions takes place, the opportunity for profit is considerable.

How to Spot Takeover Situations

As discussed earlier, any investor, whether corporate or individual, who owns more than 5 percent of the outstanding shares of a company must file a 13D statement with the SEC. Investment advisers or brokerage houses holding stock for their clients must file a 13G once they have 10 percent. This statement describes who the investors are, how much of the stock they own and what their intentions are with regard to the investment. The intent section is usually worded vaguely in order to leave the investor as much leeway as possible but still fulfill its public information responsibility.

Announcements of 13D filings can usually be found almost daily in *The Wall Street Journal* if the company is of any size and trades regularly. If one wishes to get copies of the actual 13D statement, they can be obtained directly from the SEC at a nominal cost. Those who wish to monitor large investment positions can subscribe to the *SEC Today*, a publication that lists any new investment holdings over 5 percent, the *Weekly Insider Report*, the *Insiders' Chronicle*, and *The Insiders*, all of which we discussed earlier and whose addresses are listed in the appendix. There usually are one or two good company profiles in several of these publications, with company descriptions, explanations of insider holdings and comments on earnings and management by research analysts who follow the company.

Arbitrageurs and traders follow these reports very closely in order to learn of potential takeover candidates and undervalued stocks. Once an investment position becomes known, investors must check the company's fundamentals to determine that the stock is reasonably valued, despite the recent jump in price. It is also important to analyze whether the acquiring company has the conviction and resources to make a hostile tender offer if one is required. Obviously, if the acquiring company has a long history of successful buy-outs and the assets of the target company make a good mix, the chances are good that an acquisition will take place.

On the other hand, one must also judge whether the target company could launch a successful defense against the buyer. A successful defense will depend largely on the toughness and aggressiveness of management and the resources of their company.

In a typical defensive move, the lawyers of the target company will file an injunction against the acquirer for making allegedly false and misleading statements in the SEC filing or for engaging in what the lawyers claim is an informal tender. The variations on these themes are practically unlimited.

Alternatively, the target company might claim antitrust violations and appeal to the FTC or the Justice Department to halt the tender. Such appeals are often made even if the business of the target company and the acquirer are only slightly similar in nature or if only small divisions of both companies are competitive. However, the antitrust defense does not work so well now that the Justice Department is taking a more lenient view of large-scale business combinations.

Another defense tactic is to launch such a costly legal battle that the acquiring company consents to a so-called standstill agreement. Under such an agreement the acquirer agrees to stop buying additional shares of the target company for a period of time in return for an end to the litigation.

Sometimes, if the target company's stock is selling above or at book value, the company will issue additional shares. This dilutes the ownership position of the buyer and makes an acquisition more difficult and expensive.

Most managements will be reluctant to do this if the stock price is below book, since the extra shares issued would dilute earnings to the detriment of existing shareholders. This might create dissatisfaction with an already beleaguered management trying to fend off a would-be acquirer.

Finally, in a desperation move, the company may vote to liquidate itself or part of itself rather than be taken over by a hostile suitor. This occurred in 1979 when UV Industries, a miniconglomerate, attempted every possible defense against a proposed takeover by Victor Posner before liquidating itself totally.

Another variation on liquidations is a tactic whereby the target company sells some of its valuable assets to a friendly company. The battle for Marathon Oil in late 1981 was a classic example of this. In order to forestall a takeover by Mobil, Marathon signed an agreement to sell its oil-producing properties in the Yates Field in Texas to U.S. Steel. Mobil, of course, tried to prevent this sale through legal action but was unsuccessful. The final result of this battle was that U.S. Steel acquired all of Marathon.

Brunswick Corporation, best known for its bowling equipment

and marine outdoor motors, ended up selling its most profitable line of business, Sherwood Medical, a producer of disposable medical products, to American Home Products to thwart a takeover bid by Whittaker Corporation, another conglomerate. Brunswick's managers evidently preferred corporate independence to falling into the clutches of Whittaker, even at the cost of sacrificing what had been their only growth business—a so-called scorched-earth policy.

Another defense that is becoming classic is the so-called Pac-Man strategy, or countertender. This occurs when the hunter becomes the hunted. The predator company is itself bought into by its victim company, which is trying to forestall the predator and tie him up in a legal battle and also to vote shares to try to influence the predator's management and shareholders not to go ahead with their attack. The result may be a swap of shares between the two companies and a stalemate as both companies remain independent.

Of course speculators, arbitrageurs and shareholders lose out on the premium buy-out price if such a swap occurs. Two well-known examples of this type of situation happened in 1982 between two oil companies, Cities Service (CS) and Mesa Petroleum, and two multi-line insurers, NLT and American General Insurance. Cities Service finally opted for Gulf Oil as a white knight, much to the initial glee of its shareholders and of Mesa, which had amassed over 5 percent of Cities Service. But the drama was not yet played out. Mesa, in a smart move, sold its holdings back to Cities Service at $55 one month before Gulf, citing FTC resistance, reneged on the merger. Cities Service shareholders and arbitrageurs, who were convinced the deal would go through, were shattered, and so was Cities Service management when Cities Service stock declined by almost 30 points from merger-induced levels. Many lost millions as they were forced to sell CS to meet margin calls before Occidental Petroleum finally made a lower successful tender for CS shares two weeks later.

In the NLT–American General fight, American General outmaneuvered NLT with a very innovative tactic. It offered NLT's directors a choice of a friendly buy-out of $46 or an unfriendly tender at $38. Aroused NLT shareholders finally forced NLT's reluctant management to succumb to American General in July 1982, and the two companies were merged.

There have been so many special situation takeovers or abortive takeovers in recent years that it is difficult to proffer a representative sampling. However, all of them had one common theme—they were in keeping with our basic investment philosophy of buying undervalued assets and earnings power. So when you use the checklist, one of the prime ingredients to look for in spotting a takeover is a discount to book value or net current working capital. But in the takeover game, anything goes, so there are no fast and hard rules to investing wisely in takeovers. It's a risky endeavor unless long-term fundamentals are present. Also be sure to make a determination about the seriousness of the large investor. A big investment by another company does not mean an automatic takeover, but on the strength of the coattail argument, if you buy around or below the large investor's cost, you have a good chance of having an eventually profitable investment, provided you still do your homework.

As a general rule, acquirers usually prey on companies that are selling at depressed prices, at or below book value, and are suffering trying times and perhaps temporarily distressed earnings for some reason or another. These acquirers are looking to purchase assets cheaply, perhaps in the hope of selling them off and putting the proceeds to work at a better return, or they are looking over the valley of temporary bad earnings to the time when the company returns to normal levels of profitability.

The point is that whenever you become interested in a potential takeover, after learning about it either through a tip or in an article or through some of the sources mentioned earlier, there is no excuse for not exercising due diligence and running the stock through our checklist. If the company looks fundamentally sound but is languishing at the bottom end of either its p/e ratio or discount from book value, learn whether the problem is temporary or long-lasting. Ask yourself what a would-be acquirer sees in the company. Is it a massive discount from book value that can be converted into a cash value? Is the acquirer in the same or an affiliated business of the target company where some sort of combination would produce synergistic profitability (say, by integrating its goods or services forward or backward)? Does the company have hidden assets that might eventually be sold off, thereby reducing the effective purchase price? Finally, is the company producing a sufficient return on sales, assets and equity so that it could pay its own way without large cash infusions by the acquirer?

Let's see how this works out in practice by looking at several takeovers we were involved in.

Belden Corporation:
An Exciting Product Line Spurs Takeover

Take the case of Belden Corporation, which we spotted in April 1980 with the 5 percent rule. The company was involved in the exciting growth area of fiber optics but because of a lack of sponsorship was not closely followed on Wall Street. When we started looking at the company, the stock was selling at 19, or a p/e ratio of 4½. During the previous ten years the stock had sold in a p/e range of 5 to 10, and 30 appeared to be a normal price. The 1980 recession had temporarily depressed the stock price and we thought it represented a good percentage play. Even though we weren't looking for any kind of takeover, one came along within two months. Crouse Hinds quickly acquired Belden and then in another surprise move was subsequently taken over by Cooper Industries. Meanwhile, the value of our holdings increased from $19 to $42 a share. The stock ran up so sharply because it had unrecognized glamour and had been depressed because the overall stock market environment was poor and the stock underrated. But Crouse Hinds, with a similar product line, saw the future potential of Belden's business, as did Cooper Industries. As a result, Cooper took advantage of the bad stock market environment to snap up a solid stream of future earnings at depressed prices.

The Conoco Epic

We were also involved in Conoco, but took our position in 1978 when the stock was selling in the high 20s. We thought the domestic oil stocks were cheap in relation to OPEC oil prices and liked the fact that Conoco owned Consolidation Coal, one of the top three coal companies in the country. When OPEC doubled oil prices in 1979, Conoco's earnings jumped to $9.50 from $7.58 in 1979, and the boom in all energy stocks took Conoco to above 70 a share by the fall of 1980, at which point we sold the stock.

The oil glut, the world-wide recession and increased oil conservation all helped push Conoco's stock down in the first half of 1981. We bought the stock again in the mid-50s on the premise that the oil glut was temporary and the oil stocks were oversold. Once again, we did not expect a takeover. We thought Conoco might earn between $9 and $10 a share in 1981 despite the oil glut and a coal strike. The rest, of course, is history, and we were able to sell part of our stock to Seagram and part to Du Pont at an average price of $93 a share.

Chromalloy: A Coattail Strategy That Has Not Worked

We have already touched on the pros and cons of riding on a big buyer's coattails to make big gains in stocks. This is an arbitrageur's main business, and very frequently over the last several years of merger mania there had been dramatic price increases in a single day due to the disclosure that a large buyer has accumulated a position in the stock. But there is also a perilous side to this kind of strategy. Lately, merger fever has subsided due, we think, to high interest rates, increased resistance to takeovers, lower profit expectations and a more cautious approach about incurring additional debt to make an acquisition.

In fact, there has been a pronounced trend toward partial consolidation where companies buy 20 percent or more. The Internal Revenue Service allows firms to consolidate the earnings of a company of which they own 20 percent or more. This appeals to some companies that may have a large cash trove and want to invest for the long term in the stock of another firm that is undervalued. A holding of 20 percent or so also puts the acquiring company in a favorable position for a takeover if one makes sense at a later date, since it is hard to defend a company against a firm with a large block of stock.

In the early 1980s this trend became commonplace as 13D reports, standstill agreements (where one company agrees to limit holdings) and partial consolidation moves, which can be a kind of creeping takeover, became daily news items. But if you are a small investor, it is wise not to bank on a takeover as a prime motive for investment, simply because it may be years before anything happens. Of course, you do feel safer knowing that a large investor is in the stock at prices above yours and that should the fundamentals improve, the investment could prove quite attractive. Coattail buying more often than not leads to profits, especially over a one-to-two-year period, but one should not follow these big buyers blindly. Be sure the buyer is strong financially and has a reputation for canniness and persistence. Most of all, make sure that the target company is a good value on its own merits. Even large and successful predators sometimes fail to do their homework and get caught with a loser.

Sometimes, riding on the coattails of a big investor can be less than rewarding. For instance, in 1980 we noticed that Sun Chemical had acquired a large interest in Chromalloy American Corp. for about $100 million. Chromalloy was a poorly run conglomerate, whose founder had died in 1977. His replacement was selling off undesirable businesses, reducing debt, and as a result, earnings were improving. We were in favor of such corporate pruning because of the fifty or so businesses the company was in, only three— jet-engine coating and repair, barges and petroleum services—were consistently profitable.

On the news of Sun's investment, Chromalloy's stock jumped up to 28¼ but later fell back on the repeated statement by Sun's chairman that the shares were being held for investment purposes only. While we had no reason to disbelieve Sun's chairman, we wondered how passive a role the company would play with a $100 million investment at stake. In any event, when Chromalloy dropped to the mid-teens during the 1982 recession, we decided to take a position at an average cost of 15. Sun's average cost was 22¼ and thus more than 7 points above ours. Chromalloy's basic businesses appeared to be weak but still holding up in the recession. In the fourth quarter of 1981 Chromalloy had cleaned house and set aside a reserve for anticipated losses from divestitures of business segments that had been a drag on earnings, and had lost $7–$8 million in operating losses in 1981. This streamlining and "biting the bullet" augured well for the future, we thought. At this writing, with the stock below 10, we continue to hold the shares and Sun continues to increase its position, now holding close to 38 percent of Chromalloy. We hope we will get our profit when Chromalloy's business gets stronger and Sun Chemical finally decides to do something with its investment. When that will be, we don't know.

We reiterate that patience is essential in this type of investing. Many corporations have passive investments in other companies, and traders and arbitrageurs have been sorely disappointed when no takeover occurs.

The stock will eventually increase in price, of course, if earnings improve. The bonus is the ownership position of the large investor. But the late Charles Bluhdorn of Gulf & Western was a passive investor for years in such companies as General Tire, Jonathan Logan, AMFAC and Libby-Owens-Ford, generally adding to positions during weakness in the market.

Indeed, companies such as G&W that take large passive positions in many businesses should not be overlooked as potential investment candidates, especially if they have a successful history of profitable investments. For example, Chris-Craft jumped from 13 to 38 in 1980 largely because a private investor group took over Twentieth Century-Fox, of which Chris-Craft owned 22 percent. Curtiss-Wright also made a large capital gain on the Kennecott shares it sold back to Kennecott (as we described earlier).

One final point about takeover stocks. One should never buy a takeover stock when rumors are circulating through Wall Street. Wait for the news to quiet down and for the stock to settle back a bit before doing any buying. If the stock does not drop, then don't chase it. Leave that one for the gamblers and wait for the next takeover situation to come along.

There is one final tip that could be helpful in determining whether a tender offer is going to be successful or not. When a company makes an offer to buy shares of another company—that is, offers the shareholders of the target company the right to *tender* their shares to it—the market price of the stock usually improves but not to the level where the tender offer is made. This leaves a potential profit for the arbitrageurs and speculators, if the deal is successful. In spite of the strict regulations on insider tips and knowledge, the practical reality is that takeover information does slip out to the powerful and well-connected on Wall Street. The professional arbitrageurs have their own intelligence network, which provides progress reports sometimes on an hourly basis. The stakes are enormous for some of these arbitrageurs and they use all available means to procure information. One good signal is the behavior of the options as the tender expiration date nears. If the call option is above the market price but below the tender level and stays strong, chances are the deal will go through. If the deal were expected to fail, the "arbs" would have unloaded their bullish option position or hedged by selling calls.

Had we followed our own advice we wouldn't have been surprised when the Cities Service–Gulf deal suddenly materialized. As you recall, Mesa proposed a tender for Cities Service at $45, and Cities Service countered with a bid for Mesa at $23. If Cities Service had proceeded to take over Mesa, its share price would have plunged, since its earnings prospects were poor for 1982 and it would have had to add to already heavy debt obligations. Nevertheless, Cities Service stock stayed in the high 30s, 10 points above where it sold before the tender was announced.

However, the nearest maturity call option was selling at a healthy premium, which should have been a tip-off to us that something was brewing. Playing the takeover conservatively, we decided to protect our profits and sold calls at 40 a week before they expired in June 1982, with the stock selling at 35½. (In exchange for a premium, we sold our rights to the stock for one week to a buyer who was willing to speculate that the stock would be selling over 40 by then.)

Two days later Cities Service agreed to be acquired by Gulf at $63 a share, and our stock was called at $40 immediately. A surprisingly high call premium (well above what the market indicated) was a hint that either Mesa would succeed at $45 or that someone else was lurking in the wings with a better deal. Yes, we made a profit but sold our stock at 41½ (we were called at 40 and received a 1½ premium) rather than watching the stock run up to 55 in anticipation of the Gulf merger. In an ironic twist, perhaps we were lucky. Many of our friends who held their Cities Service shares clucked away sympathetically at our misfortune for getting prematurely called in the stock. But about a month later we were doing the consoling when Gulf dropped the deal and Cities Service stock plunged to the high 20s, where it sold before the merger.

The moral of this true-life story is to respect the professionals. Rules are bent, insider knowledge does exist, and the market will generally reflect that. But even the pros get hurt sometimes, which occurred in the Gulf–Cities Service transaction, where even the insider "wire" broke down. The result—the "arbs" lost millions of dollars on paper, until Occidental came and "saved the day" two weeks later by finally buying Cities Service in the low 50s in an amicable transaction.

Chapter 8

Making Volatility Work for You

MANY INVESTORS ARE THE VICTIMS of unprecedented volatility in today's financial markets. Too often they buy securities after a big upward move and sell after big declines. How many times have we heard the lament "If only I'd done the exact opposite, I could have made a fortune"?

The average stock now fluctuates in price by at least 25 percent over a twelve-month period, even though its underlying corporate outlook may change only marginally. Table 21 shows the yearly highs and lows for the years 1977–81 of some of the stocks discussed in this book.

If you had bought at the high end of the yearly range, the ensuing price drop might be more than you could live with. But suppose you had bought at the low end of that range and sold near the high, you would have benefited from today's turbulence.

TABLE 21
YEARLY HIGH AND LOW STOCK PRICES

	1977	1978	1979	1980	1981
Burroughs	92–55	88–58	83–64	88–46	55–27
General Foods	36–29	35–27	37–28	34–24	35–28
IBM	72–61	78–59	81–61	73–50	72–48
International Paper	70–39	49–35	48–36	48–31	52–37
Union Carbide	62–40	43–34	45–34	53–35	62–45
American Broadcasting Cos.	32–24	43–23	48–32	39–26	38–27
Cessna	16–12	23–14	24–15	29–12	37–18
Boeing	13–08	34–11	35–25	46–32	44–22
RCA	33–24	34–23	28–21	33–19	32–17
Esmark	29–23	26–19	26–19	50–20	58–38

The way to get that low price is to do your buying when the stock market has undergone a major sell-off. Such opportunities now occur about once or twice a year. Rising interest rates, accelerating inflation, a recession, international shocks, fears of a credit crunch or bankruptcies all add to the volatility in the financial markets.

A glance at a chart of the New York Stock Exchange Composite Index (NYSI) for the years 1978–81 shows that there were a number of major declines during that period: October 1978, October 1979, March 1980 and September 1981. Each one of these declines was followed by a good advance in stock prices.

The drop in the NYSI in October 1978 to around 52 was followed by a rally to 62, or a nearly 19 percent advance. The October 1979 plunge to around 56 was reversed by a rise to 68.26, amounting to an almost 22 percent gain. The slump in February/March 1980 was followed by a jump in the NYSI from 53.66 to 81.29, an increase of some 51.5 percent. The late-summer decline in 1981 to 64 was followed by a rally to nearly 73.5, or a rise of nearly 15 percent. Of course, in all these instances individual stocks registered greater gains than the broad averages. We're not suggesting that one should try to predict intermediate term swings in stock prices, which is one of the hardest and riskiest strategies in the stock market. Although many financial gurus maintain that movements in the markets can be predicted, we contend that no one can consistently forecast price trends with an accuracy worth betting on. The unexpected event is largely responsible for the movement of markets, trends inevitably go further than expected, and in the short run, markets often behave irrationally.

In fact, the predominant influences on the stock market are probably the business cycle and the direction of interest rates, both of which are highly unpredictable. Interest rates are impacted significantly by Federal Reserve policy and even the large number of full-time Fed watchers are more often wrong than right about interest-rate trends. The business cycle is influenced not only by interest rates, as evidenced by the 1980 and 1981–82 recessions, but by such political actions as increased federal spending and other fiscal policy decisions.

The safer and more conservative investment strategy is to have a series of price targets for a wide number of stocks that you have already identified as undervalued. Then, wait until these targets are met, usually during a major market decline, which is when we try to do most of our buying.

However, even though a stock may have reached your target price, if the decline is severe enough, the stock may fall further. To deal with such a possibility, you should adopt two strategies: (1) Learn to identify the classic signs of a market bottom or an oversold stock market and (2) accumulate your positions in a stock over a period of weeks, or even months, which is known as dollar cost averaging.

Market Bottoms

Because a stock market bottom is characterized by selling exhaustion, an investor's major task is to determine whether all the selling is over. This is a highly subjective endeavor with no precise guidelines. However, you can look for a number of developments. First of all, see whether the NYSI, or whatever index is used as a proxy for the market, has declined 20–25 percent below its 200-day moving average—that is, its average price for the last twelve months of trading activity. (Any stockbroker and most advisory services can provide 200-day moving averages.) This is one of the classic measures of what market professionals call oversold.

Now, markets can remain oversold or overbought for extended periods of time, and 20–25 percent is no magic number. But if you do start to nibble away in that area, you are unlikely to go wrong for too long.

Another important buy signal is a market decline that becomes emotional, which implies that investors are tossing away stocks without consideration of value or price. This is called capitulation. The best way of measuring the extent of emotion in the market is to gauge the unanimity of the downside retreat in stocks. Most of the time, the majority of publicly traded stocks will go their separate way, leading a life of their own. But at certain times, in periods of euphoria and fear, all stocks go with the trend. When that occurs, the market is acting under the influence of an emotion that may soon exhaust itself.

One good way of measuring the amount of emotion in stock prices is to watch the daily new highs and lows, and the number of advancing and declining issues on the New York Stock Exchange.

Here again, no magic number exists. But it is safe to say that an environment of intense fear exists when the New York Stock Exchange records more than 1,000 declining issues a day, and some 300–600 new lows for a week or two in succession. At such times, stocks are being sold indiscriminately, which may offer an opportunity for the bargain hunter.

Another clue to look for is what professionals call nonconfirmations, one of the most useful of all the technical studies of the market. The concept here is that in order for a market move to be sustainable, everything must be in gear. Various market averages should move together (confirming strength or weakness), the breadth of the New York Stock Exchange (ratio of advancing issues to declining issues) should also follow the trend, and most important, a new high or low in an average should be confirmed by the other averages and the breadth. If it is not, the odds are that the move is bogus and misleading.

The most widely followed confirming averages are the Dow Jones Industrial Average and the Dow Jones Transportation Average, representing, respectively, the manufacturing and transportation capabilities of the nation. If one is out of whack with the other, it may imply that more goods are being produced than transported or that more goods are being transported than shipped. Of course, some downplay the interconnection of these averages, claiming that the transportation average is not truly representative of the distribution function of the nation. Airlines, which are dependent on passenger traffic, are now included in the average and many railroads are now viewed as natural-resource investments rather than transportation plays.

Nevertheless, we have found that these two averages can be useful when studied together. Market professionals know that almost without exception, a major decline in a market is followed by a "testing" of the low. The test may come a week later, a month later and occasionally a year or more later. The key to whether the low will hold, and whether stocks are a buy, is whether both averages go to a new low during the testing.

The stock market in its own insidious way often tries to confuse the public by taking the Dow Industrials (which is what most people watch) to a new low, while the Transports hold above its previous low. Of course, the Transports could "confirm" at some later point, but if pessimism is rampant and a good-sized rally took place off the first lows, one could be fairly sure that the lows will hold.

For instance, at the bottom of the bear market in 1974, the Dow Industrials bottomed at 584 in early October, then rallied some 100 points before again declining in December to 570. But while the Dow Industrials went to a new closing low, the Transports did not. Other nonconfirmations occurred during the declines in the late 1970s.

Other market tools can be used to spot nonconfirmations, such as the number of new lows and the ratio of advancing to declining issues on the New York Stock Exchange, which should also confirm the validity of a market move. If a widely followed average, such as the Dow Industrials, goes to a new low in the test, but the number of daily new lows and the number of declining issues are fewer than during the previous drop, there is a high probability that the selling pressure is abating and consequently it is a good time to buy stocks.

Let's go back to the 1974 bottom and compare the Dow Industrials to the number of 52-week highs and lows. On September 13, 1974, with the Dow at 627.19, there were no stocks at a new high and 661 at new lows. It was clear that selling had reached some sort of an extreme. Within the next few weeks the Dow rallied to 674.05, before collapsing to a new low at 584.56 on October 4. But even though there was a new closing low in the Dow, two stocks hit new 52-week highs, and only 235 fell to new lows. In other words, the Dow had made a new low, but there were 426 fewer new lows on the New York Stock Exchange than on September 13. The public, of course, was only watching the Dow and they were lured into thinking that the market was about to break down, when, in fact, the bottom had already been reached.

The much more important nonconfirmation came in December 1974, when the market "tested" its September/October low. On December 6, the Dow fell to a new closing low of 570, but the number of new lows was only 297.

Another important check is the performance of a broad-based index such as the NYSI, especially in relation to the Dow Jones Industrials. While the Dow rallied to an eight-year high in the spring of 1981, the NYSI failed to better the high it had made the previous fall. A cautious investor would have waited for a confirmation by the NYSI before believing that the stock market was about to break out of a fifteen-year trading range.

Note, however, that nonconfirmations were not a foolproof study at the August 1982 low. In early August, just before the market's upward explosion, both the Dow Industrials and the Transports fell to new bear-market lows. However, the number of new 52-week lows was a helpful tool. For instance, when the Industrials fell to 824.01 on September 25, 1981, the number of new lows rose to 504. But when the Industrials dropped again in the spring of 1982, falling to 795.47, the new lows were 327. And in June 1982, when the Industrials fell to 788.62, the new lows were only 256. Thus, while the casual observer believed the market was dropping to successively lower levels, the number of stocks participating in the decline was slowing dramatically.

Many technical analysts missed the 1982 bottom because they were waiting for the type of nonconfirmation in the averages that occurred in 1974. But the market never makes it that easy. For this reason, you should never rely too heavily on one indicator.

Another important sign of a bottom is a significant liquidation of margin debt. At the top in 1973, margin debt peaked at $7.5 billion and was cut by 40 percent at the bottom of the 1973–74 bear market. Any real market bottom must have a reduction in margin debt, otherwise the threat of such a liquidation always hangs over the market. Margin debt is an important indicator because it can be veiwed as a proxy for speculative indebtedness. In other words, before an economic recovery can get under way, the economy must be reliquified, which implies a partial liquidation of debt. Margin debt information is published monthly and can be found in *Barron's* "Market Laboratory."

Also, look for a selling panic, with daily volume on the New York Stock Exchange exceeding the level reached at the top of the previous bull market. In 1974, during the final throes of the decline, the Dow Jones Industrials dropped from 677.88 to 627.19 in four trading days. In 1970, the Dow fell from 691.40 to 631.16 in five trading days. A similar type of drop over three to five trading days on exceptionally high volume would be a classic indication of a sold-out market.

Another important sign: The stock market has fallen to a major area of support. For example, the area of 750–800 on the Dow appears to offer significant support, as the Dow bottomed at 736 in 1966, 784 in 1973, 737 in 1978, 730 in 1980 and 776 in 1982. No matter how bad the economy gets, the stock market should find major support at that level, from which could come a significant rally. How stocks behave on the pullback from the first rally will, of course, determine the sustainability of any bull move.

Those who wish to be highly conservative can wait for a Dow Theory buy signal; that is, a new rally high in both the industrial and transportation averages. After correctly calling the 1974 bottom, the Dow Theory became very popular in the mid- to late 1970s, and as so often happens, immediately lost its usefulness, as it failed to signal the 1982 bottom. It is interesting to note that the Dow Theory is most useful when no one notices a new bull- or bear-market signal. For instance, in the summer of 1981 the Dow Theory gave a classic sell signal, but hardly any forecasters or stock market analysts picked up on it.

By the same token, at the bottom of 1974–75 we had a classic Dow Theory buy signal, which was also ignored at the time. After hitting bottom in September 1974, the Dow Industrials rallied to the high 600s a number of times, but on each occasion fell back to the low 600s. For instance, the Industrials rallied from 627 on September 13 to 674 on September 19, then went back down to 584 on October 4, then up to 673 on October 30, then back to 577 on December 6. Then, finally, on January 27, 1975, the Dow broke out of that trading range to close at 692.66, up 26 points for the day on huge volume. The Transports also broke above their late-1974 rally highs. In other words, you get a Dow Theory buy signal after a major market crash, when both averages break above previous rally highs set during the basing or early rally phase.

While some might argue that the market was already 100 points off its lows, the truth is that the Dow didn't stop rallying until the early summer, when it reached the high 800s, and ultimately went on to advance for the next six years. So, most of the price appreciation was still left for the conservative investor who waited for the Dow Theory buy signal.

Another important area to watch is how the market responds to bad news. In 1974 one of the signs that stocks had already discounted the worst was that dividend cuts had little effect on stock prices. In fact, in the first six months of 1975, as the full force of the recession hit, stock prices "climbed a wall of worry" as every day the financial pages carried dismal news. Thus, pay attention to and respect a market that goes up on bad news, especially if it appears irrational at the time. The reason the market is rising is that it may already have discounted the worst and has nowhere to go but up.

Whatever the problem is in the latter stages of a bear market, investors should watch carefully how the market responds to additional problems in that area. If the problem is bankruptcies, do stocks keep falling when the next bankruptcy arrives? If the problem is high or rising interest rates, is there a time when further increases in interest rates have no further effect on stock prices, or conversely, has the most recent worry suddenly been forgotten, to be replaced by another one? Perhaps interest rates, the previous major concern, are actually falling, but no one is paying attention because fear of bankruptcies and a credit collapse are seen as the greater worry.

Another precaution is to only buy stocks when the various moving averages of the Dow give a buy signal. Basically, the concept is that if the trend is truly turning up, the moving averages—50-week, 13-week and 5-week—will start to turn up too. The 50-week moving of the Dow is the average price for the past year, and thus is a good long-term indicator of trend. The 26-week average is a good intermediate term indicator, while the 5-week average is a good short-term measure. The first sign is when the 5-week moving average moves above the 26-week average, and that constitutes an early warning signal that the trend may be changing. The real buy signal comes, however, when the 26-week average moves above the 50-week average. Because it is so hard to turn around a 26-week average, when it does break out, it usually is a signal that a major shift in direction is under way.

Each bottom has its own particular idiosyncrasies. Take as a case in point the 1982 bottom, from which was launched one of the most powerful advances in fifty years. What were the signs of that bottom? The first one, as we discussed earlier, was a nonconfirmation in the number of new lows. Second, speculation was largely wrung out of the market. For example, the ratio of volume on the speculative American Stock Exchange in relation to volume on the more conservative New York Stock Exchange had fallen to the lowest level since the mid-1970s. Third, investors' sentiment was widely bearish. The number of bullish investment advisers sank to the lowest level in more than four years. The cash position of mutual funds rose to nearly 12 percent, the highest level since the 1974 bottom—clearly indicating the pessimism among fund managers. Fourth, despite all the fanfare of sharply higher interest rates in the second half of 1982, interest rates were actually starting to edge downward a number of weeks before the market took off. Fifth, activities by insiders—corporate officers and directors, who are known to be smart buyers, especially at bottoms—had switched dramatically to the buy side.

The trouble with many technical indicators is one of degree. The extremes registered by the indicators vary, depending upon whether you are in a major bear market or a "correction" in a bull market. Thus, we are reluctant to be precise about when indicators announce *the bottom*. However, you should focus on the following:

1. How impressive is the first move off "the bottom"? In August 1982 the ten-day ratio of advances to declines was the most impressive of any rally in the past forty years. Thus, within a few days of the low, it was apparent that the market was performing exceptionally well.

2. How much skepticism meets the first rally off the bottom? By August 31, 1982, 42.6 percent of investment advisers were still bearish, despite a 100-point move in the Dow on the highest volume in history. Another sign that the rally would continue.

3. Is there skepticism that interest rates will keep on declining? During the early stages of the 1982 rally, five business and financial publications ran major articles arguing that interest rates wouldn't fall much further, when in reality the decline had just begun.

4. Does the market rally on bad news? In 1982 the first buying panic occurred when Mexico announced that it could not meet principal payments, and fears of an international banking collapse escalated. In fact, the whole last half of 1982 saw a series of terrible economic news releases: U.S. trade deficit hit a record $42.69 billion; U.S. Steel's 1982 steel shipments were the lowest since 1938; unemployment rose to the highest level since the 1930s; business failures in 1982 were the highest since 1932; aluminum producers had the worst fourth quarter since the depression; real GNP in 1982 dropped 1.8 percent, the worst performance in thirty-six years; consumption of beer in 1982 was flat for the first time in twenty-five years; in 1982, housing starts registered a thirty-six-year low; factories ran at 69.8 percent of capacity in 1982, the lowest

in the thirty-four years that statistics have been kept. Yet in the fact of the worst economic news since the depression, stocks staged their most impressive rally since the 1932 bottom. Remember: the biggest and best stock market moves occur under the guise of terrible economic news.

5. Stocks offer the best value if they are bought once a recession becomes official—that is, two consecutive quarterly declines in GNP. After all, it's a recession that causes profits—and stock prices —to decline. Thus, the best time to buy stocks is when a recession is officially announced, because everyone who is going to sell stocks has already done so. The economic numbers are generally released a month or so after the end of the quarter. If you had bought stocks at that time in the postwar period, your performance would have been excellent. In the twelve-month period following each such buy point, the Standard & Poor's 500 jumped 30 percent on an average. That calculation does not include the figures for 1982, where such gains were possible in a matter of months.

6. Is there talk of a "depression" or a repeat of 1929? Throughout the spring and summer of 1982 many articles were written on depression. If there is one clarion call to buy stocks, it is a front-page article in a newspaper or magazine about financial collapse or depression.

7. Is the market widely expected to take one more drop before bottoming? In the summer of 1982, fears of a selling panic predominated. Indeed, the very week the stock market began its historic surge, the Sunday New York *Times* ran an article about the coming selling climax. Several business magazines also carried similar stories. Imagine investors' surprise when the panic was to buy, not to sell.

While there are many other indicators that serious investors study, this list should prove sufficient. Sometimes, it is possible to make the study of the market too complicated, and a few basic rules can be more helpful than a hundred.

Dollar Cost Averaging

The very perversity of markets makes bottom picking a difficult and frustrating exercise, which is why dollar cost averaging may be a more sensible strategy for most people. Let's assume that the stock market is oversold as we have defined it above and a number of stocks have reached your target price, and based on analysis, these stocks appear undervalued. But let's also assume that you are uncertain about how much longer and lower stocks could keep declining. What do you do? Buy now or wait? Faced with such a predicament, we normally would buy half our intended position, and if stocks fell further, buy more.

The difficult part is knowing when to buy more. Our own rule of thumb is this: We will buy more if the stock slips another 25 percent from our first purchase price. (Of course, this will not happen if the stock is already at rock-bottom prices.) Such opportunities were presented to us in the spring of 1980 and September 1981, when stocks fell more than we had expected. In February 1980, for example, we purchased some shares of Pneumo Corporation at 24. The company derived nearly 70 percent of earnings from aircraft landing gear and the rest from food and drug retailing. The landing-gear business appeared stable because of increased defense spending and a new generation of passenger planes. But in the next few months the stock market decline continued further than we had anticipated and Pneumo slipped to the high teens. We doubled our position at 20, for an average price of 23. Later in the year, when the stock rose to 30, we sold out for better than a 25 percent gain. Thus, if you have confidence in your decision and the stock market appears ready to rally, dollar averaging can be a highly effective technique.

Still, dollar cost averaging is not infallible and can often be treacherous. We averaged down with Boeing in 1981, which was a mistake. We originally bought the stock at 29 and then, when the stock fell to 23, tried to average down at 26, by doubling our position. Well, not only was the market not ready to rally (it immediately declined 10 percent more), but Boeing's backlog, which moves its stock price, started to contract. Airlines canceled or deferred orders on a new generation of jets as air traffic dried up in the recession and as interest rates failed to come down. There were other political problems too, such as a cutback in Export-Import Bank funds by Reagan's budget measures and threats to certain favorable tax-leasing provisions that made it easier for cash-strained airlines to buy planes. Boeing got as low as 15 in the summer of 1982 and we had a significant paper loss. And, in fact, when the August 1982 rally commenced, we took a loss, selling the stock at 23 because we were anxious about Boeing's prospects and those of its customers, the airlines. However, the market had already discounted these fears because by year end Boeing reached 35.

Diversification

A good protection against market volatility is diversification by stocks as well as industry groups. The less sure you are of the direction of the market and the greater the probability of an extended period of market weakness, the more sense it makes to diversify.

Diversification makes sense even if your stock portfolio is no larger than $10,000. (However, $2,000 is the minimum, in our opinion, that should be devoted to any one issue. A $2,000 investment in a stock allows sufficient participation if the stock rallies.) Industry groups often come quickly into investor favor, and diversification enhances the possibility of benefiting from the latest investor fad.

Generally speaking, we would recommend diversification along the following lines:

NUMBER OF STOCKS	SIZE OF PORTFOLIO
3–5	$5,000–$15,000
5–10	$15,000–$50,000
10–15	$50,000–$75,000
10–20	$75,000–$200,000
over 20	$200,000 and above

Of course, diversification does diminish the opportunity for gains. But we would gladly accept a lower return if our risks could be commensurately reduced. Since one's ability to consistently predict the future is questionable, diversification can provide a cushion against the unexpected event.

In late 1979 and early 1980, for instance, the institutions began to invest heavily in the domestic and international oil stocks, in some cases concentrating as much as 30 percent of their portfolios in these issues. When the oil glut began in 1981, the institutions rushed to sell and the stocks declined by 30–50 percent from their 1980 highs. No matter how certain the fundamentals of a particular industry group appear, the unexpected may occur and the industry group could fall out of favor.

Portfolio diversification should be evaluated frequently, as often as once a week, depending on the market and business outlook. We constantly juggle issues in our portfolio, selling one stock with a capital gain and buying another that seems to be a better bargain. We also change the emphasis of our portfolio, depending on the business outlook. If bad economic times appear to lie ahead, we will sell stocks in which we have a gain or break even and switch into depressed issues whose underlying business will be less affected by a recession, such as food, drug, telecommunications, cosmetics and tobacco issues. Conversely, if boom times seem likely, we would emphasize those companies that stand to do best, such as some computer and seasoned technology issues, machine tools and industrial goods, retailing and housing, and building-products companies.

The Volatility of Individual Stocks

So far we have spoken only of the volatility of the market. There are also opportunities in individual stocks—namely, those experiencing a sharp decline that is unwarranted by the underlying assets and fundamentals. Such declines are usually caused by some corporate development and have nothing to do with the action in the overall market. Remember that there is a caveat to these prospective opportunities: How great an effect will the event have on the long-term fortunes of the company? And: Is the damage temporary and superficial or long-term and serious? One's success in this type of investment will hinge heavily on learning the correct answers to these questions.

We list below some of the events that can drive down the stock price of a fundamentally good company, sometimes offering a buying opportunity for the bargain hunter.

1. A merger breaks off and the stock of the acquisition target plummets in price. In such cases, the stock often falls further than is justified. The stock declines because the arbitrageurs who were betting on higher prices are selling to preserve their capital. The merger discussions should be seen as a positive because some big investor obviously thinks highly enough of the company to con-

template buying it. Once a company has been identified as a potential merger candidate, other large investors may take a look and the company could well be acquired at a much higher price.

2. Company has a major lawsuit. The key here is to determine that the lawsuit will not have a "materially adverse effect" on the company. Lawsuits for health reasons, for instance, can be particularly damaging, as was the case for asbestos manufacturers Manville and Raymark, which were seriously hurt by long litigations and settlements. Indeed, Manville went into voluntary bankruptcy in August 1982 because of the crush of litigation even though it technically was not insolvent. An antitrust suit, such as was filed against IBM, may drag on for years but have no permanent effect on the company and even brighten the picture if fought successfully, as was the case with IBM.

3. Top management is fired or quits. This may be an opportunity because the board of directors will try to put in new management as quickly as possible. Often the problem with the company was the old management, and new leadership may provide the catalyst for a turnaround.

4. Company buys another corporation with a bad record, assumes too much debt to make the acquisition, and earnings decline. This is another example of where Wall Street's short-term focus can create a good investment opportunity. Investors sell the stock because they believe the burden of debt and losses of the acquired company will penalize earnings. However, management, which takes a long-term view, is willing to suffer some near-term disappointments in earnings if the acquired company can be turned around.

Take the acquisition of Anaconda Copper by Atlantic Richfield in 1976. Initially the financial community reacted negatively. But several years later, when metals prices rose substantially, though temporarily, Anaconda's operations made good contributions to its parent's earnings and Atlantic Richfield's stock benefited.

5. The dividend is cut. Such an event will usually send the company's stock to the target price, but caution is warranted. The dividend cut could be a harbinger of worse to come. We prefer to buy the stock after a dividend cut only if the stock is so beaten down that it sells below net working capital. On the other hand, management has a large incentive to restore the dividend, otherwise their presence may be short-lived. The restoration of a dividend

can create a huge capital gain, but painful surgery on the company's operations is often necessary and there may be a long recuperation for the company's cash flow before that can happen.

6. Political event occurs that is very unfavorable to the company. Nationalizations, revolutions, elections, among other events, can all have a bearing on the performance of a multinational company. Often the initial shock drives the stock down sharply, but it can recover quickly when objective analysis indicates that the company is well diversified.

This is exactly what happened with Textron, a diversified conglomerate founded by Royal Little. Its Bell Helicopter division had a multimillion-dollar contract to supply and train Iran's armed forces, which was voided by the fall of the Shah. Textron's stock reacted unfavorably to this news and fell to the low 20s (at which price we bought the stock), but the fundamentals of Textron were still good. It sold at a discount to book value, had a consistent return on shareholders' equity of 18 percent, a steady earnings record, balanced diversification in its businesses, and debt of less than 20 percent of total capitalization.

Despite the loss of the important Iranian contract, Textron's earnings held up well, buoyed by other divisions. By early 1981, earnings were actually on the rise and the stock jumped to 38 in mid-1981 before retreating due to the effects of the 1981–82 recession.

7. Loss of a major customer or supplier. Or stiff competition enters the company's markets. A stock often drops sharply because investors fear the company will lose a major customer or worry that competition will erode profit margins or cause a loss of market share. Concern about this can often reach such an extreme that the stock falls to an absurd level in relation to book value, and the company is worth more dead than alive.

On the other hand, if the managers are smart and realistic, they may already have taken steps to alleviate the loss of a customer or market share. Perhaps they plan to introduce a new product or better service, cut costs or develop new customers.

Of course, we are not suggesting that you should downplay the loss of an important customer, supplier or proprietary edge. It may be the beginning of a rapid decline of a company. What you must ascertain is whether the company has sufficient resources to get through the tough times, as well as a history of successfully dealing with problems. Learn what management plans to do about the problem. Does its course of action appear reasonable and sensible or is it self-destructive? A cost-cutting program and the announcement of new products should be viewed constructively. On the other hand, the prospect of discounting or price wars would be a negative, even if the stock was selling at an attractive price.

Nashua Corporation was an example of a company that was seriously hurt by the loss of an important supplier. Primarily a marketer of copiers and copier paper, Nashua enjoyed a good earnings record until it fell out with Ricoh, a Japanese manufacturer of copiers and the company's major supplier. Nashua's attempt to manufacture its own copier was unsuccessful and it was eventually written off because of heavy start-up expenses and a poor environment for the copier industry.

By 1981 Nashua's earnings had dropped to around $2, down from $5.75 in 1979. Even though the stock price fell to less than half of book value, we were not sure the stock was a good buy, though initially it was tempting. The company's image was tarnished and it would take a long time for Nashua to regain investor confidence. We were particularly disturbed by the savage competition in the market for copying machines, which was so severe that it had even driven down the stock of Xerox, one of the equity aristocrats, from a high of 64 in 1981 to 37 despite 1981 earnings of over $7 a share and a discount to book value of 75 percent.

If the situation in the market was that adverse for Xerox, the industry leader, the prognosis for Nashua was worse, since Nashua did not have a strong service base and its technology was not strong enough to profit from the office of the future. In short, Nashua was an also-ran that had come to grief because of its own complacency about a supplier. In the end, Nashua was compelled to renew its arrangement with Ricoh on less profitable terms, and at this writing is still fighting for survival.

8. Labor unrest and strikes. Although such events often hurt earnings, the drop in the stock price is usually temporary and therefore presents a good buying opportunity. However, some strikes can really damage the company. The image of J. P. Stevens was tarnished on Wall Street because of a five-year battle with the textile workers' union. And the six-month strike at International Harvester proved a disaster. The company was already suffering from weak markets and intense competition, and the strike may have irreparably damaged it.

When to Sell

One of the most frequent complaints we hear from investors is that their stockbrokers tell them what and when to buy, but never when to sell. The result is that good purchases and substantial profits often turn into losses or, at best, lost profits.

To be sure, it is often easier to know when to buy than when to sell. A stock may get temporarily overvalued, but if it is a good company, with improving prospects, should you sell it? Or perhaps the market itself is giving off signs of excess speculation and there's the likelihood of a big drop in stock prices. If you have a small gain in a stock, should you sell?

Your first step in deciding when to sell is to examine your tax situation for the year. Under the 1981 tax law, the top federal tax on capital gains is 20 percent, a big improvement over the 28 percent maximum for 1979–80 and the much higher rates of the mid-1970s. Thus, you should try to hold on to a stock for one year, unless you expect a big drop in the stock market. Of course, if you have short-term tax-loss carryforwards, you could take the gain at any time because the losses and gains can offset one another.

We have five basic selling rules. Although they may appear black-and-white, a certain amount of subjective judgment should be employed in their use.

1. Sell half the position when you have a 30 percent gain in the stock, or when you have attained the investment objective for the stock, even if the fundamentals appear overwhelmingly positive.

Let's assume you have an objective of a 30 percent return before the capital gains tax, indicating a 24 percent after-tax return, excluding state and local taxes. As the stock approaches the price that would provide you with a 30 percent gain, put in a good-till-canceled order (GTC) at that specific price. You cannot watch a stock's movements all the time, and such a system ensures that half of your positions will be sold automatically. A GTC imposes discipline that prevents you from being greedy and helps lock in a self-imposed return on capital. Admittedly, this is a defensive strategy, but it does provide comfort. The remaining half of your holdings can be used to speculate on the company's improving fundamentals.

Let's illustrate how this works with Colgate-Palmolive, which we mentioned earlier in the book. Based on a $14 purchase price and an opportunity cost of 30 percent, we would sell half of our position at 18½. After commissions, we would have a profit of $4 a share, which in effect would reduce the cost of the remaining shares to 10. If we assume that Colgate might earn $2.50 in 1981, that would represent a p/e ratio of four times earnings, which is lower than any multiple for Colgate over the past decade. With this kind of strategy the stock market could have any number of large unexpected drops, and your holdings should be well protected.

If and when Colgate returns to a more normal p/e ratio of 9 on, say, $2.50 of earnings, the stock could rise to 22½, at which price we would be tempted to sell out our remaining holdings. This would give us an average price of 20 on our Colgate position, a nearly 43 percent return on investment.

2. Sell the remaining shares when the stock sells at the lowest yearly *high* price/earnings ratio of the past five years.

Our point here is that there's no need to be greedy. Perhaps a rapid increase in earnings will push the stock above its historical p/e range, but why bet on it if you already have a good profit. Caution is particularly warranted if the stock is cyclical and has a long history of moving in a wide band of p/e levels.

American Broadcasting Companies provides a good case in point. In 1981, at 27 a share, or what amounted to a p/e of five times 1980 earnings of $5.18, the stock was, we believed, undervalued. Book value was around 25, earnings were scheduled to rise slightly in 1981, and long-term debt was only about 21 percent of capitalization, the lowest in ten years.

We concluded that our ultimate objective for the stock was 40, where it would sell at eight times earnings, or the lowest *high* p/e of the previous five years.

3. Sell the stock if something more attractive comes along.

Let's say you have a 40 percent gain on a non-energy stock in six months, and along comes a smash in the energy stocks because of fears of a world-wide oil glut. Many good companies drop 25–50 percent in price and you see the opportunity to buy some real bargains, with many companies selling at their lowest price/earnings ratio in five years and at only a small fraction of their appraised value per share. In this case, it would make sense to take your profits and reinvest the proceeds in some of the undervalued oil stocks because the money could be better put to work there.

4. Sell the stock if the company performance deteriorates.

It is always wise to get the company's latest annual and interim reports to shareholders, which will give an idea of developments at the company and could call attention to a deteriorating picture.

Also, keep a close watch on the cash situation of the company. Are inventories building up and are they being financed by expensive short-term loans? Are the dividend or credit ratings in jeopardy because falling profits, high dividends and rising capital expenditures require increased debt?

Any company that mortgages its future to keep on paying dividends is probably an unattractive investment. Take the case of Chicago Pneumatic Tool, which besides tools manufactures air-pressure-related machinery. We bought the stock between 17 and 20 during 1980. At the time, the book value was 32, the current ratio was high and the yield was over 10 percent.

In early 1981 we became concerned that the company was borrowing money to meet dividend payments. Earnings dropped to $2.44 in 1980 from $3.30 in 1979, and we learned that cash flow in 1980 was $25 million, but capital expenditures and dividends were $27 million. With a recession expected in 1981, the company's business outlook wasn't good and a return to a higher level of profitability seemed doubtful. We became uneasy and sold some of the stock in the range of 19 to 22. Unfortunately, we did not sell all of it—and in early 1982 the company reduced its dividend by 80 percent and the stock price fell to 12. A setback in earnings, as we've said before, is not the death knell for a company, but it may offer you the opportunity to sell a stock and buy another one that appears to be better valued and has sounder prospects.

5. Sell when the market clearly looks overbought.

When you begin to see the opposite effect to the description we gave of a market bottom, such as over 1,000 advances a day or more than 700 new highs for a week or so in succession, discretion dictates taking half your profits or at least a winnowing out of those issues that are hitting new highs and a lightening up on those that are not participating as fully in the rally. This doesn't mean that you should sell out your whole portfolio, since even overbought markets can extend themselves. But never sneer at profits; you'll be happy you have them when a sell-off does occur. Generally, the "Market Comment" column in The Wall Street Journal will alert you when the technicians consider the market overbought. As trend predictors, technicians can be fairly accurate, although they often fail at pinpointing when the direction will change and often are ahead of the market by as much as three months. Thus, you should at least take heed of their opinions.

How to Reduce Volatility with Options

Stock options can be a very valuable tool in dealing with volatility and the question of when to sell. But in order to use them successfully, you must have a clear understanding of their risks and benefits.

Options have been traded for at least a hundred years in over-the-counter markets but only became popular with the general public with the advent of options exchanges. An option is a contract to buy or sell 100 shares of a stock at a specific price with a specified maturity. Certain terms are used in dealing with options:

call option: the right to buy stock at a certain price within a specified amount of time

put option: the right to sell a stock at a certain price within a specified amount of time

underlying security: the stock that is covered by the put or call option

strike price: the fixed price at which the underlying security is bought or sold if the option is exercised

premium: the price paid for the option

expiration date: all listed options expire on the third Friday of the particular month specified on the option, i.e., "Sears April 35" means the Sears option expires on the third Friday of April at 35

It is our belief that the purchase of a call or put option is a loser's game because options are a wasting asset. Only if the price of the underlying stock increases (in the case of a call) or declines (in the case of a put) does one have the opportunity to make money. Thus, we view the purchase of options as an outright speculation and inconsistent with our basic philosophy unless there is such a clear-cut bottoming or topping action that the temptation to buy calls or puts is overwhelming. However, as we have often emphasized, it is a really difficult exercise to recognize such a turn, and the risk of loss, no matter how sure you are, is always present. Many a professional trader who was certain of an impending turn has been proven wrong.

We do, however, subscribe to the idea of *selling* puts and calls depending on whether the market is expected to go up or down. You may not be able to pick tops or bottoms, but if the consensus is too bullish or bearish, if the technical factors we discussed earlier are in place, or if the valuation of the market (p/e's, book value, dividend yield, etc.) reaches a historical extreme, options can be very useful. In effect, we advocate a conservative and defensive strategy in the selling of calls to enhance performance.

Let's assume that the market looks as if it may be nearing a top, or political and economic events appear uncertain. It's sure to make you nervous about the direction of the market, particularly in light of some good profits on several stocks that are still undervalued. What are you supposed to do, take profits or hold on? One solution is to sell calls on the stock, assuming it has options that are traded on an options exchange.

Let's take American Broadcasting Companies as an example. Let's assume we bought the stock at around 27, a price we believe is cheap both historically and in relation to the company's expected earnings prospects. The stock currently sells at 33¾ and it is October. We are now faced with the quandary of whether to sell. Our first step is to see how much longer we need to hold the stock to qualify for capital gains. As it turns out, we have another three months to go, or until next January.

We know the objective for half of our 200 ABC shares is a price of 35, or a 30 percent gain after commissions. According to the newspaper listings, ABC calls with a strike price of 35 are selling at the following prices:

(in 100s)

NOVEMBER	FEBRUARY	MAY
1¼	2¼	2⅝

We prefer the February call because in February our ABC holdings will qualify for capital gains and we don't want to have the stock called away before then. Note that if a stock is called away, it usually occurs near the maturity of the option, when the stock is selling near the exercise price. Thus, if an investor does not want to be called away, he should only sell calls when the market or the stock has had a sharp run-up and looks ready to decline.

Accordingly, we decide to sell one February ABC 35 call and receive 2¼ ($2.25) per share. If the stock rises to 35 by February and the call is exercised, we would receive $35 a share, representing a 30 percent gain. In addition, we could keep the option premium of $2.25 per share, which is taxed as ordinary income. However, the premium of $2.25 represents an 8.33 percent return in four months on our initial investment of $27, or a 25 percent return annualized.

If ABC doesn't rise above 35 by February, we have two alternatives. Either we wait until the third Friday in February, when the option expires, or we buy back the call at a lower price and sell another call with a longer maturity. Which alternative we choose depends on what price the February 35 call has fallen to and on our views about the chance for a rally in the stock. If the option value has fallen to, say, ⅛ ($0.12 a share) and the stock might rally sharply, we would cover our option, still retaining the bulk of the premium. We would then sell another call on a longer maturity, when the stock rallied.

There are two caveats to this system that should be mentioned. First, when an investor sells a call, the investment potential is limited until the expiration of the option. Let's say our ABC stock is called and we have to deliver it. In such a case, the maximum profit would be limited to the strike price and the premium, or 37¼ (35 + 2¼). If, for some reason, the stock leaped to, say, 40, we would not benefit. In effect, we have sacrificed any upside potential beyond 37¼. Second, we are locked into holding the stock with the attendant opportunity costs (less dividend) until the option expires or until we are called away. Our money is thus "captured." Some people would not mind that, since they are satisfied with a specified capital gain or are content to stay with the stock for the longer run if they do not get called. Others, however, might have limited funds and thus may miss a better buying opportunity if it arose by the need to hold the underlying stock. Of course, they could go "naked"—that is, sell the stock anyway and hope they are not called. But this is a decidedly risky strategy and only for those with steel nerves.

Let's work through another example. Since 1975, Coca-Cola's stock has ranged from 30 to 50, and in a p/e range of between 8½ and 15. Let's assume we bought the stock seven months ago on April 15 at 32 and it is now November 15. The stock has risen to 36 and we are worried about the market, even though the company is doing well and increased earnings are expected. We would be happy to take profits at 40, representing a 25 percent gain. So, we look at the Coca-Cola 40s. We prefer an option that matures in six months so that we can be assured of capital gains treatment for the stock we hold. (However, it is possible that Coca-Cola could be taken over or some extraordinary but similar event could cause a dramatic price advance and we would get called away earlier than expected.) May calls with a 40 strike price are trading at 1½. Thus, we calculate that if we are called at 40 in May, we will have an $8 gain plus 1½ per share from the option premium, or a $9.50 profit, an appreciation of almost 30 percent. If we collect the premium, on the other hand, we have reduced our effective cost of Coca-Cola stock by $1.50 to $30.50. Note, however, that the option premium is subject to an ordinary income tax of 50 percent (plus local taxes).

Puts should be used at the other extreme—when the market or a particular stock is depressed and selling at undervalued prices. Let's see how this would work with International Paper. In early October 1981, when the stock market was near its 1981 low and International Paper was at 39, we sold IP January 35 puts at 1½, receiving $1.50 for each share. If International Paper stock fell below 35 before January 1982, we would probably be "put" the stock and would have to come up with $3,500 per put plus commissions. Yet our real cost would be 35 less 1½, or 33½, which we considered an attractive price. Of course, if the stock didn't fall below 35 by January, we would retain the premium.

Although we could have received a larger premium (2½), with a higher strike price, such as the IP January 40s, we did not want to be greedy. Let's suppose we were "put" the stock at 40. Our effective cost would be 37½ (40 minus the 2½ premium), which was a little more than we wanted to pay for the stock. Thus, when you sell puts, respect the market environment. Don't forget you may have to come up with the money, or alternatively, buy back the put at a large loss if the stock declines and you don't have the money.

A good discipline when selling puts is to use only the strike price that represents the lowest p/e for the previous five years. It would be unfortunate to be "put" a stock at a time when liquidity could be important to take advantage of forthcoming opportunities.

We believe there are many ways to trade options profitably with little risk. But the small investor should only use options with extreme caution and only to protect profits (by selling calls) or to nibble at attractive stocks near to a market bottom (by selling puts).

How to Use Stop Loss Orders

With market volatility so intense over the past five years, many stock market traders and investors are now using "stop loss" orders as a protection against some of the free falls that can rough up both industry groups and individual stocks.

A stop loss is a variation of a limit order—in effect, an order to sell if the stock declines to a specified price. Stop losses are, in our opinion, best used for the speculative stocks in your portfolio, or when the stock has reached a point where you would normally wish to sell but some rumor or potential development, such as a possible takeover, a large new order, a new product introduction or any other possible positive event may propel the stock higher. In effect, you are holding out for more based on a "story." The stock price may already have shot up past your target sale price, and if it were to decline because the expected news does not occur or proves a disappointment, a stop loss order ensures that you protect your profits. But a stop loss order is no guarantee of protection.

Let's take as a case in point—Cities Service, which we bought in late 1981 for $42. The stock had been the subject of numerous merger or takeover rumors for months and at one point rose as high as 62. Nevertheless, our investment soon fell underwater as the stock declined to 24 by February 1982, when the oil-glut story created havoc with every oil and energy-related stock. In addition, there was a disaffection among investors that no merger had been consummated.

When the stock was trading between $45 and $55 in December 1981, we placed a stop loss at 45 in case things went wrong. To our surprise, we were stopped out at 43½ on a day when an avalanche of orders hit the specialist and caused even our stop loss at 45 to be pierced. It must be remembered that this kind of selling panic occurs when speculators and institutions want to get out, and even the best thought out stop loss is no guarantee of achieving your price. This is the case because the balance of sell orders may simply outweigh the specialist's "book" and cause him to have to lower the price to a point where he can balance the buy and sell orders.

Some nervous traders actually place stop losses whenever they buy, usually because of limited capital. We would not advocate this approach unless the stop loss is well below the buying price and not just under it. A specialist can and will play games and can legally manipulate prices to pick up a point or two for his firm. If you have determined to own the stock, stick to your conviction. Do not use a stop loss if you are concerned about a precipitous fall in the market. In addition, it would not make sense to place a stop loss immediately upon purchasing a stock, since this implies a lack of confidence in either the market or your investment selection. Why buy in the first place?

Finally, many people ask: Where is an intelligent level to put a stop loss? We have already touched on the chartist approach earlier in the book and now we must pay deference to the use of the chart as an aid in clarifying a stop loss point. There are various support or resistance levels in the trading patterns of any individual stock. If you watch price behavior over a period of months, you discern this yourself even without a chart, but it is easier to fathom by looking at a chart. If you do not have access to the sophisticated charts that brokers or traders use, even a Standard & Poor's or Value Line chart will suffice. In our case, we usually ask a broker to request his house chartist to determine a stop loss point. Brokers have access to really elegant computer-aided charts and their assistance could prove helpful.

Often it is good advice to put in a stop loss at a point where the stock started to "break out"—that is, where it commenced its jump upward—since presumably whatever news made the stock take off and create new demand for it could be reversed and cause a return to the old pre-news level.

We are not entirely convinced that stop losses are that necessary and reiterate that the most appropriate use for them is when you are clearly speculating out of greed and hoping for the big event that everyone else is also waiting for.

Chapter 9

How to Use This Book
with Confidence

IT IS PART OF HUMAN NATURE to make gutsy or provocative predictions. Indeed, many reputations were made and many books sold in recent years because of some wild prediction of economic drama. But, as we have pointed out, the future is hard to predict consistently and you should not bet hard-earned capital on the probability of some economic event occurring in the near future.

Thus, the purpose of this book is not to make forecasts about what the Dow Jones Industrial Average will be at a certain date in the future. Our goal is to provide the tools for selecting undervalued stocks and to minimize capital losses during unexpected market reversals. We cannot guarantee that the stock market will have a great bull market in the 1980s, as many pundits expect, but we do expect the stock market to boom sometime within the next five years, probably when least expected.

It is important to remember that the stock market is and always has been an attractive investment, irrespective of whether a secular bull market develops in the 1980s. As we pointed out in chapter 1, between 1974 and 1982 the average stock appreciated more than 100 percent a year. Even during the virulent inflation of the late 1970s, certain stocks generated outstanding returns. For instance, many independent oil and gas stocks and technology issues rose twenty- to thirtyfold. By the same token, during 1981 and early 1982, when the Dow Industrials fell by more than 20 percent, many interest-rate-sensitive food-processor and consumer stocks fared well. Meanwhile many oil-service or high-tech stocks were losing half of their market value as the institutions conducted a year-long pogrom on them. The stock market has always been fragmented, and in a rampant bull or bear market there are going to be leaders and laggards depending on the herd's psychological attitude toward a group.

It should always be remembered that bear markets don't last forever. The worst bear market of all time—between October 1929 and July 8, 1932—lasted only a little over 2½ years. More important, that bear market was followed by the greatest bull market in history, with the Dow rising from its 1932 low of 41.22 (the lowest level in over thirty years) to 196 in early 1937. It is probable that the early 1980s, which saw the worst economic environment in fifty years, will at some point also be followed by a similar climb in stock prices.

Therefore, we would argue that investors should always have some personal participation in the stock market. While some of the market gurus adopt a black-and-white market strategy—either fully invested or 100 percent out of the market—we think the proper balance is somewhere in between. If an investor is totally out of the stock market, as one might well have been between 1978 and 1982, many opportunities would have been lost. For one thing, one would have missed the opportunities of the sharp market breaks—in the fall of 1978, fall of 1979, spring of 1980, fall of 1981 and spring of 1982—and their subsequent, even sharper reversals. As we have pointed out, market advances often occur when they are least expected—and thus, investors can not plan for them. For instance, the record-setting advance between August and December 1982, amounting to over 250 points in the Dow Industrials, caught most of Wall Street by surprise.

By the same token, being fully invested in stocks probably doesn't make sense either, except for those few occasions when the market has had a panic liquidation, such as in the fall of 1974. As we have illustrated elsewhere, stock market declines come once or twice a year and usually without warning. Thus, it is practical to always keep a reserve of cash to take advantage of the bargain prices presented by such situations.

We tried to make the case for investing in U.S. stocks early in this book, but let's repeat a few key elements here. First, alternative investments are limited. The Real estate has probably peaked in price unless inflation becomes rampant again; starting a small business is fraught with difficulties, as evidenced by the highest business failure rate since the 1930s; investments in foreign stock markets are less attractive than they were in the 1970s because of the strong U.S. dollar and political turmoil abroad; bonds are a bet on the direction of interest rates (probably the most challenging task in the whole world of finance because politics and Federal Reserve policy are the major motivating factors); commodity futures trading is enormously leveraged and dangerous; money market funds backed by certificates of deposit and commercial paper involve the risk of default; and the banking system and thrift institutions, as evidenced by the growing number of defaults by Third World countries, mergers or outright failures, are vulnerable to a crisis in confidence, collapse or both.

Given these financial risks, and the ones elaborated on in chapter 2, the liquidity of the stock market has an enormous attraction. As owners of real estate and collectibles have discovered to their horror, an illiquid or nonexistent market can be very disruptive to any long-term investment strategy.

Also, politics can have a sudden effect on attitudes and psychology, thereby requiring a sudden shift in investment strategy. For example, the inflation-hedge mania of 1979–80 was brought to a very quick and devastating end by the election of Ronald Reagan, which implied that the voters wanted an Administration that would take the necessary steps to end inflation. Conversely, the surprising upset of Giscard d'Estaing by Mitterrand threw the French franc and capital markets into a turmoil. The subsequent nationalization of companies and banks under Mitterrand is another indication of what can happen if the political wind shifts suddenly.

Alternatively, an unforeseen shock to the financial system, such as the credit controls of 1980 and the Hunt silver debacle, can drive down prices in a sudden selling panic. Being able to raise liquidity quickly during such times can often prevent a personal financial disaster.

Stocks also have the added advantage of representing an ownership position in real assets. In these days of financial uncertainty, one can't help but want to hold a portion of one's wealth in assets that represent real value. Take the recent experience in Mexico.

Between February and September 1982, the peso lost more than two thirds of its value against the U.S. dollar. Because of massive capital outflows, the Mexican government put on foreign exchange controls and prohibited any withdrawal from the country of the reported $12 billion held by U.S. residents. In effect, this $12 billion could only be converted into greatly devalued Mexican pesos. On the other hand, many Europeans who managed to escape during World War II returned to find their land laid waste and material possessions looted or destroyed. Currencies of many European governments were sharply devalued, but those who owned shares in companies that were rebuilt were able to salvage something. Obviously, these are extreme examples but they illustrate the ongoing value of stock ownership.

Some investors like to own a position in gold as a hedge against disaster. A typical recommended investment level is 10 percent of one's investable funds. Gold is viewed as an insurance policy against a sharp acceleration in inflation that turns to hyperinflation or a deflation that causes a banking collapse. Using the same line of reasoning, we would recommend investing a certain percentage of your investable assets in common stocks. This percentage may vary, of course, depending on the economic environment and whether stock prices have recently advanced or declined sharply.

How do you go about investing in the stock market? The answer, of course, largely depends on the amount of experience you have had with stocks. If you have never invested in stocks before, you will need to open up some lines of communication. The beginning investor will need a certain amount of human interaction to get started. We would suggest the following steps:

1. Develop sources of information for two reasons: first, to get some investment ideas, and second, to have someone to talk to if the market becomes irrational and your stock picks go against you. Talk to friends, relatives and acquaintances that you trust and come up with a list of their contacts who have demonstrated a capable investment record.

Next, start a relationship with a stockbroker who will also provide you with research recommendations and advice.

Also, you will, we hope, subscribe to some of the magazines and journals we have discussed in chapter 4, wherein you should be able to get some ideas on stock selection.

Drawing on all these sources, run the investment suggestions you hear about through our checklist and see if they make sense from a value standpoint. This will enable you to ask the relevant questions of your sources if you are disturbed by a certain aspect of their stock recommendation.

2. By now you should have more than ample source material—the difficulty is to develop judgment about which undervalued stocks to buy or whether a stock is really undervalued. Some people may wish to plunge right in, but the more conservative approach is to invest on paper, using a phantom portfolio for a while at least. In other words, see whether it's working for you before you actually commit your hard-earned dollars to the endeavor. Did the stocks go lower after you bought them? How did you react when that happened? Did you have the confidence to hold on through a sudden and unexpected market reversal? It is better to make your first mistake on paper so that it won't cost you any money.

One of the great banes of Wall Street is impatience. Many, if not most, investors think they have to be in the market all the time—they are afraid that this opportunity will pass them by and there'll never be another one as attractive. This is simply not the case. There are always opportunities, as one investment-letter-publisher friend of ours remarked. "In my thirty years in the business," he told us, "I've probably missed most of the major market moves, but I've only had two disasters and they were in small amounts and occurred years ago." In other words, it is important for you to develop the consistency of results first, which you can do just as well on paper as with your precious capital.

3. After you've developed some confidence by using a phantom portfolio, you can start to put your toe in the water and do some actual buying and selling.

Don't buy stocks with all your liquid assets. Start off with maybe one-third and see whether it works. If you are indeed making money and can exhibit some consistency, then gradually increase the amount invested.

Perhaps add a discount broker as an alternative to a full-service broker you may already be using. You won't get investment recommendations or research, but you will save up to 70 percent on commission costs, and if you have gathered some confidence about finding your own stocks through periodicals or contacts, this can help in saving commissions and improving performance.

4. Another way to get in the action is to join a local investment

club. Over the years, many of these clubs have generated surprisingly good results. Furthermore, it will expose you to frequent contact with experienced investors who could be a sounding board for your own ideas. If you are not aware of an investment club in your area, write to the National Association of Investment Clubs, 1515 E. Eleven Mile Rd., Royal Oak, MI 48067. It should be able to provide you the name of a local club.

5. Of course, many people don't want to have to make their own investment decisions because they don't want the responsibility or don't have the time. We hope this book can be useful for such people, too. No matter who handles your investments—broker, investment counsel or mutual fund—our book can be used as a reference tool, a quick checklist of value. Before your investment counsel buys any stock for your portfolio, tell him you want to know about it first. Then evaluate his choice in light of our guidelines. The same applies to your stockbroker or any mutual fund you are contemplating putting your money in. Let the checklist in this book be the devil's advocate for your adviser's ideas. Write for a list of the mutual fund's major holdings and see whether they are in fact valued at reasonable levels. Were the fund's stock holdings bought "right" and are they consistent with your objectives for capital preservation? *Forbes*, by the way, publishes an annual survey of mutual fund performance, and *Barron's* also regularly reviews and ranks fund performance.

Finally, for those who have previous experience in stocks, this book can also be used as a gauntlet through which you can run any recommendations, tips or investment ideas. James Thurber once said that "it is better to know some of the questions than all of the answers." If this book can keep you from buying overvalued stocks or fad stocks and participating in frenzied markets that are close to a sharp and vicious correction, it will have served a useful purpose.

We believe that the basic precepts of value do not change. The principles of an undervalued stock, as outlined in this book, are likely to remain the same for the foreseeable future. We hope that you will evaluate any contemplated stock purchase in light of our checklist of value. While we can make no guarantees that this system will provide profits, we believe that if the precepts of value are rigorously followed, you should be able to realize a better than average return and mitigate your losses in the stock market. If anything is to be learned from the excesses of the 1970s, it is that preservation of capital and a long-term investment strategy should be the predominant concern of all investors. It is our sincere hope that we have helped to provide you with a conservative strategy of capital preservation and enhancement and that you will come away from this book Wall Street smart.

Appendix

Barron's (*$55 / year*)
22 Cortlandt Street
New York, NY 10007
(212) 285-5000

Business Week (*$34.95 / year*)
1221 Avenue of the Americas
New York, NY 10020
(212) 997-1221

Dow Theory Letters (*$185 / year*)
P.O. Box 1759
La Jolla, CA 92038
(714) 454-0481

Forbes (*$36 / year*)
60 Fifth Avenue
New York, NY 10011
(212) 620-2200

Fortune Magazine (*$36 / year*)
1271 Avenue of the Americas
New York, NY 10020
(212) 586-1212

The Insiders (*$100 / year*)
3471 North Federal Highway
Fort Lauderdale, FL 33306
(305) 563-9000

Insiders' Chronicle (*$325 / year*)
Suite 1660
1300 N. 17th Street
Arlington, VA 22209
(703) 276-7100

OTC Review (*$36 / year*)
110 Pennsylvania Avenue
Oreland, PA 19075

Professional Tape Reader
    (*$245 / year*)
P.O. Box 2407
Hollywood, FL 33022
(305) 981-5963

SEC Today (*$115 / year*)
c/o Washington Service Bureau
1225 Connecticut Avenue, N.W.
Washington, DC 20036
(202) 833-9200

Speculator (*$157.50 / year*)
108 Christopher Columbus Drive
Jersey City, NJ 07302
(201) 432-8900

Standard & Poor's
P.O. Box 11370
New York, NY 10249
(212) 248-2525

Street Smart Investing
  (*$195 / year*)
P.O. Box 173
Katonah, NY 10536
(914) 232-5084

The Wall Street Journal
  (*$94 / year*)
22 Cortlandt Street
New York, NY 10007
(212) 285-5000

Value Line
711 Third Avenue
New York, NY 10017
(212) 687-3965

Weekly Insider Report (*$85 / year*)
19 Rector Street
New York, NY 10006
(212) 482-8300

About the Authors

GEORGE B. CLAIRMONT is president of Clairvest, a money-management firm based in New York City. He is a well-known Wall Street bargain hunter who, despite the volatility of the financial markets in the 1970s and early 1980s, has not had a down year since he began managing money professionally. He has an M.B.A. from Columbia University and, before starting his own investment firm, he worked at Citibank.

KIRIL SOKOLOFF is head of Street Smart Investing, a newsletter and consulting service. He is the author of five investment books, including *The Thinking Investor's Guide to the Stock Market* and (with economist Gary Shilling) *Is Inflation Ending? Are You Ready?* He was formerly managing editor of the *Business Week Letter*, senior editor of finance and investments at McGraw-Hill, Inc., an investment banker at G. H. Walker & Company and a commercial banker at Citibank.